Let There Be Light

The Inspirational Achievements of a Man Born Blind

Joe Giovanelli

iUniverse LLC
Bloomington

Let There Be Light
The Inspirational Achievements of a Man Born Blind

iUniverse books may be ordered through booksellers or by contacting:

iUniverse
1663 Liberty Drive
Bloomington, IN 47403
www.iuniverse.com
1-800-Authors (1-800-288-4677)

ISBN: 978-1-4502-6211-8 (sc)
ISBN: 978-1-4502-6212-5 (e)

Printed in the United States of America

iUniverse rev. date: 06/18/2013

I dedicate this book to those children who can't seem to compete in school, who are regularly bullied in gym classes or during recesses.

I dedicate this to those who have dreams and who make them happen even when everyone tells them that their schemes will fail.

I dedicate this book to some special teachers: How can I ever forget teachers like Mrs. DiPritoro, Miss Moody and Miss Butler: people who believed in me when I believed in nothing at all!

I also dedicate this book to all my friends who cared about me when so many didn't.

There are so many people who deserve mention, but I absolutely must add Vail Belyea to this list. Without her constant efforts to get me to start my writing this book, and her encouragement during the entire process of creation and revision, you would not be reading these pages.

My final dedication is to God Almighty. Without His help I would doubtless be dead! Even before I knew Him, even before He was there waiting for me, patiently watching and guiding me through jungles through which I could not otherwise pass!

Preface

It's April 1, 2013. (NO FOOLIN'!) What you are reading is a revised text of what I wrote in May, 2010. I made many changes which I believe are improvements to the original, as well as fixing many typographical errors found in the original printing.

I'm just about eighty-four years old. How did I get here in this retirement home, Our Lady of Peace? Has the earth really taken that many whirls?

Around me are old, framed paintings and pictures, a computer and peripherals, a music keyboard, a theremin, and a music synthesizer, "ham" radio equipment, audio gear, an iPod, and so much more. By reading this list you know that my life involves very technical things. I'll try to keep techie talk to a minimum, but so much of who I am is interwoven among these items that I cannot always separate the two. It just may be that there is some historical interest in that many of these matters might by now not be well known to the current generation. What can I say? If some of this information is boring or uninteresting to you, by all means skim through it.

In general this is not a technical book. It's a story of a person who, over time, has changed in profound ways. Although this is my own life's journey, I hope and pray that something on these pages will help a few of you as you face whatever challenges you do and will confront.

My mind is filled with memories of many past years, which is natural because I'm beginning one of my most challenging tasks: writing a book! Boy! That task forces things into my consciousness, many of which were buried and perhaps some which would best remain so!

Many of my friends tell me that I must write this book. I tell them that I don't like talking about myself and besides, I don't know how to write one. They think that I have a story to tell, and so, with their encouragement and with the help of God, I will give this venture a try.

I live in a world of the sighted. But even though I am a blind person, I do "see". So, when I write that I "see" something or someone or someplace, it's my perception and recognition that is my "seeing". And it's not, for instance, that I can hear any better than you, but have trained myself to use my hearing "to see".

Where should I begin? Maybe it should be now where I can look back on my life. That almost makes sense; so, I'll begin this narrative that way but only for one chapter. The person I have become is not the person I was. I had the usual problems of growing and maturing, but I had to deal with one thing which made growing much more difficult—blindness! You'll see that at times I was not always successful.

Sometimes it is important that a sighted person recognize my competence in a given subject. To demonstrate this I have to be something between a showman and a showoff. It's often necessary to talk about some of my achievements. I don't like doing it. Often there's simply no other way to drag a sighted person down what I know to be a correct road.

These days I welcome others to this residential community. I want each new person to understand that life does continue and that he, she (and I) can, and should, continue to keep up with new things!

Each Thursday night I play piano for an hour in our main lobby, entertaining those who choose to hear me rather than staying in their rooms watching their lives drift as television sets babble. Sundays find me seated at the organ in our chapel, playing for the worshippers. Tuesday afternoons finds me playing organ for our community hymn sing.

There is another section of the facility which is dedicated to making the lives of people suffering from Alzheimer's disease have as much meaning as possible. I'm there every Friday afternoon along with my dear friend, Vail. As I play accompaniments for her songs, she walks around to each person, trying both in song and gestures to make each one feel special.

In my spare time I walk two-and-a-half miles a day with Vail. I read; I carry out electronics experiments. I am active in amateur (ham) radio as a part of a network which drills us so we will be prepared for any emergencies to which we might be called for backup communications.

This is me, right here and right now, but how did I get started doing these things? Hmmm . . . Looks like this is the moment when I try to write a book!

Joe Giovanelli

Chapter 1

Let's get right to it. I AM BLIND! Saying that, I crammed lots of things into my life. As an 8-year-old child I knew a bit about clock repairing. I repaired radios in high school and college. Yes, college. I made my first stereo recording at a time when few people even knew what stereo was. Some years later I began writing a technical column which dealt with high fidelity sound and continued doing that for more than 40 years. For a few years I designed and manufactured high fidelity loudspeakers. I operated a successful recording studio, which included disk recording processes which I think were never done by any other blind person.

Blind. There's that word again. What thoughts does that conjure up for you? Do you think that I, along with all people blind since birth, live in a world of constant darkness? Nothing could be further from the truth. If light is taken away from you, you see very little. It is dark. It's dark to you because you have something to compare it with: the ability to see light. I have never seen light so have never experienced darkness when there is no light.

Often I've been told how much better my other senses are as compensation for my lack of sight. My remaining senses are no better than those of sighted folks. What is true is that I had to train my remaining ones in order to take the greatest advantage of what I still had. Think about a person who is born both deaf as well as blind. Obviously his hearing isn't better than anyone else's. That person must, however, use his remaining senses to a greater degree than I do if he or she is to manage himself in this world. I can appreciate what this person must have to do in order to cope. I will stay with the blind because this is my world, and, being sightless for over eighty years, I consider myself somewhat of an expert in blindness.

To give you a better idea of what blind folks have to deal with, experts say that 70 per cent of our sensory input comes as a result of what people see. How can I hope to make up for that much information loss? The answer is that I cannot totally make up for this lost input. I can get almost nothing by visiting art museums, except perhaps for information provided by lectures on whatever is being shown. I will never know the joy of seeing a rainbow, a sunrise or a sunset. Of course, when the sun is getting high in the sky, I'll know it because I will feel its heat but this is far from experiencing the beauty that sighted people perceive.

In a way my world is a rather small one. If I stand up and extend my arms out to each side and turn in a circle, my immediate, physical world ends at the point which can no longer be touched by my finger tips.

Let me amend that. Hearing extends my world beyond this. Sitting in my living room, I hear the air conditioner running to my right. This is close to twenty feet from me. The refrigerator is running in the kitchen, which is to my left. This building is very well constructed or I'd probably hear someone talking in the next apartment.

If I went outdoors now, I'd feel the light breeze which is blowing. I'd hear passing cars and a few song birds. If I'm near our entrance door, I would know when it opens because it makes a sound as it slides open when a person draws near to it.

When it's late in the evening, I can hear the sound of silence. I can sense my heartbeats. I can hear a slight ringing in my ears which wouldn't be noticed except for the absence of other sounds. In silence I can almost feel God's presence. I try to imagine how big His world is. I cannot do it. If you (who are reading this book) try this, the world you imagine won't be any larger than the one I "see!"

Now you have just a small part of what blind people can sense. No doubt questions come to your mind, like: "How does a blind person walk around a house without running into walls and furniture? How many times does he fall?" There are so many answers that I can't address them all.

I'll start with the idea that I am not very familiar with the house. If there's anyone around, I might ask for help getting from place to place. It permits me to get there fast. If nobody is here, I have to walk slowly. I might have my hands extended in front of me just a bit. By walking slowly I have plenty of time to stop if my hands touch a wall or a table. If there are tripping hazards, my foot might strike one of them, and I might or might not have time to stop. A fall under those conditions won't kill me. There's always the possibility of falling down a flight of stairs which is potentially serious. But, however, life does have risks for both you and me.

There's another sense which comes into play. Some call this "facial vision". It is more correctly called "echolocation". If I put my hand near my face, I "feel" its presence. If I'm walking slowly enough, I'll know that I'm approaching a wall and can stop without touching it. I think this has to do with sound reflections which are disturbed by objects coming between me and a sound source—even if I am not aware of an actual sound. I know of no studies about this, but I do know of a crude experiment in which the blind person had his ears covered and this "facial vision" was no longer available to him as an aid.

One question that I can't ever recall my being asked is what happens when I drop something. Can I find and retrieve it? Most of the time I can. Think about dropping a book. It will fall almost straight down. It will make some noise and, of course, I'll hear it. Hearing the book fall gives me a good "fix" on where it landed. It would be nearly at my feet so I can just bend down and pick it up, and probably do it as fast as you could.

If the object is something like a can of tomato juice and it falls onto a wooden floor, I will still most likely find it rather quickly. The can may roll when it lands. The rolling can makes a sound and if I move quickly, I may well be able to find it before it stops moving. The can might strike a wall or other obstruction. I'll hear that and know where it stopped. If a rubber ball drops, I might find it; but more than likely I won't. The ball will almost certainly roll and be soundless unless the ball strikes something while it is still in motion, I'll not likely locate it.

Remember that, like you, we have two ears. We have two because two of them can help us determine the directions of moving objects which produce sound as they go. You have this ability just as it is true of a blind person. In your case, your two eyes provide a three dimensional view of your world.

If I'm outside, I can hear a car and know from which direction it is coming and how far from me it is. If I was about to cross a street, these sound cues will tell me if I have enough time to cross safely. You see, I can also sense the speed of moving objects.

If I walk outside alone, I'll use a white cane. Sighted people know that such a cane identifies me as a blind user. By moving the cane in front of me in the proper way, I always know what lies ahead of me one step before I take it.

Moving along, I find many sighted people can be uncomfortable around blind people. They don't know how to talk to one. The person might yell because he thinks that blindness means deafness. Others just stammer and end up walking away. I try meeting these situations by breaking the ice—asking questions of the sighted persons, thereby putting them at ease. They answer the questions and discover that it's possible to talk to a blind person as they would chat with anyone else. If I hear someone walking by, I'll say, "Hello." That simple act will often be all that's required to be an ice breaker before the person has time to notice that I'm blind.

The one really pet peeve I have runs like this: I'm in a restaurant with a friend. The server takes my friend's order and asks: "What does he want?" A lot of my friends know to tell the server words to the effect: "I don't know what he wants. You'll have to ask him." I used to get really irritated but now I kinda laugh to myself.

Frequently I was asked if I work and was this work done in a "sheltered workshop". They would be lost for words when I said that I was a recording engineer and wrote for a leading magazine which dealt with high fidelity sound. Such people are often nonplused by this.

If you were interviewing a blind person for a job, would you be likely to hire him? I don't know what you personally would do, but I can say there is about a seventy per cent unemployment rate for blind people, even when they are well qualified for a given position. I knew this but even so, I tried for positions for which I was eminently more qualified than the sighted competitors who were also applying for that position. Am I bitter about this? No, but I am a realist as you will learn in later chapters.

Despite those grim statistics, I was gainfully employed as the owner of a successful sound recording business. During my recording work I met people of all ages. Quite a few of them were drifting, finding no life's path. It was my privilege to show them the possibility of doing the same sort of work that I was doing or steering them to allied fields.

I have told you that I have been sightless since birth. If there is any advantage to my situation, that advantage is what I have over those who lost their sight in later life. Such a loss of sight can be the result of many factors. I have had some experience with those whose sight was lost in defending our great country. Remember that 70 per cent of what a person takes in is the result of what his or her eyes see. When that much of a person's input to life is suddenly gone, they might not find it easy to locate food on their dinner plate. They cannot tell what time of day it is. If they drop something, they will likely not be able to locate it and pick it up.

Their senses must be trained to do things which were taken for granted before losing their sight. This is so traumatic that many such people give up and many turn to suicide as their only escape. It takes a great deal of personal courage and a competitive spirit for these folks to "suck it up" and re learn how to live life.

Later I'll have a bit more to say about this, but I will say right now that in order to help these vets, I somehow had to attempt to walk in their shoes. This was one time that I had to imagine how a sighted person functioned prior to his loss of sight so that I could have an idea how to be helpful in his world.

From what you've read up to this point, you can see that I have accomplished quite a bit. But the road was never easy. You'll see it was some time before I realized that I was different; I was blind. Many people tell about their happy childhood. Mine was not at all happy. Even when there were bright moments, sadly I didn't recognize them at the time.

Nothing is as rewarding than guiding lost souls to do something worthwhile. That's why I'm telling you of these things. I'm not bragging, but stating these things in hope that a reader will feel the call to help others. I also hope and pray that a reader or two might be inspired to overcome his own situations which may be weighing them down.

Chapter 2

Let me tell you my story, which began before I arrived. In December, 1901 my dad, Anthony Joseph Giovanelli, was born in a little town in southern Italy. His father was a wine and olive oil taster, and Dad could have done the same thing when he grew up. Even before he was born, his oldest sister came to America to seek her fortune and to walk on streets paved with gold (or so the shipping line advertised). Despite not knowing any English, she worked hard even when ethnic discrimination was extreme. She saved enough money so she could bring the rest of her family to this country. Dad was 6 or 7 years old when he came.

I don't know very much about Dad's family life, but I recall an amusing incident which he told me. Apparently his Mom wanted him to learn various chores around the house, including grating Romano cheese. He enjoyed eating it as he worked; so, his mom insisted that, while he worked, he whistle!

His education ended after the 8th grade because he had to start working. A lot of his early jobs are unknown to me, but I know that he worked as an iceman and a machinist. He was good at that work, but his career ended dramatically when a gear broke loose from the lathe at which he was working and circled his leg, neatly cutting his pants leg off but not touching him! Of course his mother ended that career. Eventually he learned a bit about real estate and was involved in selling some expensive property on eastern Long Island. There were tennis courts on the property, and, because he was a natural athlete, he quickly learned the game.

Meanwhile, in October, 1905, my mother, Elinor Darrow, was born in the small hamlet of Easton, NY. She was a farmer's daughter and naturally had to learn to do farm chores. Her education started in a one-room schoolhouse. Eventually she went to what was then called a "normal" school and graduated with teaching credentials.

She landed her first (and only) teaching job in a school on eastern Long Island, not far from where dad was selling real estate. Mom was not at all interested in sports but she happened to be watching a game of tennis and met dad. As I gathered, she was swept off her feet and it wasn't long before she stopped teaching, they got married, and the newly-weds moved to Florida.

If you consider this for a second, you'll see some inherent problems in their relationship. Dad loved sports and was outgoing and fun-loving. Mom was bookish and introverted. Dad's love of tennis, baseball, and then later on, golf, was to her nothing more than a boy playing and not doing man's work. Dad had no love of books so often made remarks about how Mom couldn't do anything but keep her head in a book.

Dad was raised as a Catholic but actually only started attending mass in later life. Mom had a Quaker background and had Methodist instruction. All went well enough until her pastor criticized the clothes she wore. She seldom set foot in a church from that time on. I can't remember the first time I was in a church! It could have been when my sister, Mary, made her First Communion. The words were strange because the service was in Latin. I didn't know the significance of the experience.

Shortly after moving to Florida, the newlyweds put a down payment on a plot of land on which dad planned to start a truck farm selling vegetables. He always had an eye for good produce.

On January 11, 1928, my sister, Mary Elinor Giovanelli, was born. And then on April 10, 1929, I, Joseph Anthony, arrived on the scene. I can't say that my arrival caused the Great Depression of 1929, but that event did mean trouble for our family. The local bank failed so all the family savings were gone. There was no money to pay the mortgage on our property, so there was nothing left for us but to move North, back to Brooklyn, NY, where my dad's family lived. Mom's family still lived on a farm in upstate New York. There were no chances of finding work there. It was hard enough to find work in Brooklyn, but the odds of finding a job were lots better there. Mom stayed home to raise Mary and me; Dad found odd jobs here and there. Money was tight, but Mom really knew how to stretch a buck!

I don't remember much of these times, but I do remember that we moved into a basement apartment which I think was rent free because my folks took care of the coal furnace and did all the repairs to the property.

When does a person begin to have complete memories? I can only remember a few scraps—snapshots as it were. Looking way back, there was an old and sullen man sitting on an equally old wooden chair. The veneer was chipped in a few places. I found out eventually that he was my dad's dad, slowly dying from prostate cancer. The part I didn't remember nor understand was that Mom was forced to care for Dad's father since Dad's family did not help with this care. For whatever reason, they just assumed that Mom would do what was necessary. This was grossly unfair to her, and it made her extremely bitter. This situation was just one more strain which my sister and I were caught in the middle of.

Reaching further back in those dim recesses of memory, I was on Mom's lap. Her arms were around me. I must have been asleep because I can remember waking up and finding myself still there and feeling a warm, calm, and peaceful feeling. I got up, not knowing that this would be the last time I'd experience anything like that. Mom must have thought I was old enough not to need that kind of closeness. I didn't think about it much then. At some much later time that repressed experience would come into play.

I can still see my bedroom, which was right next to the coal bin. I tried to play in the bin but found out about dust, and Mom kept me away because of how I could get my clothes dirty! My sister played with the girls in the neighborhood but somehow I wasn't making friends with the boys, and didn't know why. I hadn't yet understood the difference between me and other kids.

Meanwhile, Dad got work driving a truck, delivering flowers for a local florist. This would be the start of better times, but Mom didn't know it then.

Even before Mary started kindergarten Mom taught us to count to a hundred. I still recall that if we went past 100, we figured that the next hundred would be a hundred a hundred. When Mary started going to school, umom would take me along. I was a year younger than Mary so wouldn't start school yet, but even so, as we walked, mom would show me the red light signal boxes, mail boxes and fire alarm boxes. She taught me to recognize by touch, the large, raised letters. I quickly learned to read "Traffic Control Box New York City," or the one which said, "In case of fire, open door and pull hook way down". She wouldn't let me pull it though, and that was disappointing!

Mary started kindergarten as I said. While Mom was teaching me to read, I sure remember Dad showing me how to tell time by removing the glass which covered the clock face and explaining the numbers as they relate to hours and minutes, as well as the position of the hands in relation to the numbers. He also showed me how to use a screwdriver and pliers so I could do small mechanical tasks. By feel I found the indentation in the screw and learned how to fit the head of the screwdriver in and turn it, feeling the turning with my hands. I learned that nuts used on bolts had several sides, and the pliers would hold on to those and could then be turned to tightened the nut on the bolt—or take the nut off.

These were important lessons because I became fascinated with clockwork and found out how to open up things which would have been better to be left closed. I remember opening a switch box and learning about electricity and electric shocks the hard way. I bravely closed that box and learned that electricity could be a friend but that it does need to be respected.

Then there was the lesson that Dad taught me indirectly. He had an expensive pocket watch, and I thought I'd like to see what was inside its case. I forced it open and bent the sections holding the gearing. The watch was beyond repair! Dad walked into the room and asked what I was doing.

"Nothing," I said and laid the parts on the dresser—not realizing that he knew what I just did. I got a pretty good spanking, I mean really good—and he ran out of the house. Sure, I deserved it, but I wondered how he knew that I put all the broken parts on the dresser. I knew there was something not quite right, but I could not imagine what it was. That puzzled me how Dad could sometimes know things which I could not know. I can't remember when my parents told me that I was blind and how that fit into the puzzle.

My next mistake was the time I threw a stone and accidentally broke a window. I figured I could blame the Smith brothers because

Mom didn't like them. I got another spanking! Mom knew that I was the culprit, but how did she know that? She told me that she saw me. I didn't know that word, but I made the connection between that event and the one where dad knew that I destroyed the watch. I gradually realized that this "seeing" was something that most people did but that I could not do. "Hmm," I told myself. "This must be why the kids didn't want to play with me. Yeah, I realized that I was different, and blindness was what made me that way!

When I think back on ruining a watch, breaking a window, this next little caper was the crowning achievement in those early child days. Brother! If I had been caught this time, it could have had consequences for both me and my folks!

Everyone was out—including the tenant on the first floor. I knew that this tenant stored things in our basement area. I wanted to explore what was there. Somehow I just knew there was a treasure if I could only find it.

Indeed there was! I found an elaborate music box. That looked like real fun, and it was! By that time I knew more about looking into a mechanism without destroying it like I did with Dad's watch. I found that the arrangement for winding it up was broken. I made a temporary repair and partially wound it. What a glorious sound! There were little drums, and a great music box—not like the little movements found in jewelry boxes. This one had lots more notes. I let it run down and just in time. The tenant came home. If she had gotten there just a bit sooner, she would have heard the thing playing, and I'd have been in trouble again. That was too close for comfort. So despite my wanting to get back to it, I left that box alone!

Many years later when I was well out of college, I happened to meet the lady. I dared to tell her about my experience with her wonderful music box and asked if she still owned it. Alas! Someone bought it for the internal parts. If the buyer was a dealer, it would have been obvious to him that he could have repaired it and sold it for quite a bit. Knowing what I know now, I have to guess that he would have been able to sell it for at least two thousand dollars.

Chapter 3

Mom, Dad, and probably my sister each knew that I wasn't quite like other people. Mom was a school teacher by training, and she wanted me to be educated just like my sister Mary. One of the things a good teacher learns is to know how to find information on any given subject. She read all she could about the education of blind children. By checking with the New York City Board of Education she found that there was a school in Brooklyn (Public School 93) which had some resources for educating blind children and how to meet their special needs. This was a regular public school with the addition of a "home room" to which blind or partially sighted kids would go so they could get the special skills that are essential, such as learning Braille and working with arithmetic.

Perhaps I should stop to tell you that partially sighted people are sometimes considered to be legally blind. That condition is met if the person can vaguely see an object at a distance of twenty feet while a person with average sight could see the object at a distance of 200 feet.

I must have been six years old when I started school. Memories of those early days are hazy. I can tell you that the school was not near home. I had to get there by trolley car, which took about 20 minutes each way. Mom had to take me there in the morning, go home and do whatever needed doing, come back and pick me up and then take me back home. It was a very long time before I realized what a sacrifice she made in order for me to get an education. She'd have to do even more later.

In the beginning I met the other kids who used the home room. When I think back on it, it was like a one-room schoolhouse with children of all ages from early grades through the eighth grade. Not all those kids were very nice, and I learned which ones to avoid. Melvin and Elwood really were mean and I was afraid of them. Later I learned that I had good reason for my feelings.

On the other hand there were some very nice ones. I'll never forget Dorothy. She wasn't always patient with me because I didn't know things which she thought I should. Even so, she was special in some indefinable way. Generally she treated me great. Then she started missing more and more school days. Eventually she just didn't come back. I heard about her headaches, her upset stomachs. Then I was told that she had died as the result of a brain tumor. I cried like crazy; I just couldn't believe that I'd never hear her voice or touch her hand again, though it was so nice at the time. That sort of contact would play a part in later life.

Just about that time George Gershwin died from that same malady. That made me very sad. I liked his music and knew that we lost an irreplaceable giant! Only now, as I recall, that sadness was also because of losing Dorothy!

The home room teacher was Mrs. DiPritoro, who was really an excellent person, absolutely dedicated to her work. Quite soon she introduced me to Braille. There are two basic ways to write Braille—one which employs what is called a Braille slate. The other is to use what's known as a Braille writer. The slate is very slow compared to the speed of a Braille writer. (For information about the Braille system or the methods for working out arithmetic problems, see appendix A.)

The plan was, I think, for me to start with the Braille writer immediately, but alas! When I was shown one of these devices, my curiosity got the better of me and I started to dismantle the thing. Obviously Mrs. DiPritoro made me start instead with the slate and stylus. (See Appendix A.)

I didn't know why I was in school; so, I didn't behave very well. I seldom did what I was told to do. I'd ask everyone I could if they had any old clocks for me to mess with. I told you that Mrs. DiPritoro was dedicated, and one day she said that if I'd pay attention and do as I was directed, that she would give me a couple of clocks! Wow! I wanted them, and worked very hard so I'd get them as soon as possible. While doing all of this, I got really interested in what I was supposed to learn. I enjoyed some of the stories in the Braille books, so I read them and was always ready with my assignments. The day finally came when the clocks were given to me. Of course I was excited, and enjoyed learning a lot about how the gears worked to move the hands around the dial. By then, however, I was so interested in schooling that I continued to work hard.

There came a day when I left that home room for the first time, and entered my regular grade with sighted students. After my daily Grade work I would return to the home room for more specialized training in learning more about Braille or about arithmetic. I can't remember what I was supposed to do in those Grade classes, but apparently I was given oral tests, which I passed in a way. You'll see that this "way" was not a good one. The way the grades and seating were set up, I didn't get to know the sighted students except for one or two who were assigned to take me back to the home room.

Three years went by, and Mrs. DiPritoro was promoted and left us. Mrs. Burns was her replacement and was a nice lady but didn't have the forcefulness needed to run this home room. I became her pet, and some of the kids started hating me because of that.

It became obvious to my mother that something was wrong. The various teachers just passed me along from one grade to the next without regard to how much I really learned, so Mom knew I needed to go to a school which was better equipped to handle blind students. I had a terrible premonition that this change would not be a good or happy one.

Chapter 4

You know how it is with books: there are flashbacks. In this chapter I'll share some of mine.

I'm back at just about the time I started going to that public school. I remember the time when I first visited my grandparents and "seeing" the farm where Mom grew up. I remember getting there on a Hudson River Night Boat. I loved the breeze, the motion of the boat. We docked in early morning and were met by a man who drove us to the farm.

I had to nap on a horsehair sofa that day—and it was itchy. I remember when I first had to walk on the grass. Barefoot or not, the change in the feel of walking was scary, and I wished I was somewhere else! I had never felt grass under my feet until then. I guess I was at Grandma's for a month and I gradually got used to the house and yard and learned about life without indoor plumbing and running water. I really began to love that farm and my grandparents.

At the farm I met Aunt Avis, Mom's sister. I'm trying to find a way to describe her. I can't tell you what she was wearing nor the color of her hair or whether she was fat or thin. I can tell you that she didn't wear perfume and that she smoked lots of cigarettes. She did a lot of reading, just like Mom did. She was assigned to bathe me; after all, I was a little kid and knew nothing about rustic bathing. It was kinda like a sponge bath. She really scrubbed me good and hard! I guess I got clean, even if I seemed to lose all of my skin!

Each year I would see her, and I wasn't sure that I liked her much. I used to ask her lots of questions, like "what makes a thunderstorm happen?" She gave me a general idea of the process. I also tried her on radio questions, but she had no answers. She told me to listen to a program called "Science Forum," and all my questions would be answered. It was only broadcast on a local station, but each summer I listened to that show religiously. It was truly an education. I remember one show in which the audience was introduced to experiments conducted by the Bell Telephone Laboratory. Two microphones were placed in front of a symphony orchestra and the sounds from those two mikes were transmitted by telephone line to a distant city. They called the result "binaural sound". We could only hear about it; we could not hear that sound for ourselves. The people on the show said that the sound of the orchestra was just as it would have been heard had we been present in the room in which the musicians were performing. In time this process would become very important in my life.

There were so many things to experience, like riding in the rumble seat of Grandpa's car. Sometimes Aunt Kitty and Uncle Arthur would come to see us. Uncle "Art" was Mom's brother; Aunt Kitty was his wife. I liked Aunt Kitty—she made the best blueberry muffins (and I still think so). She also understood how mechanical things work, which was fascinating to me. Uncle Art was a tease. I didn't understand teasing but eventually did. Over many years I learned to do it, much to Mary's regret. And yes, I must confess that I still resort to it with my friends.

I lived with my grandparents during many summers. I learned to pump water to fill Grandma's washtubs. I learned about milk and cream and how they were separated by means of a machine called a separator. It was a centrifuge, and the arrangement by which the separation worked involved a cone-shaped structure made from many parts which had to be removed first from the separator, disassembled for scalding and then reassembled prior to putting the unit back into the separator. I loved working with that; I could do it faster than grandpa could. Grandpa gave me that job because it made his life easier, and it gave me something important to do. It's necessary that the separator parts rotate at a rather precise speed as noted by an alternate ringing and tapping sound. The space from one to the next sound had to be even, and I could get that absolutely right. Eventually Grandpa gave me the job of doing all these things on my own with no supervision. I mean to tell you, that was the biggest thrill of my life at that time.

During an exploration of the house, I came to the parlor. In it there was an old pump organ. How could I have guessed that it would be significant? I figured out how to get sound from it, and was able to pick out melodies. That was fun, but somehow I knew there was more than melody in music. I knew that I should play more than a note at a time. But what were those notes? Any that I tried didn't sound right, and that kept me from playing that organ with real enjoyment, but I spent quite a bit of time each summer "messing" with it.

I didn't realize how necessary it was for me to spend those summers in that quiet, rural place!

Back in Brooklyn I learned how to go around my block. I suppose it was Mom who taught me how to do it. I would go around in a counterclockwise direction. This meant that I would stay near the buildings on my left. By using "facial vision" I could sense the building. Sometimes I'd put my left hand out to check for doorways and where the building began again. I could sense the corners most of the time. Sometimes there were clues such as a hedge or a high stoop. Maybe it was halfway around the block where there were some wide, open spaces. These were garages, and I was taught to listen for cars which might be coming in or out of them.

What was under my feet was important. If I stepped on a large metal plate which gave a bit as I stepped on it, I'd know this was a cellar entrance to one of the buildings. Sometimes the cellar door was open, and I learned to know that because my leg would hit a bar. That was a guard used to keep someone from falling down the steps. I learned how to walk to the right of this for a couple of steps before I could move back to my normal path. Eventually I'd get back to my own front stoop. Now I could make the circuit with no help.

It was wonderful to leave the house, make a left turn past the drugstore, candy store, garages and some houses. What a feeling it was to be able to go into the candy store and buy penny candy and come back home without help. That was a small step about living independently, but there was so very much more to unravel. One day I tried to learn how to use roller skates, starting with just one skate. I accidentally ran into some people! They sure didn't like that, to say the least. That was the end of my roller skating career!

I didn't know what Mom went through because of me. More than one person told her that she must have been a real sinner or she wouldn't have had a blind child! "You probably had syphilis," they'd say. Folks would tell me that I didn't belong on the street, and that I should be in an institution! I didn't know what that meant, but it upset me nonetheless.

We had a radio, and early on I became fascinated with it. Where were the people whose voices I heard? One day when my folks were out, I moved the big radio cabinet out from the wall and crawled behind it to find the people. What I saw were hot glass bottles or bulbs near the top of the box. Under the main part of the radio I saw a structure which held a cone-shaped piece of paper, and the paper was moving ever so slightly as people talked. This made no sense to me, and from then on I wanted to solve the mystery of that magic cabinet.

I got hooked on the programs of the time: Don Winslow of the Navy, Terry and the Pirates, The Green Hornet and a ton more. I listened to soap operas and started imitating the way some of the women on those shows talked. This set off alarm bells in Mom's head! She talked about that new school that I'd have to go to.

I remember Sundays. They were special in an indefinable way. There were just a few cars running in the streets. There were lots of church bells. Sitting outside on our front stoop, the sounds, the silence, and just the entire ambiance were mystical!

One incredible day presented me with my first big mechanical challenge! Dad dropped our alarm clock. That was a virtual catastrophe, given that we were living in The Great Depression and Mom wasn't sure we could buy another clock. In any event the clock was broken so I ended up with it! I opened the clock and found that the balance wheel was out of its pivots. I got dad's pliers and loosened one of the pivots so that I could get one end of the balance wheel shaft into its hole. Now there was clearance enough to get the other end of the shaft to slip into the other pivot point. I had to line up the wheel with the lever so the wheel could be pushed by the lever. (For more details about my thought processes about the working of that clock see appendix B.)

When I knew I had it right, I tightened the pivot which I had previously loosened. The clock worked almost perfectly. The ticks should be evenly spaced, one to the next, but, because the thin restoring spring had been bent, the ticks were uneven. Nevertheless I proudly handed it to my parents who were absolutely shocked that I managed all that! Ya know what? When I look back on that, I still wonder how I managed to do it. I was only 8 years old! I can hardly believe that the clock incident happened in 1937! Here I am now, in 2009. It's astounding to me that I can recall that event when it happened so very long ago. But I digress.

The routine of school was by now—well, routine ... Home Room to a normal class and back.

More fun awaited me the next year. Dad gave me a crystal radio set kit. The parts were supposed to be mounted onto a small board, which I didn't have. Dad explained how the parts were wired together, and I completed that small project in a rather long time, but I finished it, even though the parts were hooked together loosely!

Dad ran what he called an aerial and a ground wire into my bedroom because in order for this crystal set to work it had to be connected to them. I connected the earphones and put them on. I thought I heard something but wasn't sure. I was told to slide a ball across the coil winding. I heard a station! I was also told to move a rather stiff wire (a"cat's whisker") around the surface of what Dad called a crystal, to locate a place where the radio station would be heard at its highest possible volume. I then found that I could slide the ball along the coil and could then hear two or three additional stations. My dad said that radio stations were picked up out of the air. I didn't yet understand what the ground was for but I figured out that it was the aerial which somehow attracted the stations. That was wrong but what the hey!

It wasn't really a "whizz bang" moment, but it gradually came to me that our big radio cabinet worked like a crystal set ... that there were no men hiding in dark corners. When hearing the loudest stations, I could stick my finger into the hole at the center of one of the earphones and feel a piece of metal vibrating. I put that together with what I learned about the "big radio". The vibrating piece of paper and the vibrations inside the headphones were, in some way, the means by which the sound was heard. I was learning something concrete about how radios worked!

About that time, a radio repair shop opened and it was right next door. It was easy for me to find so I often went there just to stand around and hear the techie talk between the owner and his assistant. The owner was a kindly German fella named Walter Schmidt. He showed me things, such as a tube tester. I didn't understand what it really did. When our radio quit working (right in the middle of an episode of "The Lone Ranger") Mr. Schmidt came to our house to repair it. Mr. Schmidt was a real genius. He repaired it, of course, but he went beyond that. He knew that this old set could sound better than it ever had. What he did in order to make our set sound good was to add something which was many years ahead of its time. When he finished, the radio sounded unbelievably rich. Previous to the repair I barely heard the bass tones in music, but after the repair the bass was solid. Also, there was a sweetness to the sound which I had never heard. I was completely overwhelmed by the tone of this radio. More than ever I wanted to know about radio and good sound!

One day when I went into his shop, he had a real surprise for me. He gave me a table radio which actually worked! It was mine to keep! That radio could be tuned slightly above the top end of the AM broadcast band and at that point I sometime heard people talking about technical things which sounded interesting, but I had no idea what they were really saying. They talked about "modulation transformers", "signal shifters", and lots more things. What I was hearing were "hams" discussing their equipment. I wanted to be just like them. On another visit he showed me a small box which he said was a way to send out radio signals to all the houses in the area. He had a phonograph connected to it and he was playing the largest disks I ever saw. They were 16 inches in diameter!

Meanwhile each Saturday evening all the neighbors could hear strange sounds coming from the radio shop. I could tell there was a large crowd cheering about something. There was a guy speaking—shouting really. Mom said the speaker's name was Hitler, and she wouldn't let me go into that shop again.

I had my tonsils removed about then, and Mr. Schmidt came to our house to wish me well. He was crying with joy about something going on in his country. I suspect now that he was overjoyed about the take-over of the Sudeten Land (then a part of Czechoslovakia), which led to the start of World War II. Because Mr. Schmidt was so happy, I also began to root for Germany!

I was a pretty self-absorbed kid then so never knew that things were actually looking up for my family. Between runs delivering flowers, Dad hung around the flower shop watching how flowers could be arranged in different ways to form bouquets, funeral blankets, corsages and more. During a very hectic time at the shop Dad asked if he could try his hand at floral arranging. He proved to be really exceptional. He drove the truck less and stayed in the shop more. He got a slight pay raise.

Mom thought that she had to start working so she could save money "for a rainy day". Around this time the country of India was a huge topic in newspapers and magazines. The turban was becoming fashionable. She found that there was a shop near where my school was that gave out piece work making these turbans at home. She got the job and she bought a sewing machine so she could do more piecework than she could sew by hand. Maybe I'm all wet, but I think she had to make twenty dozen of these each day. I still remember the large box of cloth which was already cut according to the proper shape. What she had to do was follow a pattern which showed how to sew each turban. I don't know much more about that, but I remember that she took a couple of classes from the Singer Sewing Machine Company so she could do her work with as much speed and accuracy as possible.

I remember getting on the trolley and Mom would be carrying a box of the completed garments. If you really want to appreciate what Mom was going through, think about this. She spent eighty minutes a day getting to and from my school. She had to cook meals, clean the house, and do the piecework. Then there was my sister, Mary. She was getting more irritable almost by the day. I guess she was ten years old and was losing weight and was down to sixty pounds. Our doctor found that she had a digestive disorder which prevented her from properly absorbing food. She had to go on a special and strict diet. To make meal planning simpler, we were to a great extent, on that diet. I had no idea what really was going on in our family. I needed to think about more than me as the center of the universe.

One of the things which my sister Mary could eat was something I never had before—grilled cheese sandwiches. I loved them. They were made in a waffle iron. Making grilled cheese sandwiches was the beginning of my learning to cook.

I remember that equipment. I remember that you couldn't put the sandwich into it until a little arrow moved to the word "bake". I couldn't read the word but I could recognize the position of the sliding arrow so I learned to put sandwiches into the waffle iron when the arrow was at the right place. I learned to listen for the way the cheese sizzled. I learned that when the sizzling had gotten to sound at just the right loudness, the sandwiches were done. If I waited too long, the cheese would dribble out of the sandwich and the griddles would be a sticky mess—which I didn't know how to clean up.

There were many more lessons over time. Our gas stove didn't have a pilot light. The flame had to be lit using wooden kitchen matches. I learned how to strike a match on the rough surface of one of the burners, turn the gas on, and then bring the match near the burner. I'd hear a slight "wuushs" and feel heat. That's how I knew the flame was lit. Using the oven had its own set of hurdles. The heat scared me. Lighting the oven burner gave me the shakes because I had to light the match and bend down so I could move it into the oven and hope I was near enough to the burner so the gas would "catch". Over lots of years I learned how to boil water, how to fry hamburgers, how to use a timer to aid in figuring out when a food was cooked. In addition to using a timer, I learned to tell the state of a food by the way it sizzled and by its aroma. I learned how to set the temperature by the position of the pointer on the knob which set the strength of the flame and how to place a pan on an oven shelf without getting burned. I learned to use pot holders to protect my hands from coming into contact with the inside of the oven.

Much of the way we blind people cook is by the sound or the smell of the cooking food. I learned how to prepare a complete meal. Doing this was hard and I avoided doing it if possible.

It was the summer of 1938 I guess, when I went to Grandma's farm, and Mary went off to a special hospital for kids with her stomach condition. What a great summer it was! I learned to ride one of Grandpa's work horses bareback! I had the separator to work with. I had that parlor organ to play (or try to). I got to know some of the kids from neighboring farms. That was great—except for a couple of times when they would tease me by hitting me lightly and then run away. I even got a couple of clocks. These had gongs which struck the hour and pendulums which hung from little hooks and I found that the speed at which the pendulums moved determined how accurate these clocks would keep time. I figured out how the gong would sound the correct hour.

The kids showed me how to use Dixie cups and a length of thin wire to make a crude "telephone". If we kept the wire real tight, we could carry on a conversation as I talked into one cup and my friend would talk into the other. I think we could talk as much as 50 feet apart; then after that the sound was just too blurred. A thin thread worked better than the wire.

Grandma read stories to me from the Bible. I thought they were the same kind of stories I already knew about, like "Hansel and Gretle", "Snow White and the Seven Dwarfs", "Hans Brinker and the Silver Skates", etc.

I really did enjoy that time; it was probably the nicest time I ever spent up to that point in my life. Do ya know what the best part of it was? My sister and my folks weren't there. I didn't have to share anything with anyone!

Aunt Avis was there as usual, and I could tell her that I was still listening to "Science Forum". Aunt Kitty and Uncle Art were there quite often; they only lived thirty miles from the farm. They had a car like Grandpa's and I got to ride in the rumble seat and feel the wind rush by as we drove. It's too bad we don't have cars like that now. I guess the closest thing to riding in a rumble seat is riding in an open convertible, but the rumble seat is better, at least it was in my memory.

Sometimes I'd go to their house. I can still taste Aunt Kitty's blueberry muffins. As I said earlier, I've never had better ones! On one magic day she showed me their Victrola. She showed me how to play records and I was captivated. Just a few years later I'd own a much smaller version.

There was still a bit of summer vacation left when I returned from the farm. I spent a few days with folks from Dad's side of the family. They lived in a bungalow near the ocean. I was afraid of the sand when I first went there but I learned not to mind it at all by the time I went back home.

My aunt Esther was the matriarch of that family. Could she ever cook! You should taste her spaghetti! ... that great tomato sauce spiced with garlic, basil, parsley, and a ton of other things. Somehow it didn't matter how many people she had to cook for. Usually there were seven or eight of us there, but one day Aunt Esther found that we were going to have 30 people that night. She shouted orders to each of her children in her Italian accent: "Marie, you's gonna grata the cheese." Josephine, yous-a-break up the spaghet," and so it went. How could it be that she had enough food and how could 30 people fit into those tiny rooms? Well, us kids ate on the porch, and lots of people ate in shifts.

The family next door roasted marshmallows which I'd never had before. What a way to end the summer! Over many years our family and lots of Dad's relatives spent many happy hours there, building memories which would last a lifetime. One wonderful memory was our July Fourth visits. The neighbors and family members chipped in so my Uncle Dominic could buy fireworks, and I don't mean those little peewees. Many were huge "shells" which sounded like cannons. He was taught to handle fireworks safely back when he still lived in Italy.

This would be my last year in public school. I had no idea that I wasn't learning anything—but that fact would catch up with me in horrible ways just a year later.

Nearly two months passed. It's the last Sunday of October, the night before Halloween. As usual, I was listening to the radio. "The Mercury Theater on the Air" was just starting. Orson Welles said that we were in for a special dramatization of "War of the Worlds". The plot centered around an invasion by Martians. We heard a dance band and it was interrupted by a news flash about the invasion. Despite the fact that the initial landing took place in a small town in New Jersey, there was a reporter there to bring us the terrifying news. How could he have gotten there so fast? Well, anything can happen in a radio play; I heard of that sort of thing quite often. The program ended because the hour was up, when all the Martians were killed by birds.

Even before the show closed, I heard lots of noise in the street outside our home. Mom and Dad came home and told me about the fact that we were at war with Mars. Later I heard about panics in various parts of the country. I thought about this: "It couldn't be that people were acting crazy because of a good radio play?" Sure enough, it was that play which shook up the Nation. I began to think that it was really easy to insight a mob into a frenzy. Isn't that what was happening in Germany when Hitler was ranting and raving!

Almost two months went by. It was the Christmas Season. We saved a few pennies so we could buy a present for each of our parents. Dad set up our tree, and Mom showed Mary and me how to decorate a tree. I couldn't handle putting the roping and the lights in the best places for a good effect. I had no trouble with hanging the ornaments. I learned to place them randomly which usually made for a good show. Mary also helped with them. We shared in putting the tinsel on. Eventually the tree trimming became a tradition which lasted till 1980—the last Christmas before Mary died from the ravages of cancer. She was only 51!!

Another part of that tradition was listening to "A Christmas Carol," as broadcast each year starring both Orson Welles and Lionel Barrymore. In those early years one of the stars narrated and the other played Scrooge. It wasn't long, however, before Barrymore always played Scrooge. I think our whole family was riveted to the radio for the full hour of the show. As time went on, the sponsors reduced the show to just a half hour, and much of its magic was lost.

We had those traditions but we were never really taught the full and exact meaning of that special day. Lots of times Dad took Mary and me to Midnight Mass. I don't think either of us wanted to go, but after we came home from the Mass, Dad broke out all kinds of great Italian cold cuts and pastries, and Mom would make hot chocolate. Doing these things became yet another tradition. In fact, Mom's hot chocolate is still fondly remembered by some of my cousins. It was so hot that we were all sure that it would never get cool enough to drink!

Often we had really great New Year's Eve parties. I remember one in which Dad introduced me to whisky on the stroke of midnight. He wanted Mary and me to know about what the adults drank because he believed it was important for our education. Occasionally he would offer us a small glass of wine. I think he did us a favor. He wanted us to taste these things at home rather than learning about them from strangers. I love a shot once in a while to this day. I think that because of the way Dad introduced them, we learned to savor them and not have too much liquor. We often had lots of Dad's relatives in for fabulous, Italian dinners. Mom wasn't Italian but she sure did learn how to prepare the food. She learned a lot from my Aunt Esther.

Time moved on relentlessly till the dreaded day when I transferred to a boarding school for the blind. When I look back on that time, I still have no idea why I knew that the school would be traumatic. Was it because I was afraid of most new experiences? Would my life have been different if I had no fear or premonition of problems? Had I looked forward to a new situation, would this have made my experiences with the other kids different from what they turned out to be? I'll never know so all I can do is tell you how things were for me and show you what I eventually overcame.

About that time, however, I got a hold of some old telephones. We didn't have one, but I had heard about them. I played with them. I had a battery and figured out a way to connect two telephones together so I could talk to my sister who was in another room. I didn't know how to make the bell ring so that Mary could know when to pick up the phone.

Time never stopped. I could almost feel it pulling me down to some mysterious and terrifying place. I'm 10 now. I have to say goodbye to Mrs. Burns and the few friends I made in good old Public School 93. Yes, I was going to a new school, and I just knew it would be big-time trouble!

First, however, there was this summer of 1939 to get through and all the time dreading that new school. There was one really bright spot though. I think I'm right when I tell you that the first New York World's Fair opened. Our whole family crowded onto the Long Island Railroad train which took us to the Fair grounds. There were merry-go-rounds, not the little ones which were sometimes on the streets, but big ones with great music coming from complex machines. There were many educational exhibits. Because Mary and I were born in Florida, we were taken to the Florida Building. I have to say that all I can remember was the great "ices" they served. Dad took me to the Italian building. I couldn't appreciate the fine Italian art works, but I was fascinated with the history of flight from the viewpoint of pioneering Italian aviators.

I saw many wonders, but two stand out. One was the RCA building. A movie was running which showed the various aspects of something called "television". Pictures could be sent right to our homes with no wires connecting the house with the studio. The description of the way pictures were transmitted and then converted into pictures was over my head, but I got enough of an idea that this was a special kind of radio. Outside the theater, there was a man demonstrating a very small, battery-operated radio. They let me look at it and tune in various stations. I remember that it was housed in a metal cabinet. I remembered that set for many years because one of the guys in my college dorm had that exact model radio and he asked me to repair it for him.

Then there was the Bell Telephone Laboratories exhibit. What I remember was a demonstration of speech performed on a machine. The demonstrator typed on a keyboard and what he typed could be heard as words and sentences. Just by changing inflections, the machine changed the meaning of a sentence. Think about this sentence: "She saw me." Merely by changing which word was accented, the sentence would have three, different meanings. What practical purpose was there to such a machine? I'd find out perhaps forty years later.

My folks enrolled me in a summer camp in New Jersey for blind boys. I'd been away from home before, but never stayed with complete strangers. The first day I was there, kids welcomed me by inviting me to go on the big merry-go-round. It was a platform suspended on an axle about two inches from the ground. There were four bars radiating from the center to the outer edge of the platform. Four people could stand on it and hold onto a bar while the merry-go-round was moving. To get it going we had to grab a bar and run as fast as possible and then get on to the platform. When I got on the contraption, the other guys were still running in order to get more speed. It was too much for me, and I flew off and hit the concrete real hard. I was shaken up but otherwise was fine. I was really embarrassed and got the feeling that this was just the beginning of things I wasn't good enough to handle, and I was right!

There were many activities including swimming. I already had learned to hate and fear the water. Making matters worse for me, the walk to the beach was on a narrow pier so it was possible to fall into deep water. I couldn't move because of fear, and lots of kids were backed up behind me. They started pushing and that made it worse. Nobody cared that I was in trouble. I don't even know how I eventually got off that pier. Now I was forced to walk into the water. A counselor handed me what he called a "flutter board". By holding onto it I was able to stay afloat. I kinda liked that feeling, but I never did learn to let go and learn to swim. To this day I only know a little about doing the "doggie paddle". Then there was the wrestling match. When my turn came, I had no idea what wrestling was. Within a second after the start of the match I was pinned. I was humiliated in front of everyone. That month in camp dragged by. The camp was built on marshy, swampy land. No way to count the mosquitoes! Because of the constant dampness, clothes were never dry. When Mom saw my clothes and how mildewed they were, she said she'd never again send me to that camp, which was just fine with me!

There came a day shortly before the end of the camping season when a violent storm came through the camp. The roads were flooded. I can't recall why but I left my cabin to get a feel for what was happening. I walked a few steps through the slush and I heard a boy crying. I went over to him and found him kneeling in the muck. I touched him and noticed he had on a jacket and tie. I asked him what was wrong and why he was kneeling in the mud. He said that he was supposed to go to church and was told that he couldn't go because the bus couldn't pick him up. He was asking God to forgive him. He had been taught that he must never miss church. He thought that he committed what he called a "mortal sin". I didn't know what that was but I told him that it seemed to me that God wouldn't be mad at him because there was no way to get to church. Nothing I said was any comfort. I left him still kneeling and crying. His name was Albert Peroni, an orphan who lived in a religious school for the blind. Just a few years later I would become more involved with that pathetic boy.

On the last night we had an awards banquet. I had learned some camp songs and was asked to sing them. I actually got some applause! Awards were given out; I received one for "good sportsmanship". I almost laughed because I wasn't a good sport, but just tried not to show my real feelings which made the counselors think I handled things bravely.

I couldn't wait till I got to my Grandparents' farm. Even there I was not able to shake off that feeling that my future in the new school would be bleak. I performed the various chores I'd learned to do. Added to my list was pulling weeds. I learned to know what was or was not a weed. It was hard work, but I really didn't mind. There were hay rides, but I didn't like them. I'd always have a headache and I couldn't breathe easily. Mom thought I was trying to get away without going on these rides. I finally figured out, years later, that I was allergic to hay and grass.

One day I was sitting on the front porch, seated in my favorite rocker. Grandpa was sitting with me waiting for somebody. The man arrived and talked earnestly with Grandpa. As I think about that time, it's a wonder he didn't ask me to leave. He was talking grown-up stuff which meant little at first. Eventually the visitor told Grandpa that many of the local farmers were starting a co-op. It would invest in modern machines which each farmer would use when his crops were harvested. It would mean less work for each farmer and would also result in greater production. It sounded great to me, but what does a kid know? Grandpa was a wonderful man, but he was fearful of anything new. He knew horses and mistrusted gas-driven machines. He turned down the chance to join. I felt terrible, but a kid doesn't have much of a say, does he?

We often took trips to local points of interest or to great places to have picnics. Some of my cousins came to the farm for a visit and, during a drive to a picnic, my cousin, in the car ahead of us, called out for us to stop and listen. He opened the door. His radio was on and Winston Churchill was speaking from England, declaring war on Germany. I can't say I understood the full significance of this, but it was a rather sober picnic. Talk was really subdued.

Chapter 5

We came home. It was a special weekend. My family and I went to look at an apartment. We were still living in that house in which my bedroom was near the coal bin. Just from this fact you can see that our family's finances were improving. The apartment was small—just three rooms. I don't remember the sleeping arrangements, but I knew it would be crowded. It was on the third floor of a four-story walk-up. I didn't think I would like that apartment, but, like everything else in my life at that time, I had no say about it. Come to think about it, I simply couldn't handle any changes. I'd miss the little backyard where Mary and I played. I'd miss the little storage shed where I kept some of the things I played with. To add to this awful time, I would be going to my new school at the end of the weekend. I knew that when I came home from that school, I'd be living in a strange place. Well, nothing I could do about that.

The day came! I was on my way to the school: The New York Institute for the Education of the Blind. I did not yet know that I was beginning my new education in a school which has a rich history, dating from 1831. Many people of note got their start in its halls, such people as Fanny Crosby, the famed writer of hymns. Her most beloved of them all was "Blessed Assurance".

The school was far away in the Bronx. The trip took an hour and a half each way by subway and a bit of walking. What that meant was that my folks couldn't take me back and forth each day, so I became a boarder and would be staying there from Sunday evenings to Friday afternoons!

I had to learn how to navigate the grounds because the school was not the way you might think a school should look. It was a campus that sprawled over 14 acres. The property was surrounded by a high fence and it could be entered by means of two or three gates. Most of us entered through the main gate. It was a walk of perhaps 50 feet into what was called an arcade. (This was a covered, concrete walkway with large concrete pillars supporting its roof.) If you turn left and walked into it, you would arrive at the dining room. A right turn brings you to a two-story dormitory building. This is where the younger kids like me lived. The second story consisted of a second dorm for somewhat older kids. If you walked nearly to the end of this arcade, there was another dorm building similar to the first one, and this housed the older guys, those in high school.

I don't remember the exact layout of the grounds, but as I recall, there was a T in the sidewalk just a few feet before you got to the arcade. Going to the right took you to the four-story school building. A left turn brought you to what was usually referred to as "the girls' side". What I have described is what's called the upper school. Somewhere on campus was the Lower School which was both the dorm and school building for the kids in grades 1-4. In another part of the campus there were some chicken coops and kennels which were there to aid in teaching animal husbandry to those who wanted such education.

Like the public school, this school had both blind and partially sighted students. These sighted kids fell into the legally blind category. I was amazed at how those kids could handle whatever sight they had. Their small amount of sight gave them a huge advantage over those of us who were completely blind.

That first full day seemed OK. I ran into a few of the kids who were at that summer camp. I began to get acquainted with my teachers. I was given the same assignments as the rest of the kids in the 5th grade class. My reading was very slow. Oral spelling was a nightmare because I could hardly spell any word correctly. Kids tittered with each misspelled word. And although not always true, it was the sighted kids who gave me many of my problems. "Yes," I thought, "this is worse than I imagined it would be."

Gym was—well, I don't know how to put it. There was a running track which the kids handled great except for me. The kids found me to be an easy mark. They'd roughly throw me around and I had no way of stopping them. I tried asking the gym teacher for help, but all he said was that I'd have to get used to it. Before each gym class we had to change into a kind of uniform called a "gym suit". My shoes wouldn't work well on the gym floor so I had to wear sneakers. I tell you this boring stuff because it took me forever to change into this apparel. That always made me late for the class, which meant that the boys and the teacher were always on my case! I had to do extra running as punishment. You'll see that I had a similar situation the next year.

As I walked around the grounds, the kids teased me: I remember them telling me to walk slowly because there was a lake which I could fall into. There was no lake, of course.

I just didn't know anything about dormitory living, like making a bed. I did like listening to the radio with the others after supper. The radio was smaller than mine at home. There were those voices coming out of a much smaller box than ours, but because of the crystal set and the other radio that Mr. Schmidt gave me, I had some clues.

I'd been here less than a week and I felt lost and alone. What more will happen to me?

During those first few days at the school I heard the guys use words I hadn't heard and didn't know what they meant. I was so relieved when that first week was over, and I was on my way home on the subway with my mother. It came to me during the trip that I could ask mom what a couple of those words meant. You had to shout to be heard on those noisy trains, so I shouted: "Hey, Mom, what does fuck mean?" I was told later that lots of the passengers heard my question, and mom got lots of stares while waiting to hear how she would respond. I only remember that her definition was vague, and that it was a word people didn't use. Well, she couldn't be right because lots of the kids were using it!

What a relief it was to be back for the weekend—even though I came into a new home. I tried to tell Mom that I didn't want to stay in that school, but all she said was that I'd just have to tough it out. She didn't tell me how! There was one good thing, however. Dad ran an aerial from the roof into our apartment and our radio worked better than ever. There were lots more stations which I could listen to.

On that Sunday night,—the start of my second week—just before leaving home to get on the subway and that long ride back to horror, I heard the radio program called "The Shadow" for the first time. It captured my imagination. He was like Superman (who I also had heard), and I wanted some kind of hero, someone to take me away from that school. I invented someone and made up stories about him. At first he was "Captain Al". He eventually became "Al Sulivan". Sulivan was intentionally misspelled because he was not Irish; he was a Martian! That was kinda fun, but really he didn't exist and I had to take whatever was to come. Even though I had been in church a few times, I had not learned that there was a real Hero waiting for me to find.

The next week was like the first. I couldn't make friends for some reason. A new kid came into our dorm and I figured I'd try to make friends with him before he had a chance to find out what the others were doing to me. Confidently I said: "Hello, Lewie."

His immediate response: "Go fuck yourself." There's that word again. Even though I didn't know its meaning, the tone of his voice told me that I didn't make a hit with him.

I can still recall an evening when our house mother, Mrs. Macumber, set up a nice place for me to study. Some of the guys came along and chased me away from there. Mrs. Macumber came along a bit later and saw that I was in a far less comfortable place and wondered why I moved. I could tell she was annoyed and there was no way to explain it. Yeah, it probably seems to you, reader, that all I had to do was to tell her why I was forced to move. I just couldn't tell her what happened. (I think that it was shame which kept me silent.) Recalling that difficult time, in retrospect, I should have been able to express my problems to others. Had I been able or willing to do so could have saved me much anxiety.

Somewhere along the way I met a real great guy, Louis Mitchell. He never bothered me. In fact, he was always kind. We were friends almost to the time he died many years later. I can still recall a day at the start of gym. I was about to change into my gym suit when I found Louis lying on one of the locker room benches. I asked him what was the matter, and he weakly mumbled something which I couldn't hear. I ran to the office where the gym teacher hung out and told him about Louis. I stayed with him till the teacher came to check out the situation. It turned out that Louis had pneumonia. Thinking back, I realized that this was one of those rare times when I was able to think of somebody other than myself.

I don't know what to tell you now. There were some good things, such as the morning assemblies, where a mighty pipe organ was often played. Then Fridays we had a period in that auditorium where the Senior Chorus was practicing. All those voices accompanied by that organ! I was wowed! In my wildest dreams I could not imagine that one day I would play that organ or sing in that chorus, but, as seems to happen, I'm getting ahead of myself.

There was a group music lesson, taught by a wonderful teacher, Miss Gillman. I learned some of the basics of reading Braille music and how to use it to learn a simple song and then how to play it on the piano. She'd often play a recording of a classical piece and that gave me a chance to become aware of that musical genre.

I found that there was something else, very special. No, great! On Thursday nights, our house proctor who was the science teacher would entertain us with simple experiments. I was excited about those, and I could show everyone my crystal set. That proctor explained in very basic ways about radio. One Thursday night he showed a couple of us a simple way to test whether a radio tube was bad or good. Much of the time this test could quickly determine the proper operation of a tube. I didn't always understand what he meant, but I could begin to see that there was a real answer to radio's mystery, and I knew that I would find it.

I remember an experiment in which we learned that by wrapping a large amount of wire around a bunch of nails and connecting the ends of the wire to a battery, that the nails would become magnetized. I tried this when I got home one weekend, and wow! The nails were magnetic as long as the coil was connected to the battery.

It was great to have a chance to experiment, but weekends which I hoped could bring me peace did not always produce it. My parents were so different from each other and those differences often resulted in bitter quarreling. After some of those weekends I was almost glad to get back to school.

There was an older boy, Harry Sutcliffe, who, like me, was mistreated quite often. He handled it better than I could. We gravitated toward each other. He was studying radio and electronics. It was terrific that this course of study was available in that school. Could it be possible that I could take that course? Harry reached a point in his studies where he learned enough to become a licensed amateur radio operator. He patiently explained some basic principles by which radios worked.

Sometimes when I was home on a weekend I would hear Harry talking to other amateur radio operators (hams). That was really exciting.

I wanted to learn enough so I'd be a ham. And I knew that if I was to become an amateur radio operator, I would have to learn the International Morse Code. Another of the older guys had what he called a "code buzzer" which would allow me to practice code as I learned it. I told him that I would trade my crystal set for the code buzzer. He thought that was a great idea. I knew he would know how to use the set; he seemed to know quite a lot about how radios worked.

It was a great day for me, right? Well, one of the kids was somewhat of a problem—something indefinable to me at any rate. One of his problems was that he would steal stuff from other people's lockers. My code buzzer was stolen and never recovered. That was a crushing moment. I didn't have the code buzzer nor the crystal set! I soon forgot what little I learned about sending and receiving Morse. It was one more thing to hate about this school!

I was in the fifth grade at the time. Miss Moody was my teacher. On a certain day she had a "science corner" which was for the students who kept up with their assignments. I could hear the kids doing experiments, but I never was with them because I never kept up with my studies. It just wasn't like the way it was in Mrs. DiPritoro's home room. She made learning fun even though the regular grade instructors didn't teach me anything as I've already told you. I couldn't tell Miss Moody that I was always afraid and that kept me from concentrating on studying. Along with that, I was really behind where I should have been if I'd gotten better training in those public school classes. Weeks came and went. I'd seldom get an assignment done. I'd make excuses like how I forgot what the assignment was. Everyone knew I was lying.

Who could I tell? Our main house proctor was the Dean of Boys, but how could I talk to him—tell him how I felt about being bullied or just the possibility of it? That proctor was a gossip. I'd go by and find him near the main switchboard gossiping with other teachers about what other guys told him in confidence. No, he couldn't be trusted. No way was I gonna talk to him. Some days I'd get an upset stomach as gym period approached.

On one certain Friday I was walking with Mom to the subway on my way home. My legs gave way and I fell. I had a hard time getting up and started crying. I managed to get home but couldn't think straight. I'd start crying again. Mom saw what was happening. I was having a "nervous breakdown"! I don't remember much about that episode except that I was glad that I didn't have to go to school for a while! I remember going to a clinic for evaluation but that is all I recall about this time. It was several weeks before I could go back to school. I was a little calmer then, but nothing really changed. I had to try to make up the lost study time.

The end of the school year was coming up. How can I ever forget that last full school day? One of the guys asked me to walk with him to where there was some kind of a gadget he thought I'd want to see. That sounded good; I was more than surprised at his apparent interest. When we got to wherever we were headed, there was a bunch of other guys there. They grabbed me and undressed me just to "check me out". They really didn't do anything, but even so, I felt, well, violated. I guess that's the adult word. I was shaken up, but the next day some of those guys came to me and said that I was initiated into a club of some sort. I never heard about that club again.

So there it was, my first year. I knew that I had eight more years to be at that school because it ran through high school. My problems were not over during summer. Mom enrolled me in the school's summer camp, Camp Wapanacki. I could look back on last year's camping experience, and a year in that awful boarding school. Some of these same kids would be at the camp so it would be more of the same. Like the school, there was no cost to the campers. Both the school and the camp were supported by a combination of state funds and privately raised money. Money could easily dry up if there was any significant scandal. This is why there was a separate boys' and a separate girls' month for camping. No coeds, no hanky-panky! The camp was in northern Vermont, deep in the woods. The country was hilly because of its nearness to the Green mountains.

We got to the camp on our school bus. It was a long ride, covering a distance of perhaps 350 miles. During the trip kids would sing camp songs and some pop songs of the day. When I got off the bus, I found myself at a rambling, two-story building which housed the kitchen, dining room and "rec hall," and the infirmary on the second floor. A porch ran around the outer perimeter of the building, running right down to the boat dock and the beach.

If I stepped off the porch, I could make a left and follow a rough-hewn rail cut from long tree branches. It was a long railing with breaks at various points, showing us where individual cabins were located. If we continued following the railing to the top of a slight rise, we'd get to the latrine in which there were the bathroom facilities plus showers. There was, however, no hot water!

The cabins had little furnishings. All I can remember is that there was a table in the center of the room. As you walk through the door, there were a couple of double bunks on each side. We campers got a bit of exercise if we had to sleep in the upper bunk. What living arrangements we had were serviceable if not quite like home sweet home. I had to learn all of this, and I found things a bit confusing at first, but learning all of this was nothing compared to getting around the school campus.

In retrospect I don't think the camp was as bad as the school experience was. Sure, there was the taunting but not so much physical abuse. There were fun things, like telling stories around a campfire. There were the Wednesday hikes into town, 6 miles each way. Getting there was OK, but coming back was rough because there was West Hill, a pretty steep climb. I don't know now how I made it.

There was swimming, which I often didn't go to even though I was supposed to. We were taught how to row a boat, and I was quite good at that! There were free times, and I often spent time in the camp library listening to a talking book. That's nothing more than an early form of audio book.

The camp was quasi military. We had a bugle sounding reveille, followed by a personal inspection and then there was a flag raising ceremony in the morning and flag lowering at night. There were cabin inspections at unannounced times. The food was hearty and quite good, especially the ice-cream we had on Sundays after the noon meal. The ice-cream was home made in a contraption filled with ice and salt. The ingredients were in a large barrel which had to be hand cranked. Let me tell you, that was hard work but I can't remember anyone's complaining about it because the reward was terrific.

After a few of those Wednesday hikes, I was toughening up and could manage that hike a lot better than the first time. Quite a few years later, while attending that same camp, I broke the official record for hiking back from town but I couldn't tell anyone about it... again I'm getting ahead of the story.

Camp ended and I could get back to Grandma's farm. What a relief! I got to hike to the local general store with my sister. It was only a couple of miles away and, after those hikes at camp, that walk was nothing. This time my sister, Mom, and Dad were with me at the farm. Dad showed me a bit about how to drive a car just so I'd learn something new. That lesson might have saved lives. One evening Dad drove us to Anderson's Dairy for some ice- cream cones. Mom and he got out of the car and were walking to the dairy. Mary and I were in the back seat. We were parked on a hill. All of a sudden the car started moving, gathering speed as it began rolling downhill. I can't believe that I did this, but I immediately jumped over the back of the front seat, fell into the front seat and jammed my foot hard on the foot brake. My folks saw the whole thing. They could never have gotten back to save us from a disaster. For once, I, yeah, I, was a hero! Why couldn't I recognize that I had done something noteworthy, something positive? Otherwise I can't say there was much new about that summer except that I could get kind of recharged before the next school year- one which began with a terrible shock!

Chapter 6

On the first day of classes I learned that I was not promoted to the 6th grade. I was assigned to what the school called an "ungraded" class. This class was actually designed for students who were mentally retarded. (Political correctness would say that the class was for the "mentally challenged".) To me it's the same thing. At first I was dejected, but then I really liked that class. I could do class work in a breeze. The teacher was Mrs. Stein, a gal from Germany. She didn't always know how to pronounce some English words, but I always was able to help her with them.

She and Miss Moody got together. Miss Moody wanted me in the 5th grade again; I'd rather have stayed where I was, in the ungraded class. I felt like I was really somebody in that class. No way that I could have understood the ramifications of this, but Miss Moody believed more in me than I did, so I would be in the 5th grade after all.

There was more to it than being left back. As I said, the school was divided into two divisions: the Upper and the Lower Schools. The upper School used to start at the 5th grade level, but this year Upper school started at 6th grade. By returning to the 5th grade, I would be moved to the Lower School with "the little kids". So being left back wasn't the worst problem; it was leaving the big kids and moving in to be with little kids. My mind churned because I wondered if I could even keep up with them.

On the last night before I moved to the Lower School, Gene, one of the guys who made lots of trouble for me, came to me. He told me that he was sorry for all that he had done. He said that, when I returned to the Upper School, he would try to help me. He seemed sincere enough, and indeed he was.

The next morning I cleaned out my dorm locker and moved into new quarters. I got to meet many of the younger children, including some who would be my classmates. One of them was Robert Graves. He lived perhaps 300 miles from the school so he couldn't even go home on weekends as most of us did. The only time he could go home was for summer vacations and long Holiday breaks. Bob and I got along very well and our friendship lasted until his death many years later. I got along very well with most of the guys and girls, but there still were a few who would bully me. Even so, it wasn't too bad compared with what I took during the previous school year.

Because of spending a week or two in that "ungraded" class, I missed some early lessons. There was a class called "eurhythmics". This was a combination of gym and music. We'd march around the large classroom in time to music. Then there was singing—not songs necessarily. Sometime the teacher would sing a note and say what it was. Then she would call out a note and we'd have to sing it. We had to sing something like "lu lu" on these notes. The students did this with no problem. Because I missed the first few classes, I didn't know that the teacher had previously showed the kids the relationship between notes. It wasn't difficult for them to find any note based on that relationship. Believe me, this is much easier to do than to describe. If the teacher started with C, and asked the class to sing a G, they could do it unerringly. I wondered how they could memorize all those notes.

Unknowingly I was about to do something very important. I set out to memorize notes. I'd strike any key on the piano and then check what key I hit. I knew the basic layout of a keyboard so doing this was easy enough. As I did more and more of that, I got better at correctly identifying whatever note I randomly struck. Armed with that knowledge, I could sing any note the teacher called out. I was keeping up with everyone! What I hadn't learned was that the other kids could sing a note because they learned the relationship from one note to the next. I knew nothing about relationships between notes, but I didn't have to because I could sing any note as I'd memorized their sounds. Later I found out that I could do something which most musicians could not do because I had what many called "perfect pitch". It really isn't perfect, but at any given time I could come very close to a note that was called out. This gift is both a blessing and a curse which I'll get to later.

I got into other troubles related to Eurhythmics. Before we got to the class, we had to change into special uniforms. This reminded me of the gym suits which I couldn't manage last year. I've forgotten the details which made changing into the uniform so difficult. Thus I can't describe them. What I do recall is that I had one hell of a time getting them on and off. Add to this was that I'd get lost in the building trying to find the classroom. The girls gave me grief about that—except for one: another Dorothy. (Remember the one that I knew in public school?) Although a nice person, she didn't figure in my life until some years after my leaving that school.

Like the previous year, gym was very traumatic for me. This was especially true when it came to the horse. This horse was the kind that you might see gymnasts use in Olympic competition. We only had to perform relatively simple maneuvers. One was to stand so that I could hold onto each of the pommels. I was supposed to use my arms and legs and propel myself over the horse and land on its other side, still holding onto the pommels with my hands behind me. I could do that occasionally. Then there was a slightly harder maneuver which I think was called a "half wolf". Here the idea was to hold onto one pommel with both hands and jump over the horse in a way similar to what I did using both pommels. I can't remember managing that one!

During that same class we were expected to walk on what was called a "balance beam". This was a strip of wood about four feet long, suspended an inch or so above the floor. I don't know how wide it really was, but to me it seemed as though it was only a quarter of an inch wide. It might really have been two inches wide. I was terrified of this. While standing on it, I felt like I was ten feet off the floor. Looking back at this, I can't imagine why I couldn't get it into my head that this was actually very close to the floor, so, if I fell off, nothing would happen to me. I think these tasks occurred twice a week and not in the other two gym classes.

Another thing which was taught in Lower School gym was a game called "kick the can". I was really very good at this game. The game was like baseball except that, rather than batting a ball, the players kicked the can. The can was flattened so it was easier to kick. For some reason I was good at that. Kids wanted me to be on their teams. That game gave me the only joy in gym. I don't know how I knew where the bases were, but I sure did know it then. I was one of the best players!

Sometimes the gym teacher gave demonstrations for teachers from various schools to show what we did in gym. I was left out of most of the demos except for "kick the can". I also remember that "we played a modified kind of volley ball. We played it while on our knees. We had to hit a ball over the opponents' net and defend against balls coming over our side of the net. I was quite good at that one, too.

The class work was going quite well. There was a Braille dictionary in that classroom, and I read it whenever I had spare time. I even learned how to interpret the diacritical marks which were the keys to the proper word pronunciation. I found that it paid to read the introductions to books because that's where I learned how to use those marks.

Like the preceding year, gym was causing me to become more and more anxious. My mother took me out of the Lower School for a time so that I could avoid another "breakdown". When I finally returned to school, things appeared to be the same. I still had to attend gym classes. I dreaded those times when I'd have to work with the horse or the balance beam, but I was not asked to do this nearly as often.

There were times when the gym class would put on other demonstrations which included even more events than those I previously mentioned. I asked the teacher if I could be excused and she would not do it. There were various groups of kids doing different tasks which included quite advanced work on the horse, the balance beam and the trapeze. Somehow the only ones I was asked to participate in were "Kick the can" or volley ball. I was really surprised at this, never thinking that the teacher was instructed to have me participate in only those events which I could handle without stress.

How I really loved music appreciation classes! The Eurhythmics teacher read biographies of some of the more well-known composers and played recordings of their work. I got perfect scores when it came to recognizing the pieces and their composers and also recalling facts about their lives.

That school year was ending and I actually did make a few friends along the way. Some of them lasted well beyond my school years. Near the end of that final term in Lower School Dad bought me a radio—one which was much better than the one Mr. Schmidt gave me. Over the course of time that radio taught me much about radio's inner secrets.

Best of all, I was promoted to the sixth grade—and with good marks!

Chapter 7

Early summer I'd have to go to Camp Wapanacki again. It was almost like a reunion: seeing some of the guys from the Upper School as well as seeing some from the Lower school. I really have little recollection about the next few camp seasons, other than not looking forward to them. Anyhow, after the camping was finished I went to my grandparents' farm again and to me it was luxury. I remember listening to the radio there and finding a morning show devoted to classical music like what I had been taught in Music Appreciation class. I listened to it whenever possible.

Then it was back to school; September, 1941. (I'm 12 now.) I was in the sixth grade and my teacher was Miss Butler who taught us whatever we needed to know and more. She read stories of Greek mythology and other famous classical tales. As a part of English class and spelling, she drummed the meanings of prefixes and suffixes into our heads and explained how these were the building blocks which formed words. We learned to figure the meanings of many words which we had not read nor heard simply by analyzing their spellings and using our knowledge of prefixes and suffixes. That knowledge stands me well to this day.

There were always those damned gym classes, but I found that if we were doing something that the teacher thought was doing us good, he would not necessarily convene a formal class. Naturally he did have some classes in which we played baseball on a real diamond. I think the dimensions were smaller than professional fields but everything was in proportion. The rules for this game were modified. The ball we used was a large, rubber one. The teacher was the pitcher for both teams. There were no trick pitches. The idea was for the ball to come in on a bounce a couple of feet in front of the plate. It would, of course, bounce up and cross just in front of the batter. He had to time his swing in order to make contact and hopefully hit far enough to get on first base or better. You guessed it. I seldom made contact with the ball. It was bad enough that if I hit it at all, I was allowed to take first. If there were an odd number of people in the class, I was not chosen for a team. I was the score keeper. Because I really liked baseball, I had no trouble keeping everything straight.

Gym and other classes became more difficult when two new students were enrolled in our school. They were Melvin Wilson and Elwood Chambers, boys I knew from my days in Public School 93. These boys were just plain mean-spirited. They tried to bully nearly everyone. It was fortunate that they did not remain in our school for long. One day on the playground these boys pulled out knives and threatened to use them! Teachers saw this, and the boys were summarily dismissed.

Early in the school year one of the families in our apartment house was moving and gave us its old, upright piano. As with so many things, I had no idea this was an important event. What a surprise that was—coming home for a weekend and finding the piano. I spent lots of time sitting at the instrument and picking out melodies such as "Drink to Me Only With Thine Eyes" or "Believe Me, If All Those Endearing Young Charms," etc. I could pick out the melodies, but I couldn't figure out what notes should be played along with the tunes. I got a few chords right, but these were simple songs so it was easy to get some of it right. It was something else again if I tried playing some of the pop songs of the day. Sure, the melody wasn't hard to figure out, but I never got the background right, and it was discouraging.

After that weekend, it was back to school. As I got to know more of the main school building and the various classes being taught, I learned that there was a radio room in which the electronics teacher had lots of gear, including amateur transmitters and disk recording equipment. I would sometimes get near the room's closed door and hear great sound coming from some of his equipment. One day I opened the door and started to walk in. I was so anxious to meet the instructor and see the wonderful world of radio gear he had. Alas! It was not to be. There was a mike stand which held a very expensive microphone. I knocked that stand over! The instructor was very unhappy. He asked who I was. I told him and was immediately told never to come near his room. It was gonna cost him one hundred dollars to have that mike repaired. I found out that he taught radio and electronics to a few students when they entered high school. Would he remember me? Would he accept me as one of his students?

I was taking piano lessons from a rather cold lady, Miss Thode. She was rough on me; she would not tolerate anything but perfection. Like any other piano student, I had to learn scales and the precise way they were to be fingered. There were other exercises. I understood what was required, but I was not measuring up. Then there was memorization of music which I had to read using a special music notation—very different from the staff music notation used by sighted musicians. I had learned how to read Braille music two years earlier, and I remembered much of what I had learned at that time. Reading the music was one thing; memorizing it was something else. I did poorly.

You may remember about Gene, who promised to help me when I got back into the upper school. I didn't see much of him while I was in the Fifth Grade. It turned out that Gene was studying with Miss Thode, and he had no problem with her. I told him about my trouble with her. He admitted that she was tough, but he said that he could easily remember what he read from Braille scores and was a quick learner of all the exercises and scales which are necessary for a person wishing to play the classical repertoire. I must say that he was really good. He could even play jazz—including some of the songs which I could not figure out beyond playing their tunes. He would eventually show me, directly or indirectly, how to figure out those background chords.

Every piano student had a practice period each day. This was UN supervised time and I was expected to work on whatever was taught in the actual lessons. The practice room assigned to me was right next door to the radio room. I'd often hear beautiful music or the instructor operating his ham gear. These things distracted me from my practice time. When I either came to practice or left it at the end of the period, I'd often run into that instructor. I'd timidly say "hello" and he answered me more or less civilly. I found out that his name was Bob Gunderson. I asked a couple of times if I could come into his room and learn something about his equipment, but the answer was always no.

The school had a good library of Braille books, and I found one about the basics of radio receivers. I borrowed it and read it, but somehow most of it was above my head! What a disappointment! My mind was just not mature enough to grasp these concepts, but I could not know that, of course.

One of the classes assigned to me was singing in the Junior Chorus, and I did quite well. The teacher was pretty easy-going, and I found it easy to learn the various little tunes which we would be expected to sing in Morning Assembly. Yes, this was in that same room where two years earlier, I heard the Senior Chorus singing to the accompaniment of that magnificent pipe organ. The chorus teacher usually accompanied us, but at times my piano teacher did it and also taught some of the songs. She was not easy-going, but I managed to do all right.

And there was typing class. It was no problem learning the many parts of the machine as well as the layout of the keyboard. After learning all of these basics, we had to do simple exercises by which to become more familiar with the keys and to increase typing speed. The exercises were to be typed in rhythm with music which was played on a phonograph. The music was just a bit too fast so in order to keep up; I had to hit some keys even if they were the wrong ones. I never became really accurate, but I could type rather fast. I understood that typing would be the best means by which I would write letters to others. Some blind people have learned to write with pen or pencil, but I never did master that skill, so typing would be very important despite my not being as accurate as I wanted to be.

Along with regular classes there was religious Instruction. I can't remember how it was that I attended these classes. These instructions were according to Catholic doctrine. We started with basic questions, like "Where is God?" Answer: "God is everywhere". I could not conceive of that. We were taught about praying and that God hears and answers these prayers. I wondered how God could hear prayers when he had to listen to so many prayers at one time! We learned about the life, death and resurrection of Jesus Christ. We were told that during the time that He was dead, that He was buried in something called a "sepulchre". I never figured out what that was or where the sepulchre was.

The course ended when we were sufficiently prepared to receive Holy Communion, Confirmation or both. Those of us who had studied went on a bus to a special church, and it was there that I made my First Communion and was confirmed into the Catholic Church. On that bus was a guy named John Kogler. We went through those religious instructions together, but it was on that bus trip that we became very good friends. You'll meet him again a bit later.

When my Dad found out about my confirmation, he began taking Mary and me to Children's Catholic services. I had no idea what was going on. The priest spoke in an unknown language and even sang in that language. There was the smell of candle wax and incense. Little bells would ring. Eventually I figured out that those were preparing us for Holy Communion.

Getting back to school again, there was always gym class. It wasn't as bad for me as classes of past years, but I was always nervous whenever I attended one of them. I did learn a couple of judo holds but was not a proficient wrestler. Our school was rightfully famous for its wrestling teams. Our guys wrestled against regular public high schools and would often beat them in all weight classes. Some matches took place out of town.

On one particular day in gym just before our team was to travel to Georgia for a match, the gym teacher had all of us sitting on the floor as he talked to us in a way which was unlike anything he had ever said. He told us that our team would not be going to Georgia. He said that it had to do with something called "Jim Crow". I never heard of that, and I'm not sure if any of the rest of the guys had heard of it. The instructor told us about something I surely didn't know anything about. He told us that some of our team members were African-Americans and that the Georgia school wouldn't wrestle with any of them. The only way that our team could be invited was to leave the black kids behind. The instructor said that this was absolutely unacceptable, so the team would not go unless all its wrestlers were permitted. We were told that the racial problem was extremely serious in our country. He wanted to be sure we knew that some of us were of different skin colors and that this shouldn't interfere with any friendships in the school. We were all equal.

I knew none of this but I knew that some guys had different speech patterns from others. I eventually learned to identify skin color by the way some kids spoke. Blind people don't know about color. We all got along all right. Certainly none of my problems were because of someone's skin color. It wasn't until early high school that I learned about prejudice on a personal level.

That school year of 1941 rolled on. On a Sunday in early December I was listening to the Brooklyn Football Dodgers playing. The game was suddenly interrupted by a news flash, followed by a news report coming via short wave direct from Hawaii. Webley Edwards was describing the Japanese attack on Pearl Harbor as it was happening. I remember the reporter's name because I used to listen to that same man as the announcer on a program known as "Hawaii Calls". It featured music from the Islands. It sounded different from what we heard from our local bands, and I was really taken by it.

It was a somber mood when I got to school that night. There wasn't a lot of chatter. As young as we were, we did understand that a national tragedy had occurred. Monday's classes were routine, but during lunch in the main dining room, a radio was brought in so we could hear the President of the United States and that famous speech in which he said: "This is a day which will live in infamy." WE WERE AT WAR—not just with Japan but with Germany and Italy. This hit me hard because I remembered that nice radio repairman, Mr. Schmidt. I suddenly knew why my folks would never permit him to come into our home. I didn't want to think that he was the enemy, but I couldn't draw any other conclusion.

I won't give you a blow by blow account of every school situation. Whether for good or bad, my life was settling into a routine.

On a February day in 1942 I had what I suppose could be called a defining moment. It was a Friday. The school day was over and I was waiting for someone in my family to pick me up. Quite a few of the guys had already left. Bob Whitstock was still there. He was one really nice person. He could well have been the smartest kid in the school and he was in my sixth grade class.

He challenged me to an Indian wrestling match. There are a number of variations of that game. (I wish I could draw a picture because it would save some words.) Anyhow, the variation used was something like this. We were seated opposite each other and our arms were extended and our palms touched each other's. After a count-down we grasped hands and the idea was to see if one of us could push the other's arm flat.

No way can I really express this. All I know is that when he squeezed my hands, there was something really calming, comforting and peaceful during that moment. There was something about his hands which was, well different, and special! Perhaps it was a kind of energy which was transferred from his hands to mine.

Don't ask who won the game. All I can say to you is that as I was going home I felt better than I had in a very long time! Hold on before you judge what you just read. This was definitely not a sexual experience!

For the first time since starting classes in that school, I was anxious to get back because I wanted to tell Bob what happened and how I felt. When I found him, I told him about that very brief encounter and what it was like. I felt, well, energized and at the same time, at peace. I hoped he would hold my hands again.

He was very quiet. The wait for him to say something seemed endless. When he did speak, it was in a very quiet tone. He said that he was willing to hold hands on a very few occasions, with a total time limit. When that time ran out, he said that he would never do it again. He did seem to understand that it was a great help, and it was the only reason that he would consider holding hands at all. He chose the places and times. Eventually his time limit ran out. Before it did, I felt lighter and happier; I could ignore any bullying situations.

Once Bob was no longer willing to help, I gradually fell back into just, well, getting along but with little joy. Maybe it was worse because I had a taste of freedom from those oppressive feelings. I didn't mention my need to anyone. What I did was to shake hands with some of the other guys, but that feeling of peace and freedom didn't come over me. What made Bob's hands so special? Could it be that Bob had the ability to transfer some healing force? The school went on and this new discovery was of no use!

A month went by and I sensed some restlessness among many of the students. Something really big was brewing! Bob asked me if I'd join what he called a "strike". He talked about the fact that we (the students) didn't have any representation.

It was a week or so before Easter. Morning Assembly was convened as usual. A few of us refused to leave our seats. The principal, Dr. Frampton, (whom we all hated) was in charge on that fateful morning. Assembly was dismissed. As people filed out of the room, the others remained seated. One person shouted that we wouldn't leave until our grievances against the school were addressed. The principal immediately shouted to one of the proctors: "Take down the names of these students and send them all home!" Bob was among those "rebels". Well, inasmuch as I really didn't understand what the whole business was about, I quickly got out of there before my name could be taken.

I guess that Bob was the youngest of the guys, but there were some who were in high school. Indeed, the halls and classrooms were emptier than usual. A hush fell on everything. Would these kids come back? Would I ever see Bob again? It was more than that hand holding incident. He was my friend. I was sad to the point of tears. I stayed away from people so they wouldn't see me. One of the bullies came along and asked what was the matter. I told him about Bob's being dismissed. What he said amazed me. "Boy, you must really be a good friend of his. You're so upset!"

A week went by and none of the guys came back. There was a rumor going around that some were back and having a meeting with the principal. Then I saw for myself that all of those who were dismissed were back. In one of the assemblies the principal explained that there would be some changes as to how the school was run. The way it was, if someone did something wrong, he or she would have been suspended or expelled. Now there would be a merit system. Slight misbehavior would earn one demerit. If a person got ten demerits, he would be called to the principal's office and might or might not be dismissed for a while. If that student kept getting into trouble and earned too many demerits, he would be expelled. A Student Government was also set up so that many problems would be referred to that body for judgment rather than going directly to the principal.

One of the grievances was that it was important for boys and girls to learn how to act with one another. What the principal called a "Social Hour" would be arranged so that for about forty-five minutes after supper, boys and girls would mingle in the common lobby. Every once in a while dances would be held so people would learn about being with each other. There was to be a sort of mini prom in which a guy would invite a girl to the dance. Each would dress up, and the guys would give the girl a bouquet.

These were unbelievable concessions. I really didn't know many girls except for seeing them in our classrooms. Now we could meet and get to know them. I went to a few of those Social Hours. Can you guess what happened? Sure you can. None of the girls seemed to like me!

The year ended, and then another month of the school's summer camp. There was nothing new about that summer's experience except that there were three major events.

The first was a run-in and a big fight with a guy named Nario. I gave him a good tussle and vice versa. It was a draw. Then we wondered how we got into that little fracas. We became life-long friends. We still get together or talk on the phone to this day. It never occurred to me that I was getting stronger and that I was learning how to defend myself.

The second event was that I began to attend Sunday worship services in a little Catholic church in a nearby town. The priest was very informal. When someone came in late, he'd interrupt whatever he was doing and greet that person warmly. I wanted to know more about the God Whom I had learned of in Religious Instruction. It wasn't my time to know Him! After the service, I enjoyed riding on the camp bus and being away from camp for a while.

The third major happening was a letter which came from my sister. She was at my Grandparents' farm, and the news she brought me was not good—not at all! Even in upstate New York, that summer was brutally hot. Even so, as was his way, Grandpa was toiling in the fields, working under a blazing, noon sun, with a horse-drawn reaper. He had a stroke. It was a miracle! The horses led him home. I don't know all the details except that he partially recovered. He could walk very slowly. No longer could he do farm chores.

When the camping season was over, I went to the farm and found Grandpa. He could talk properly; the stroke didn't affect his speech. Despondent! That's the best way to put it. He sat by the window, watching his cattle and horses being taken away by the farmer who bought them. I think this was the worst summer I could remember! I was seeing grown-up problems. It was a time when I felt another's burdens and felt helpless to do anything about Grandpa!

While witnessing all this, I remembered the co-op which could perhaps have saved Grandpa from this tragedy. I knew that the co-op was a success. In fact, I got to know the son of the co-op leader. He took me to his farm and showed me how one machine could milk several cows at one time. They put a rubber gadget on my finger and I felt the suction come and go, simulating the milking of an udder!

While sometimes Mom and her father didn't get along very well, this catastrophe pushed them together at the time he needed comforting and practical help. Time on the farm dragged by, something that never happened. The day before we returned to Brooklyn, Mom took my sister and me around the house and the property. I couldn't imagine why she did that but she eventually told us that this would be the last time that we would live in that house. With Grandpa's stroke, my grandma could not handle the property and it was going to be put up for sale. I was told that the price for all 80 acres plus the house and the out buildings was $3000. I asked mom if, among all the members of hers and dad's families whether we could raise that money so we wouldn't lose that wonderful place. She said that it was not possible. I couldn't imagine a summer without that house and all of its memories.

Chapter 8

I guess there was a week between my coming back to the apartment in Brooklyn and my going back to school. I used some of that time to play with the radio dad gave me. Not that I knew what I was doing, but somehow I came up with a way to increase its ability to pick up distant stations. You'd be bored by the details, but it all came about because I ruined the radio's loudspeaker by trying something which destroyed the tiny coil which was used to move the speaker's paper cone. I hooked up the wires which were originally connected to the speaker to an old earphone using a long piece of wire which was neatly coiled up. If I moved that coil of wire near some of the tubes, I could hear more stations. If I moved it too close, the earphone would squeal so I had to back the coil of wire away from the set to just the right distance and all would be amazingly fine. I'm not altogether sure how this worked to this day, but I later learned about a kind of radio in which a similar principle was used.

I found, too, that if I connected the set's antenna wire to the house radiator that I could hear lots of stations. Because of the nature of that radio, I was flirting with danger, (I could have gotten a nearly lethal shock) but nothing happened and I went on blissfully unaware of the potential problem.

I tried to take my mind off the loss of my grandparents' farmhouse and my going back to school, but I couldn't completely do that. I couldn't forget that experience with holding hands and knowing there was no way to repeat it.

I didn't catch on that I was getting physically stronger and that I was learning important lessons. My church visits had no obvious effect on my life.

All too soon I was on the subway on my way back to school and the start of the seventh grade. I was 13 years old. The way the school day worked was like this. First there was morning assembly. This began with the ringing of a bell about a half hour after breakfast. The assembly usually consisted of the singing of a hymn, the recitation of a "Memory Gem" (which I never bothered to learn), followed by any announcements related to the school day. One of the staff then read from a newspaper, giving us important headlines and a summary of sports events. We were then dismissed.

The rest of the day was divided into periods. There were 3 periods in the morning. Somewhere between periods was recess. After the third period there was a break for lunch and time for study or whatever, before the remaining periods. I don't remember the afternoon schedule, but there were either three or four periods. Again, sometime between periods was an afternoon recess. And after the last period we had time to play or study. In my case, I found as much time as I could to listen to the radio.

After the evening main meal there was a bit of free time in which we could either go to the Social Hour or do whatever we wished. Then there was evening Study Hall.

Once that was over, we had some free time before our mandatory bedtime. That time depended on our ages.

All of the seventh grade studies were taught by the same instructor and in the same room. I remember the teacher, Mrs. Athearn. She was a kind lady whom I liked. She was not a forceful personality so really didn't have complete control over us. It was fine while she was there, but when she could not be, a substitute would come in, and she was also not a strong personality. You know what must have happened before I get to tell you. I remember one day in particular. The kids ran wild. One of the guys got hold of a magnifying glass and, because he had partial sight, he could catch the sun on that glass and focus it on someone, burning his or her arm or maybe causing a page to catch fire. I was sorry about the events of that day. I really think that had Mrs. Athearn been in greater control, the substitute would have had an easier time of it.

On this day the guys and gals got out of hand to such an extent that the ruckus could be heard all the way down the corridor! I was not involved. Perhaps I could have been but I had to watch my step;

I'd already earned a few of those demerits I told you about earlier. No matter what I did do or had not done, it was reasonable that I'd never be believed! As I said, in this instance the guys went too far. What a complete mess! The substitute teacher was in tears. Dr. Frampton, the school's principal, came hurriedly into the classroom and boy, he was a formidable presence! We were told that each of us was to write a composition, apologizing to the teacher and present each of our compositions directly to her.

Well, I was not among those who carried on during that mess. No way was I gonna admit to something in which I was not a part. I was not going to apologize for something that I didn't do—even when we were all told to do just that! How could I say I was sorry when I had nothing to be sorry for? I wrote my version of this apology, telling her how sorry I was for the way she was treated. I said that I understood how terrible she must have felt, and I knew she was a blind teacher and I knew what it meant to be mistreated. I told her what a nice person she was and that she was a really good teacher of Braille. I said that there was no way I could apologize for my actions because I was just an onlooker. I had nothing to be sorry for because I didn't take any part in that session. I signed my name and handed it to her, knowing she would not believe a word I wrote and that this would lead to more demerits and that I'd be sent home for a time as penance.

I was wrong. A few days later she summoned me into her classroom and thanked me for writing such a nice composition and thanked me for caring enough to write down my feelings. Here it was just a few days into the school year and I already had such a close call!

Mrs. Athearn had no problems of her own with that class. She wasn't a great teacher but I think she gave us reasonable assignments. In my case, it was a matter of not being interested in learning anything and so half the time I didn't turn in any home work. Because Mrs. Athearn was so lenient, I always got away with that.

I had other classes besides the basic ones. There was gym; maybe I really didn't have as much trouble in it, but I couldn't tell the difference. I did a little running on the track to increase my endurance. I found the weights and learned how to use them. I pumped more and more iron until I could pull up the whole stack of weights. I never found out how much weight that was, but I was amazed how easy it was getting to be in pulling them up. I did that only so the gym teacher would not convene his exercises, wrestling, or whatever he might have wanted to do that day. As long as I was busy and the rest of the guys were doing something, not too many real gym sessions were held. Maybe the teacher was a bit lazy. I don't know. What I didn't know was that I was doing myself some real good by building muscles.

There were those piano lessons. I did learn a few scales and a couple of what could be called "baby pieces" but was not making good progress. I had another class that year called "Elementary Music Theory and Ear Training". There were many facets presented. One exercise was having to write down the notes of a tune without referring to a keyboard. We had to think about the tune and what we heard in our heads.

Remember that in the lower school I developed a sense of musical pitch, so I could readily write those tunes down. The teacher, who was a strict and formidable lady named Gertrude Martin, was amazed that I handled such assignments easily. There was so much to learn, like the names of the chords on each note of a scale. I never took notes because once I heard about these things, I had them committed to memory and I have not forgotten any of that to this day.

The seventh grade subjects are the ones which one would take in any school. There was a little difference in one special way. One period each week Mrs. Athearn would bring a table radio to class so we could hear something called "The American School of the Air". It presented subjects in a dramatic format. I don't remember one single broadcast, but I do remember that this table radio had a remarkably good sound. I wondered how this was obtained. I'd had the idea that if a radio was to sound good, it must have a large loudspeaker and be housed in a large cabinet. I can't remember how it happened but I got a peek inside the radio and found everything to look like the innards of most table radios of the day except that the loudspeaker was—how can I say it? Well, if its paper cone was pushed slightly, it would move much more than any loudspeaker cone I'd seen. Could this one fact explain that great sound? Had I but known it, that simple idea with some refinements would be used in a leading brand of high fidelity loudspeakers just a few years later! This idea lay dormant.

I spent more and more time with John Kogler, whom I mentioned earlier. Both of us learned the Morse Code from one of the older guys.

I tried to learn it a couple of years earlier but I just could not grasp anything more than how to send and receive numbers 0-9. But now I had the whole set of symbols down, and I learned it all in twenty minutes!

John and I learned that dots would be sent by voice as "dits". Dashes would be sent as "dahs". Thus, the letter "A" which would be written as "dot dash" would be voiced as "dit Dah". With practice, John and I could talk using Morse rather fast. We knew that if we were to become amateur radio operators, we needed to be proficient in Morse. Because we had a way to "speak" in Morse, I didn't need a "code buzzer".

I still had a couple of years to go before I could officially begin my study of radio and electronics at this school, but I wanted to learn something more right now. On weekends and at other odd times I experimented with earphones and found that not only could they be used to listen to sound, but if connected in the right place and in the right way, they could serve as microphones. I knew it was a step, but I wanted to know what vacuum tubes did and how they worked. Remember when I tried borrowing a science book from the library and failed to understand the concepts behind vacuum tubes? I borrowed that same book and looked at the relevant sections. When I read about vacuum tubes this time, it read as though I was reading a story. I understood quite a bit about radio, more than I thought. John was not capable of understanding the principles in that same book.

I have no idea what I was supposed to learn in that seventh grade, but I was learning things which I use to this day. I should have been excited, but I wasn't.

Something was missing in me. I couldn't relate all of the little pieces which were coming together. I still had no really defined personality.

Except for John, I didn't have close friends. I thought Bob Whitstock would be one of them, but he moved in a different plane. He was always reading books which would help his Seventh Grade studies and wasn't wasting any time. I didn't dare talk to him; I had to avoid him because the only real help I needed was what he could not offer. Bob became a member of the new Student Government. Even though there were older boys and girls who were also involved, Bob was elected President. Why did he get good grades? How could he have done so well? I was always on the outside looking in. He enjoyed being with girls up to a point, and I really didn't get to know any of them.

Once in a while I'd go to a Social Hour, but I had no idea how to talk to any of those girls. I guess most Seventh Grade guys weren't really interested in girls, but they did find it possible to talk to them even though they had to pretend not to want to. That really didn't bother me though and this probably was just as well at that time. It was going to matter big time later, but perhaps not quite in the way you might guess.

Gym was getting easier to tolerate—but it was not without trouble. It wasn't long before I was getting an occasional upset stomach. Finally it got to a point where I was sent to the infirmary for a checkup. I'm not sure that the doctors found anything wrong, but it did offer me an escape. This might not have come to my mind except that there was a nice girl there, Claire Goldrick. She was interested in music and liked listening to the radio. It was refreshing talking to a girl! She did complain of occasional headaches. I understood that well enough because I had some here and there.

After I was released a couple of days later, I hardly ever saw Clair. Well, I did on rare occasions over a couple of years. When we met, gone was that nice person. She was not liked by other girls and guys, and I wondered what was going on. One day one of the guys told me that she went to the hospital because of a really bad headache. Alas! I would not see her again. The headaches were the result of a growing brain tumor, which also caused major personality changes. She died soon after that, and I remembered how Dorothy (from Public School 93) suffered from those headaches. She was lost to me all those years ago.

The year moved along; it now was late Fall. When I came home one weekend, Mom said that Grandma and Grandpa were coming to live with us for the winter. Here we were, living in a three-room apartment—all four of us. Where would they sleep? How could they keep from being in each other's way? As I expected, Mom and Dad got into pretty good arguments over this. It looked as though home would be a war zone, just the way school so often was. In the end it all turned out fine, although it didn't immediately seem that way.

The owner of the florist shop where dad worked died and so dad was out of work. At one time this would have been a tragedy, but it was war time and jobs were plentiful. My cousin, Al, was working for a firm specializing in the manufacturing and installation of Venetian blinds which were becoming immensely popular. Dad got a job with the company where Al worked. Dad was a good mechanic. The company was expanding to where it was picking up government contracts. One such contract involved substantial work at military bases in North Carolina and Virginia. Dad was sent down. His new salary was way above anything he had known. The talk at home was rather heated, mainly related to his wanting to move the family down where he was working. Mom said no and no definitely meant "No"!

Just about the time my grandparents were gonna come live with us, Dad went down to Virginia to install blinds in the Pentagon, and later in a couple of Marine corps bases being built then. Meantime Mom also found work with the U. S. government. Her salary was also better than any which she had earned at other jobs.

I remember going back to school the week before my grandparents were to arrive. I didn't do anything during that school week because on the Sunday evening when I got back I asked one of the guys to show me how to make a flying tackle. He was completely blind and nevertheless could do that with ease. He always had an incredible amount of coordination and a sense of where his body was even when he was in the air. During the lesson I fell and twisted my knee so badly that I could barely walk. John Kogler tried a bit of walking with me, hoping the pain would fade away. It didn't.

I ended up in the hospital. Most of those who were there were grown men. I heard them talking about all kinds of things, including the conquest of ladies. Well, by then I'd learned quite a bit about "man talk" or maybe it really was "boy talk". One guy's story was fascinating. He jumped out of a window because he thought he could fly. This was so interesting compared to the much less adventurous life I led. I asked him to tell me more about this because I thought I'd like to fly. He said that people really couldn't fly, but he thought he could because of something he was taking. He told me about how great it felt after taking whatever it was. I asked him if he had any of it that I could try. He told me in no uncertain terms that he would never give me any of what he called "dope' and he scolded me big time. He said: "Never look for it anywhere, and do not try it. It's false and it makes you do dumb things like thinking you could fly and then jumping out a window." To me he was really a man in the true sense of the word, so I took his advice because he knew so many grown-up things.

I stayed there for almost a week and was eventually picked up by my Mom and somehow got home. I had a cast which immobilized my knee, so I had to walk with that leg straight. It was painful and hard to walk that way. Even so, it was so great having my Grandparents there. I didn't mind that Grandpa took over the family radio and listened to the war news all the time. After all, I had my own radio! My Grandparents learned their way around our neighborhood and where the stores were. They relieved Mom of some of the shopping and cooking. Grandma was a really good cook. Weekends were more exciting than I'd known. Just having these people around made me feel better.

It was terrific going back to school and being excused from gym for a couple of weeks. I was relieved, but somewhere in the back of my mind was that feeling I'd had when holding Bob's hands. I did my best not to think about it.

The weather was getting milder. It was almost time for Grandma and Grandpa to go home to their new house which was located about a mile from their old farm. Before that happened, my radio stopped working. I knew how to check tubes and knew which one needed to be replaced. Grandpa said he'd buy me that tube. There were a few places nearby which might have it. We went out together, walking slowly because that was all he could manage. He was determined to try any possible shop, but that tube was not available. The war made radio tubes very scarce. I was out of luck. My faithful radio could not be fixed.

They left, and I was lonesome for sure. Well, with Dad gone, at least there wasn't too much squabbling. The school year dragged by until summer vacation.

Then there was summer camp. I have no recollection of that particular camp season. I do know that on the last night of camp there was an awards ceremony as there always was. Lots of the kids got their "W" (for Camp Wapanacki) patches, but I didn't get one. There were other awards, but I didn't get a single one. I tried not to care. In my heart I knew I didn't deserve any awards.

After that I went to live with my grandparents in their new home. The house was such a disappointment. There weren't as many rooms and many were very small compared to those rambling rooms in that great old farmhouse. Nonetheless there were rooms enough for all my family and, when necessary, a guest or two.

There was no room for that parlor organ that I loved. It was relegated to a rather large shed which was attached to the house. Yeah, there was the organ, standing on the dirt floor, along with some gardening tools and, of all things, the outhouse which was more convenient than the one on the farm. Gradually I got used to going to the shed and messing with the organ. I got used to the layout of the place. The whole place didn't seem like home. Could I love it here? Could I still find peace here?

My Aunt Avis visited for a week or so. She didn't have to wash me now, so I liked her a little more than before. She liked some pretty "high brow" stuff on the radio, like "The Bell Telephone Hour". I didn't really like that at first, but I grew to enjoy it more as my appreciation for music deepened.

The first thing Grandpa wanted me to do was get his old radio working. He was grumpy from inactivity and not being able to hear the news. I examined what had to be done. Other than finding a wall plug so I could give the set its vitamin "E" (electricity that is). The next thing was that there was no antenna. Grandpa found me some wire, quite a length of it in fact. I had to trudge through some of the tall grass around the house to see how I could put up the antenna. I saw that the only way to do that was to find some staples and run it along the house wall. So I ran the line through the Window and around the house, nailing as I went. I tried the radio and my antenna worked as well as what Grandpa had used on the farm. He was overjoyed.

But the time came to leave, spend a bit of time at home, and then back to that damned school—And the start of the Eighth Grade. Not much really happened that year, but those things which did occur were memorable and important.

Chapter 9

It's now September, 1943; and I'm starting the eighth grade. I'm back here at school and nothing has changed. It's the same old drill! Sure, the characters are different, but it's all the same.

My eighth grade teacher is Mrs. Wright. She's a different sort from Mrs. Athearn—a bit tougher and has a regional, but American, accent. Everybody here talked about her and how she lost her husband. He was the principal, and beloved by all. His story was told very often. It was some time in 1939. The big school bus was just outside the main gate. Mr. Wright was standing on the steps of the school building, calling the names of the boys and girls who were to board the bus. Without warning he pitched forward and fell down the entire flight of concrete steps. He was dead before he hit the ground. In the midst of doing what he loved, he was hit with a massive, killer heart attack. It was quite a long time before the students felt normal after such a great loss. After hearing about those events, I wondered why his wife stayed on to teach.

She was not a strong teacher, and we sometimes could get away with being a bit slack. The problem was that we never knew when she would come down hard on anyone who didn't turn in home work. She had marvelous stories to tell us about Monsoon rainstorms in India where she was a missionary. I didn't know what that was, but I gathered that she and her husband were dedicated to that challenge.

Something else changed. My voice deepened to the point where I could no longer have the vocal range necessary for me to sing in the Junior Chorus. Now I was going to sing in the Senior Chorus—that same chorus which I heard so many times either when they practiced or when the chorus appeared in Christmas programs, graduation exercises and in some other times. I could not imagine that I'd be lucky enough to be singing with them.

The pieces we sang were a lot more difficult from those I sang in Junior Chorus. Not only was the music more difficult to learn but we had to sing in Latin or Spanish. I remember that some pieces were so difficult that I could not memorize them when the accompanist played my part on the piano or organ. I asked for the actual note names. By a combination of both hearing the part and hearing the names of the notes themselves, I could usually learn my part quickly. Unfortunately lots of the members thought I was showing off because none of them ever asked for the notes the way I did. They never did believe me that I was doing that because I needed to.

We were good enough so that churches would ask us to perform. I recall that when I first came to the school, the chorus was invited to perform at Carnegie Hall. That concert included Lauritz Melchior singing solos, and it was all done with a full symphony orchestra! The concert was recorded and I heard that recording. Now I was in that same chorus. Would I ever have such an opportunity?

A few weeks into the school year I got a really good surprise. Bob Whitstock (who by now was called "Whitty" by most of us) showed me a portable phonograph. There were two phonograph records in the case, and Whitty showed me how to play them. One of them was a Capitol disk featuring the pianist Freddie Slack, his orchestra and Ella Mae Morse. She sang "He's My Guy". The other side of the disk was "The Doll Dance," with Slack on the ivories. I was really taken with that recording which I still have and cherish. It's remarkable that the record didn't wear out from the number of times I played it. The biggest surprise of all was that Whitty gave me the phonograph! I guess you could say that it was the junior of the old phonograph that my Aunt Kitty had. That phonograph led to something both bad and good.

Meanwhile, John Kogbler and I were still "talking" Morse Code. He was older than I; so, he was just starting high school. He was in the radio class that I so very much wanted to attend. John would tell me some of what he learned. As time moved along, I found that John was not learning things correctly. He so much wanted to be a part of this, but he just couldn't get a handle on it. He had to drop out of the course.

As I told you, so much of that year was the same old drill. There was gym and there were those piano lessons. I was doing a bit better but not making the progress that Gene was making.

In my free time I listened to the radio but with a difference. Many of the guys wanted to hear more "pop" music than I did. One of those guys was Richard Kupferle who we called "Kuppy". When he heard something he really liked, he'd very strongly encourage me to listen. Quite often it was a Capitol recording featuring Paul Weston, Johnny Mercer, the Pied Pipers, Jo Stafford, and Margaret Whiting. I don't know if Kuppy ever studied music, but he had an innate understanding of what he was hearing. He'd tell me to listen to how the orchestra changed keys. I was really getting hooked on the sort of music that Capitol was recording.

On weekends at home I tried to play some of the tunes I had heard. I had no trouble with the tune, but my background chords were simply wrong and I had no clue as to how to make them right. I spent more time at the piano than ever. It was lucky that I did because Mom was thinking of getting rid of it because I hadn't been playing it much.

During one of his trips home Dad installed venetian blinds in our apartment. The apartment house was heated with No. 6 heating oil and that produces lots of soot. Mom showed me how to dust the blinds, and it became my responsibility to do that every weekend. I was given an allowance because of this. I also had to dust the furniture. No doubt I spent some money on candy, but I saved some, a quarter at a time.

I understood that it just was not possible for Mom to do everything around the house because she was working. The way I remember it, she was working nights and sleeping in the day time. Because of these things my sister, Mary, had to learn to pick me up on Fridays. It meant I could not leave with the other kids. Mary couldn't get on the subway until her school day was over so the soonest she could get there was at about 4:30. I kind of liked this in a way because the school was quiet and it seemed that the place was my domain and not that of the teachers or the bullies. What a feeling that was! Of course too, I was always glad to be home.

I almost never felt real peace within me—nothing like when I held Whitty's hands. I finally decided that I had to talk to someone about this, so I confided in John. He said that he might be willing to hold hands, but his hands didn't impart any of the feelings I so much wanted. He thought about it and then said, "Ya know what, Joe; maybe you should try girls' hands!" You can see how slow I had been on the uptake. After two years, I never considered that possibility. Would a girl's hands feel, well, right?

Every so often the school would take some of us to a movie, and that time was coming up. It was January, 1944. I was feeling so many emotions. I wanted to be noticed. I wanted to get into that radio class. I just had to do something, anything. It was January 19, the day to go to the movies.

I couldn't stand the waiting. I wanted a better tone arm to use with the portable phonograph Whitty gave me. The one on the machine weighed too much and it was ruining records. What I needed was a lighter one which produced a tiny amount of electricity rather than converting the motion of its needle (stylus) directly into sound. There was one which would do what I needed and I was determined to have it. During a recess I sneaked into the room where the machine was. I brought a screwdriver with me so I could remove it without damaging anything. I removed it and stuck it behind all of my books which were stored in a special place made for us to keep our textbooks. I hoped it wouldn't be missed or found between then and Friday when I could get it home. I was nervous about what I'd done because it was wrong, and I knew it.

Now it was just after the evening meal and we were going to be loaded onto the school bus which would take us to the theater. Could I somehow meet enough girls and find one with just the right hands? It dawned on me that there was a place where all the girls had to pass in order to get on the bus. It was nervous time for sure. I had to force myself to say hello to each one as she passed and shake hands with her. A few girls came along and none had what I was looking for. I began thinking this was a bad idea. Suddenly there was Marjorie. I couldn't believe my good fortune! Hers were incredibly powerful—way better than Bob's! Somehow I managed to stick with her and maneuver in such a way that I could sit next to her. The one thing I don't recall about that evening was the name of the films which were playing.

Marjorie was more than surprised that I held her hand and asked why. I whispered a few words about how important this was, and she seemed to consider it. She let me keep her hand for the entire evening.

The bus ride home was incredible because I felt so much at peace and relaxed and yet energized.

The time between then and Friday went by at lightning speed. On Friday morning someone noticed that the tone arm was missing from one of the phonographs. One of the teachers asked if I'd heard of anyone talking about stealing that tone arm. "Stealing"! I never thought that I stole something. I told that teacher that I did not hear about anyone stealing anything. Was that a lie? I never did hear about anybody taking anything they should not have taken. Of course, I hadn't heard anything like that because no one else knew about the missing part. I could tell she wondered about me all the same but she never quite said anything. She did say that whoever it was who took that unit, did so with some skill; she knew I was pretty good with mechanical things.

I got the device home and was never really suspected, at least, I didn't think so. I put it away very carefully to let time pass before I would try connecting it to my wind-up phonograph.

Back in school I started to think about writing short stories. I asked Mrs. Wright if I could take home a few sheets of the special paper needed for writing Braille. She let me take some. In fact, she told me to help myself whenever I needed it.

I started going to those Social Hours. Often Marjorie was there and sometimes she wasn't. When she was there she would sometimes let me hold her hand. My grades were improving. The school year was coming to a close. Marjorie was becoming less and less available.

There came a day when I was summoned to Dr. Frampton's office. I was uneasy, very uneasy. If a kid was asked to go to that office, it usually meant that he was in deep trouble. I had no idea what trouble I could be in. I was in a study period at that time, and Marjorie was there. I told her I was in some kind of trouble and would she meet me in the hall for a couple of minutes. She knew what I needed because she understood that a command performance with the principal was bad stuff. She was there just the way I needed her to be. I felt much better as I walked into his office.

He confronted me with the fact that a lot of school supplies were missing, including Braille paper from Mrs. Wright's room. There were a number of other items and I knew I had nothing to do with any of them. He mentioned that tone arm which was found missing some months earlier. I didn't deny taking it—well, not exactly. I simply said that I'd thrown out better junk than what I was asked about. I found out later that he called Mom to his office to ask if I had brought anything suspicious home. She told him that she knew I'd sometimes bring Braille paper home, and it was with Mrs. Wright's permission. The matter was dropped.

I knew that I deserved some sort of punishment, but I escaped a very close one. I made up my mind that I would never do that kind of thing again. I guess I could have been cocky and figured that I could get away with it again, but that was not how I felt. I had another chance and I understood how important this opportunity was. It must be that there was a purpose to this.

Around this time those of us who were Catholics were expected to go to morning mass. To me that meant confessing my sins so I could receive Communion. Even though this was a weekday, a priest was available to hear confessions. I entered the confessional and said the appropriate prayer for confession. I told the priest what I had done. Apparently my sin wasn't important because he gave me a minimum of penance. To tell you the truth, I didn't think the priest really listened to what I told him.

It's the beginning of June, 1944. All the war news was looking good. We were winning in the Pacific theater but much more still needed to be done to make victory assured. The same was true in Europe. It was widely reported that a massive invasion of France was scheduled, possibly for the sixth of June. Rumor had it that the invasion would be covered on radio. It would be past bed time; so, I couldn't listen on the living room radio.

I thought about building a crystal set. I learned a lot about radio even then and I thought I could build a crystal set which was better than the one I traded a few years earlier. I don't want to bore you with too much, but the radio used a better tuned circuit than the one which made use of a sliding ball which effectively changed the number of turns on a coil of wire. I was collecting radio parts by that time so I had what I needed and got the crystal set built pretty quickly. I needed an antenna. I ran a wire from one bed to the next. I needed a ground so I used the radiator in the dorm for that. The set performed very well, with some real loud stations. In a way it was all for nothing. I heard the very beginning of the news coverage and promptly fell asleep!

Only two weeks remained of the school year. Formal classes ended for us eighth graders. We were facing something unfamiliar to us: The New York State Regents exams. These were tests administered statewide at the same time of day. New York State prepared these tests. Even the teachers did not see the test questions until the envelopes were opened at the appointed times.

I was scheduled for two tests. I know that one was Typing. I don't remember what the other was but the problem was that they were both scheduled to be taken at the same time and that was impossible. Instead I would take one at its proper time and a special time was set for the other exam. Between the first test and the specially scheduled one, I could not speak to any one so there would be no chance for cheating.

The typing test was very difficult. I had taken and failed it twice already, but unlike the first two which were given by the typing teacher, the state now changed this to a Regents exam. It was more difficult than what the teacher had taught me. It was more than typing perfect copy. I had to compose a proper business letter. It had to be formatted just right. Then I was presented with a document which contained columns. I won't go into the details of how to fit all the columns on their lines and with all the starts of each column aligned perfectly, one above the other. I never could get that right.

A day or two later I reported to the eighth grade room and was told that I did well on one exam, but I failed Typing again! There was no way for me to repeat the course, so the failure had to stand. I cried like mad! I really had tried my best. Mrs. Wright tried to say funny things to cheer me up, but I just couldn't be comforted. I was a failure again. It would be held against my record, and I'd have to work harder to get better grades so that failure wouldn't be considered so important. I think I managed to have another session with Marjorie which took some of the sting from that day.

The school year ended. Then there was summer camp. The effect of Marjorie's help stayed with me, but gradually diminishing. I knew I'd see her next year. There was nothing remarkable about that season. Awards Night came, and like other years, I didn't earn any.

After camp I again visited my grandparents. Their presence in my life gave me peace of mind and of heart. I saw my Uncle Arthur and Aunt Kitty again and that was a treat. Aunt Avis came for a short visit.

Most radio programs didn't remain on the air very long, so it surprised and pleased me that "Science Forum" was still on.

Of course, I played the organ and the experience didn't completely satisfy me. I experimented with the "stops" and discovered that the sound of the organ could be modified considerably. Unfortunately the organ began to exhibit problems such as notes which might not sound as loud as they should; some didn't play at all. The shed was a dusty place so dust could easily get into the instrument. Parlor organs work with a vacuum to produce their tones. The vacuum would pull dust into their vitals.

When I returned home, there was a week or two before school resumed. This was my chance to work with the tone arm whose origins you know about. I removed the original, heavy one which was on that portable phonograph and replaced it with the better one. I connected its wires directly to my headphones and was pleasantly surprised when I played a record that the sound was heard in the headphones. It wasn't very loud, but it was much clearer than what was heard when listening to the original tone arm.

The next step was to see if there was a way to hook it up to the family radio. I didn't have a complete idea of what to do but I knew I should connect it to an amplifier tube. I did that and it worked very well indeed. I couldn't leave it connected or the radio would not work. Listening to the phonograph was a chore because of the need to connect it each time I wanted to play it. My sister and I started buying recordings to augment the two I already had.

Chapter 10

It was early September, 1944. I was getting off the subway and walking with Mom for the 6 blocks back to school. Mom started walking back to the subway. As I walked through the main gate, I was moving into a different dorm because I was now 15 years old and starting high school.

The school day was somewhat different from what I had known. There were the same number of class periods and recesses. The main difference was that for each class subject I had a different teacher and each teacher was in a different classroom. An important difference was that I was finally able to take the radio class with Robert W. Gunderson, the radio teacher. Yes, I finally made it!

Bob Gunderson was one of the most amazing people I've ever known. Although blind since birth, nothing kept him down. He had many patents to his credit. During World War II he worked in the prestigious NBC recording studios. Later he worked for several firms as a designer of radio receivers both for civilian and military uses. He developed equipment by which a blind technician could test radio equipment as well as a sighted technician. He understood better than most blind people that if they were to compete for work in the sighted man's world, they had to be better grounded in their chosen fields than the sighted. He was as critical of his own work as he was with his students. He took what he did very seriously and he expected that his class members must do the same or he would drop the student from the class. As you'll discover, he was both tough but fair.

This class had two parts. One was held in the Science room and consisted of lectures about radio theory and practice. The second part was devoted to hands-on lab work where we learned to identify parts or to dismantle some old radios which were beyond repair but could yield parts which we would use later. This lab class was held in the basement of one of the dorms. It was equipped with work benches and all sorts of storage cabinets which held radio parts. The classes were never held in the Radio Room—the one from which I was banned so long ago. Some of the students did get to see that room, but I was still persona non grata there.

I still had gym and piano lessons. I looked forward to Social Hour, but Marjorie was not always there and not always willing to spend time with me.

If you look back over your life, you'll come up with some funny vignettes which meant nothing then but still remain with you.

For instance, there was a science class all Freshmen had to take. The material was a snap. The teacher, Dr. Nichols, was explaining how an object could radiate from something warm and move to a cooler object. The instrument used to check whether this, in fact, was true is known as a "radiometer". Each of us was to place his hand on it and the teacher would watch it and indicate whether or not the vane inside the unit was rotating. The teacher asked us to guess in advance who was the most radiant person in the room. I confidently named Marjorie as my guess. Others made their choices. When she placed her hands on the device, the vane turned at such a speed that we could hear the slight noise that it made. She was the only one who radiated with power enough to make the instrument register that way. Everybody wondered how I could be so confident. I never explained it.

There weren't many high spots in this year, but two stand out. In English class we were assigned to read the classic, A Tale of Two Cities by Charles Dickens. As I read it, I tried to imagine living at the time of the French Revolution. Travel was done via horse or on foot. There was no electricity. As the story of life in London and Paris unfolded, I was caught up with the characters. There was romance, intrigue and heroism. As we neared the end of the book, the teacher told us that we were not to read the last chapter. Wouldn't you think this would have made all of us curious enough so that we'd read it? Just the way the teacher told us not to read the chapter was so compelling that none of us did, even though we wanted to know how the book ended.

When the class convened, the teacher made no introductory

remarks. He just read the chapter, acting out all of the parts. Everyone was captivated. We were there when Sydney Carton stood under the guillotine and said, "It is a far better thing I do than I have ever done. It is a far better rest I go to than I have ever known." The bell rang, signaling the end of the period. Not a word was said as we filed out of the room. I suspect that almost everybody had tears in his eyes! This was one of the most poignant experiences I ever had.

Then there was the second highlight which had a lasting significance; it determined my life's work! It was the middle of the morning, and I was supposed to be practicing piano. Beautiful music was emanating from the radio room. I recognized Fred Waring and his Pennsylvanians. I opened the door and stepped in very quietly I thought. At that very moment a pager bell went off. It rang in a particular pattern. The page was for Mr. Gunderson to go immediately to the principal's office. He was making a recording on a disk for Mr. Waring. He couldn't leave the recording but, at the same time, a summons to the Principal's office had to be heeded. Mr. Gunderson knew I was standing there and said something like this:

"Joe, come in here. I have to go so I'm gonna show you how the recorder works because I need you to finish the recording in the proper way." He rushed through all of the many steps involved in monitoring and then finishing the recording. Then he said, "If you do this right, I'll show you around this room and teach you how to run everything here. If you mess up, you'll never see this room again!" With that, he ran hurriedly down the hall.

I won't try to explain what was involved in those steps, but it was complicated and it had to be at precise times and in the right order. I wasn't sure if I could keep track of it all, but I didn't have time to think about it. I did what was required, and then lifted the cutting stylus from the surface of the disk and shut down the system. At that minute the end of period bell rang, and I had to go to the next class. Mr. Gunderson had not yet come from the Principal's office; all I could do was sweat it out, wondering if I did things right.

I didn't see him until the next radio class. He announced to everybody that he entrusted me with an important project and that I did everything exactly right! I was so proud and excited I was "bustin' my buttons!"

He began giving me private lessons about disk recording and the many problems which can occur during the making of a phonograph record. Recordings at that time were made on specially coated aluminum or glass blanks. He had lots of blanks and he told me to experiment with as many as I wanted to because he could always get more. Then he gave me a spare key to that room, which I carried till I left the school. The hardest thing I had to do when I left for the last time as a student was to return that key!

Along with that, Mr. "Gun" (as we called him) gave me books to read so I could obtain my license as a radio amateur otherwise known as a "ham". I still had my regular radio studies, which was no problem. Doing my other class assignments was another matter.

On weekends I would do some experimenting and tinkering. I also went to church with Dad. He had returned home by then. I got to know all the priests, especially Father Martin.

School moved on and Marjorie was less and less helpful until she and some other girls wanted to put on a radio play for morning assembly. She asked me if I would help with the radio setup and sound effects. Once she knew I would help her, she was more available to help me. I could see that Marjorie was only going to be of very temporary help!

The guys also planned to do some sort of dramatic presentation for morning assembly so wanted my help. I don't remember the whole business but for some reason I could not help both groups. The guys gave me a hard time over that, but the girls asked me first so there was nothing they could do. They got over it once the plays were performed.

There is little more to say about that first high school year. I didn't work too hard on any assignments except for those related to radio and electronics. In that subject I got to the point where I could take some lab projects home and build simple apparatus and come to school the next week and show Mr. Gun how it worked. Most of the time he was pleased.

I was careful with my weekly allowance because I had to buy a tool box and some small tools, including a soldering iron. All of us in the class had to learn how to solder, despite the high temperature of the iron (over 400 degrees F). Mr. Gun wanted to toughen us up against accidental contact with the hot tip of the iron. If he heard somebody say "ouch" or some such thing, he'd offer to step on our toes so we wouldn't notice the feel of that hot tip. We either learned to be careful not to touch it or to keep quiet if we did. I didn't like to solder a connection, but it was all in the game. I worked at it but never was really good at doing it. I would at least get the connections to hold even though I often used more solder than was necessary.

It was often required to drill holes in wood or metal, which was tedious when using a hand drill. Dad had a power drill but he wouldn't let me use it at first. I recall a weekend when I had a project to do and holes had to be drilled so parts could be bolted into place. Since Dad wasn't home, I decided to teach myself to use his power drill. I marked one of the holes with something that looked like an awl (called a center punch), making a little depression in the metal which would hold the drill bit in place before drilling. I was pretty sure that it would be even more necessary with a power drill. I plugged the drill into a wall socket, placed the bit into the depression, pressed down a little and turned the drill on. No problem at all. It was a piece of cake. I drilled all the necessary holes and assembled the project. When dad came home, I showed him what I had done and told him how much easier it was because I used his power drill. He saw I wasn't hurt and the neat job I'd done. He never again kept me from using the drill.

I had to use that drill because one of the other guys in the class was already using one, and I didn't want him to get ahead of what I could do. He was a really good mechanic, probably better than I was. That was John Wahlen. We got to know one another quite well and often helped each other with radio projects.

There wasn't anything notable for the rest of that school year, as I remember; but summer camp was something surprising! Most of the camping was as usual. What made it different was that Gene was at camp, and he got a group of guys together and formed a jazz quartet. Gene wrote an arrangement which was easy to sing. I sat in on a couple of their rehearsals. Gene played each part separately so the group could learn them. That quartet sang the song just the way I knew the music should sound. I was able to memorize all the parts. I made sure to think of each part quite often until I got back home.

I couldn't wait until I got to our piano. What I heard as the guys sang those parts was what I was looking for when I played. It took some time stumbling over the keys but I finally could play the entire arrangement. The Song was "DREAM" and it sounded just the way I hoped it would. To begin with, I never had played in the key of B Flat before. Now I could play that one song in a basic way. What about other songs? I tried playing one. As I did, I recognized that a couple of those chords from Gene's arrangement could be used in that song. Slowly and painfully, I was on my way!

Meanwhile the war was continuing. It's April, 1945. It looks as though the war in Europe is almost over, but the Pacific theater is very active. We might win that War, but it seemed like many men on both sides of the conflict would die. We heard all of this via radio news reports. With all of this, the news didn't seem real. I know that I heard the news but I couldn't feel a connection to what was taking place. After all, our nation was isolated. No way could the enemy attack our shores!

It was a Saturday morning. Both Mom and Dad were at work. Mom was doing her job in the Postal service and dad was working in a renowned florist shop. Mary and I were home. I don't know what she was doing, but I was playing phonograph records. In the midst of this we got a telegram from Grandma. Grandpa died on Friday evening!

Mary and I talked about this and knew we must get in touch with our folks. We didn't have a phone. Mary had the work numbers for our parents and she went to the apartment house superintendent to use his phone. She came back and she said that we had to pack suitcases for the sad journey to Grandma's house. I already learned how to pack a suitcase because it had to be done each week before taking the subway ride to school. I packed my duds and Mary packed hers and those of our folks. We knew that when they got home, we were headed to Grand Central Station to take the train to Albany.

Yes, it was a somber time but somehow I couldn't really feel the grief that I should have. All I could think of was that in April the reception of distant stations on the radio dial would be good.

On the train Mary and I talked using Morse Code, figuring that what we said couldn't be understood. Well, there was a navy man sitting across the aisle from us and he knew the code. He laughed and said that our secret was safe with him. You already know that I was proficient with the code but you didn't know that, as a high school student, Mary could and did join a youth program offered by the Civil Air Patrol. That's where she learned to send and receive Morse.

We got to Grandma's house in late evening. Grandma told us that Grandpa had been in failing health for some time. He could no longer go to bed at night but had to lean back in a recliner which was his favorite chair when listening to the war news. He listened to it almost continuously at that time. He ate very little. On Friday night, however, he asked his wife for a cup of cocoa. She made it and by the time she came into the living room to give it to him, he had died peacefully.

Although I could not really feel grief, it was the suddenness of his passing that really hit me. I guess I was just plain stunned. Much of the following day was taken up by funeral preparations. I think Mom knew I wasn't reacting the way she thought I should. She made me go up to the casket and touch Grandpa. On rare occasions I had touched him while he was living, and noticed that his skin was wrinkled. As I touched him this time I felt his skin as wrinkled, waxy and very cold!

"This is what death feels like," I thought; and it somewhat unnerved me. Other relatives or family friends had died, but this was the first time that it was palpable to me. I never cried the way people thought I was supposed to. I knew I wouldn't see him again, but it wasn't until I went to Grandma's house and he wasn't there that I could feel a sense of loss.

Aunt Avis, Aunt Kitty, and Uncle Art came to Grandma's house that evening and we all went to eat in a small, country restaurant. I walked with Aunt Avis. She was so different from how she seemed in my earlier years. She spoke to me as an adult and as an equal. I was part of the family and I never noticed it before that night. Aunt Avis sat with me in the restaurant and I just had to take her hand. I did and she let me keep it. This whole business of death unsettled me. Could my aunt help me again? I filed that away.

Then it was Sunday and the funeral, followed by a graveside service in a rural cemetery. It wasn't like a city cemetery where there were grave diggers. It was manned only when there was a burial and handled by local men who were not paid but volunteered their time. If a death occurred in winter, the ground would be frozen so the coffin would have to be stored in a cold place till the ground thawed in early spring. Then the remains could be buried. I would get to see this a few years later. I don't remember much more. Everyone said their good byes and we went our separate ways. I would be heading back to school.

A day or so later, VE Day came!!! The war was over in Europe. My first thought was how Grandpa missed the victory. I found this to be more of a devastating time than the rest of the events related to his death and funeral.

When I went back to school, the help and peace I got from my aunt Avis was still with me, but, as always, its effect diminished with time.

Time dragged by and there were final exams and the year was over.

Of course, there was summer camp, but I knew that when it was over, I'd be back with Grandma. What would that be like—without Grandpa? I couldn't imagine that for a part of the time it would be just the two of us.

That camping season was really tough. My friend, Nario, was there and Louis Mitchell. Their friendship wasn't enough. I still had problems with some activities. Right now I don't remember what they were!

Now here I was, getting off the bus which took me to the little house near the city of Troy, about 20 miles away. It had been really hot in Troy but it was refreshingly cool at Grandma's. I think my sister, Mary, was with us. In fact, she and I took the train from Grand Central Station in New York which stopped at every station along the route. We finally got to Troy. I remember that this was a somewhat silent trip because some time earlier I confided in her about holding her hands. She had hands which could have helped me, but she was outraged and things were never quite the same between us. We got along, but there was always a kind of wall separating us.

We finally got to Grandma's house. We were welcomed warmly as usual, and it felt good just to be there, even without Grandpa. It wasn't easy for Grandma, but we tried all the harder to do things for her.

She gave me a new and potentially dangerous job. It was to fill the kerosene stoves in the living room and in the kitchen. The tanks which held fuel were made of glass. When placed on the stove in its proper position, the oil emptied a few drops at a time from an opening in the bottom of the tank. It was removed from the stove with a handle like what you'd find on a mop pail. It was mounted so that when lifted quickly, the tank would flip so that the opening was on top and no fuel would drip. I'd carry it outside to where the huge oil barrel stood. I'd hold the tank under a faucet mounted on the barrel and turn it on.

The hard part was to be sure not to over-fill the tank in order to prevent oil from spilling. Grandma would watch me and say when to stop filling the tank. Next I had to line the tank directly over its receptacle on the stove and turn the tank fast and lower it into place without spilling oil. Fortunately I never spilled a drop even after repeating this process many times over a few summers.

I got to see Aunt Kitty and Uncle Art a couple of times on that visit. I learned that Aunt Avis was also coming to stay for a few days. I would be glad to see her, especially because we had that helpful time at Grandpa's funeral. She helped break the sadness of that time.

I made a mistake telling my sister about holding hands, but do I dare try telling Aunt Avis how much she could help me? Yes, she seemed to be willing enough to hold hands during that evening at the restaurant, but this was an entirely different thing. I needed her to be willing to do the same a lot more often. It was a scary thing if it went wrong. What would she do? What would she say to my folks and Mary? If, however, if it did work out, Well...

She arrived, and we talked a little about this and that. Mary was a voracious reader just like Aunt Avis; thus, they had much to talk about. I would just have to bide my time and hope for the right moment to ask for her help. Meanwhile I had the radio and the organ to work with. It was amazing how some of those jazz chords sounded when played on that organ. There were a few bad notes in the instrument, but the organ could really sound good overall, so I spent quite a bit of time playing it.

Then one night as Aunt Avis was going into her room to retire, I followed. I asked if she had time to talk to me and if what I said could be kept just between us. She seemed as though she was one who would keep her counsel. I explained my problem and if she could hold my hands when possible. She never hesitated. She immediately let me have them, and a powerful wave swept over me. I felt so elated and relaxed. I wondered how she decided to help me so quickly. I found out much later that she knew I was a disturbed child and when she heard about that, she somehow understood that this could be the key to something good for me.

One time we were alone. She seemed distant and aloof. What had I done? As before, when she went to retire, I followed and apologized for annoying her. I was really upset. I surely didn't want to bother the only person who would help me. I started crying, and she put her arms around me and said that I did nothing, but she was troubled by the realization that Grandma, her mother, could not stay alone in that house over winter. Aunt Avis was wrestling over whether she could or should have her stay with her in Buffalo (where she lived). She wasn't used to being responsible for anyone but herself and, in her heart, knew she had to take her mother in. I was sorry to see what was going on, but was surprised and relieved that for once I didn't mess things up!

I had at least a temporary solution to the major thing which so dominated my thoughts.

One time when I was listening to the radio, President Truman announced that an atomic bomb was dropped on the city of Hiroshima (in Japan). As days went on, another bomb was dropped on Nagasaki. Many reports of the horrific effects of those were reported: There was a mushroom-shaped cloud with each explosion. There was the searing heat which could be felt far from each explosion. People were in agony. Many were immediately nauseated and quickly succumbed to radiation. I could picture all this. It was almost like I was there, right in the middle of the terror. For a couple of years I had many nightmares of those tragic events.

Summer was ending, and it was time to return to Brooklyn for a week and then go back to that school I hated so much. At this same time, my Aunt Kitty gave birth to a little girl, Alice. It would be a few years later that Alice and her own family would play a significant part in my life.

Chapter 11

When I got back to school, it was September, 1945. We had a new guy in our dorm, Herman Foster. One day when I went into the living room, there was Herman at the piano, playing all sorts of great jazz. I could recognize some of the chords he used but not most of them. I asked him if he would teach me some tunes. He graciously did so. He had me play the tune, stopping me whenever I played a wrong chord. I learned a lot from a few of those sessions. I began to create a set of flexible rules which I could use when playing other songs. Herman was, to say the least, a colorful character. Whenever I played something the way he knew it should sound, he'd invariably yell, "Get back from that!" His enthusiasm was so contagious that it spurred me on to make me accomplish more.

Occasionally I'd see Gene, and he showed me how to play with some "fills" rather than just playing chords. His musical abilities were becoming more obvious. Miss Thode and he got along just fine!

Me, well, I was finally at a point where I was learning a piece by Bach which may have been a minuet. In any case, I learned some of the music but it was a bit much for me. Miss Thode played the piece for me so I'd know whether I was reading the music correctly. I started to play it according to what Bach thought was best, but only up to a point. I saw some jazz possibilities and composed my own version. I did not try writing it using Braille music notation. I memorized it. When my next piano lesson came up, rather than playing what little I knew of the real score, I played my version. This was my last lesson.

She said in angry tones, "You're dismissed! I've suffered long enough. You have no talent." I was at once relieved, but at the same time I knew in my heart that I could have applied myself and done much better.

I often wonder if I had liked her as a person, whether I might have accomplished more.

I looked for Marjorie. She would not help me! I knew I must not dwell on her. This was my sophomore year, and there was more homework. I was starting to notice that others had personal problems and I wanted to help. Robert Graves was in high school and wasn't doing well. He was close to having to go into the retarded class, just what I had done for a short while several years before. I hadn't lived up to my potential, but Bob Graves did, and yet it was barely enough to keep him in high school.

While I was waiting for a member of my family to pick me up to go home, Bob was obviously very sad because he lived so far from his home that he could not go there most weekends. I wondered if I could bring him home with me on some weekends. I asked if he'd like the idea, and he was overjoyed.

This wasn't as easy as it sounds. First I had to check with Mom. She liked the idea because she knew Bob a little bit when she took me to school and met him along with some of the other guys. The second problem came up when I asked the school officials about taking him home. I was told that I could do it if his parents gave their permission. Bob had to write a letter asking if it was all right. It was, so, on various occasions, Bob would come home with me.

I don't recall what we did in most cases, but I do know that it was great having someone to "hang out" with. One experience told me something of how his mind worked. I was showing him some radio experiments I was doing which required the use of earphones. The weekend ended and all was fine for the next week. When I went home the following weekend, I planned to do some radio work which involved those phones. I couldn't find them.

When I got back to school, I asked Bob if he could remember where I put them. His reply was, "No, I didn't steal them!" I told him that I knew he hadn't but hoped he could remind me where I might have put them. He said that he thought they were under my bed. When I got home, there they were. You can imagine that in a three-room apartment, space was at a premium. Putting things under my bed was the only way I could keep a few items on hand. I knew right away that Bob was very sensitive and I'd needed to be careful how I handled him.

I had to choose words carefully, trying to anticipate how he might look at things before I said something to him. It was a challenge, but I was able to avoid upsetting him.

Having Bob home with me on some weekends made me notice another boy, Albert Peroni. He recently started attending my school. If Bob's problems weren't serious enough, Albert was in far worse shape. He had no family other than a brother who was in the Marine Corps, and Albert didn't even have his address. He had to stay in the school all the time. He would go to Camp Wapanacki for a month but was at a virtually empty school for most of the summer and for times like Christmas.

Albert Peroni! Where did I hear that name? My thoughts drifted back to the first summer camp I attended. There was Albert, kneeling in the mud, crying inconsolably because he could not go to church!

Al was really bright and joined the Radio class a year after I had. He was a fair pianist and he learned the Morse Code easily. I began to wonder if a person with musical talent was more likely to learn the Code more easily than those who were not musically inclined. Over time I found that to be the case.

I arranged to bring him home some weekends. Because he was in Radio, he could enjoy some of the experiments I was running.

My life was changing in many ways, but I didn't know it. I still needed Marjorie's help which was seldom available.

I was still working with Herman who liked good sounding radios or phonographs. He knew I had a piano so was willing to work with me. Herman was a truly amazing person. Although totally blind, he could travel around New York City using the subways. I had not yet learned how to do that.

We had a date at my house for part of a Saturday afternoon. All that remained was to check with my folks. When I asked them, they flatly said that he couldn't come and Mom made sure that I had something else to do so Herman couldn't visit. I had to tell him that the trip was off. He was quiet for just a short time and said he understood. I had a vague idea—no, a strong idea—that Herman would never be allowed in our home just because he was Black! I knew Herman understood what was going on; doubtless he'd had lots of experience with prejudice. Truly, I'm not sure if it was prejudice on Mom's part or fear that the neighbors wouldn't take kindly to having a Black kid in our apartment. I have a reason why I don't think this was a prejudice thing because a few years later, both my folks liked having Louis Mitchell come to visit. Louis was one of the very few friends I had made when I first came to the school. I must have seen him over the course of my stay, but it wasn't until the end of high school that I remember spending much time with him.

The year dragged on. I was getting better at playing piano but still not really good. I tried playing in the dorm living room so I could be sure to remember all that I learned to date. Most of the guys laughed when they heard me play.

The first half year was over. A new course of study was introduced which was designed to acquaint us with basics about business, common sense items which might come in handy when we entered the working world. It was Called "Introduction to Business," taught by my former typing teacher.

Marjorie made it plain that she wanted no more to do with me, and I just had to do something about that. I used my "movie strategy" to check out the few girls who were in the class. I shook hands with them, introducing myself. There were a couple of them who I did not know.

One of them, Eilene, had really incredible hands! Yeah, they were even better than Marjorie's! How could I ask her for help? I can't recall exactly how it went, but in essence, I asked if she would be at Social Hour. She came, and in an attempt to play it cool, I told her about a person who needed her help and that he needed to hold her hands. Of course, it was a dumb approach. Eilene saw through it immediately and turned me down cold. She'd have nothing to do with that idea and with me. Here was a person with incredible possibilities, and it was already lost before I got out of the starting gate. I'd have to hear her voice in that class, and it was a really beautiful voice. I ventured to see if she would change her mind. It wasn't gonna happen.

My grades still were not good, close to failing in fact. I still was doing very well in the Radio course. I continued to study for my amateur radio operator's license, even though at this time the Government had not begun issuing new licenses. Unexpectedly Mr. Gun told the class that the Government was again starting to issue licenses and that we could prepare for the exam in earnest.

It was early March, and Mr. Gun said I was ready to take the test. The night before taking the test, Mr. Gun wanted to give me a Morse Code test at 13 words a minute which was the speed of the test I would have to pass the next day. By that time John Kogler and I had talked in Morse so much that we could send or receive at a speed very nearly fifty words a minute. Mr. Gun sent the code for about five minutes, simulating what I would hear during the real exam. I copied everything fine. It seemed so very slow that I fell asleep during the test run! Mr. Gun had to wake me up when the practice test was done. Even so, I didn't miss a letter! He was really surprised because he'd never had this happen with one of his students.

I couldn't help thinking of Marjorie or even more, Eilene. I so wished I could see either of them, but I had to force that idea out of my mind and pay attention to the business of passing that ham license exam. The exam was held at the local field office of the Federal Communications Commission; it is this body which issues these licenses. Mr. Gun and his wife, Lilian, took me, along with a couple of others to the examination room. Lilian had to write down what we dictated as we copied Morse Code. I was so nervous that I missed two letters. Fortunately, I still passed that part of the overall test easily. Then she read the test questions to us, one person at a time. It was nervous time for all of us, but we all passed. It was only a matter of a few weeks' wait till our licenses arrived and we were able to put our equipment on the air.

Mr. Gun was nice enough that he built all the equipment I needed in order for me to get my station running. My license and my government assigned ham call was W2PVY. I still hold and use this call, which I've had for more than sixty years! The following Saturday Mr. Gun and one of his friends came to my home and set up an antenna on the apartment house roof. On April 6, 1946, I nervously got on the air using Morse Code and talked to my first "contact".

The rules were that I'd have to wait a year before I would be able to talk to other hams by voice. It also meant that I'd have to take a more advanced exam at the offices of the Federal Communications Commission. If I passed it, I would have all of the privileges available to "hams".

A week or so after I was licensed, Albert Peroni and some of the other guys in the class got their own licenses. We arranged to see if we could communicate with each other. That attempt was only partly successful. Even so, it was a blast. We were encouraging one another. There's something about obtaining amateur radio licenses which places us in a fraternity. Personal problems are forgotten. As we talk to strangers, each helps the other even when we have not and probably never will meet face to face. There's something about being in the radio hobby which changes us. We don't know that ahead of time; it just does. I mentioned Harry Sutcliff earlier. Ham radio changed him from an introverted boy who lacked confidence into an out-going and well-adjusted guy. Family members started to look at me differently just because I could talk to people without using a telephone even though I was only using the Morse Code.

I taught John Wahlen about disk recording. Between us we came up with an idea that we could record some of the talented folks in the school and sell them recordings. We probably charged a quarter or fifty cents for a recording, but our little venture took off. And we were making a little money which we needed in order to purchase radio parts. John wasn't great with the principles behind radio's operation, but he was a really good mechanic—so we complemented each other occasionally.

The school year was coming to a close. John and I were called to the office of the Assistant Principal, Paul Mitchell. We couldn't guess the reason. We were told that we could no longer sell recordings to the other kids. Some parents complained that their children were spending too much on our recordings. Apparently they were spending more money than their allowances. Our reactions were pretty much alike. We had only bad things to say, feeling we were being held back by a system which didn't see that we were trying to do something different. Looking back on this, there was a tendency for the school to hold people back if what a student did wouldn't fit into its preconceived models. We could not see that some parents had reasons for their complaints. It was the students in the ungraded class who were not responsible in the way they handled their money. I hated it that rules were designed for those who were slower than others. Some of us saw it as unfair that the least capable were going to keep us from doing things.

Meanwhile I still needed either Marjorie or Eilene, and I could not have their help. The blow of losing our little enterprise made that problem worse. Added to that was that some kids hated seeing us succeed. Isn't this so often true that those who do very little try dragging down those who are doers rather than trying to emulate them!

The school year finally ended, and I had to go to summer camp. After the years of going there, I still couldn't like it. Even though I had a few more friends, it still wasn't easy for me to participate in camp functions. Why should this year be different?

As long as I live, I won't forget the bus ride which took me to the camp that summer. There were two buses taking us. Because the trip was 350 miles, there were a couple of rest stops which would permit us to stretch our legs. One stop was really great because it was at a little restaurant which served wonderful ice cream! This day I ordered and consumed a pint of that "goodie" (which cost 19 cents!) and then was going to the bus with some others. From out of nowhere I heard Eilene's voice say hello to me in a rather icy tone. Why was she there? I found out that she and another girl were hired as dish washers so they could earn extra money. I spent the rest of the ride in silence. All I could think about was how hard camping was, and there was Eilene who might have made my life so much easier and I wouldn't have that help.

The camp was pretty much the way it always was. There was something new though: a talent show. I don't remember everything about that show. I don't think I tried playing piano. There was a rather new kid in school, Alfred, who was pretty good on the instrument. He could do some good, technical things but didn't have the sense of harmony which I was developing. He had an arrangement of a song, "You Won't be Satisfied Until You Break My Heart," and he asked if I would sing it, while he accompanied me. After a couple of run-throughs, we worked well as a team so I reluctantly decided to work with him in the show.

Then came the night of the show. I was sitting on the porch of the Rec Hall. Eilene and another girl from the school, Leah, were talking together when two older boys went up to them and started making really raunchy comments about them. The girls were trying not to react, but the guys just talked more trash. I couldn't see those girls being treated that way. From what I knew, they were about the least deserving of this.

I did something totally uncharacteristic. I ran over to where the group was and told the guys to shut up and get the hell out of there. I expected them to gang up on me because that's how things would always go. Rather, they shut up and meekly walked away. I was nevertheless uneasy because I knew they'd get even somehow. They never did. Despite my fear, I knew that if that happened again, I'd have to act in the same way.

The show was on a Saturday night. One of the entrants was Eilene. She sang three songs with no accompaniment. They were all tunes that I knew and loved. I wish you could have been there. Eilene had the voice of a professional singer. I regret to this day that I never made a recording of that incredible voice.

The next morning some of us piled on the bus to go to Sunday services. Eilene sat next to me. As the bus was pulling onto the road to town, I just had to ask Eilene if she would change her mind. It was just too much for me to have her sitting right there. Her answer, "Not in public." Was this a partial change of heart?

"Eilene, there's no place that isn't public!" She took my hand for the whole ride to church and also on the return trip. I couldn't believe it. I wanted to thank her, but nothing I could say seemed good enough. She was encouraging.

Eilene made herself available at any suitable time. We were not sure how the counselors would view our actions and, as for me, I sure didn't want to lose what I had. During one of those times I asked her what changed her mind when she was so obviously adamant. Was it perhaps that I stopped those two guys from talking trash? No, it was the song I sang, "You won't be Satisfied Until You Break My Heart". It's a pretty lousy song, but something in the lyrics made her stop and think.

Camp life improved somewhat because I really tried to join in and work hard. Awards night came and went, and, as usual, I received none.

The next morning was the time to get on the bus and head for home. I didn't want to leave. I wondered if I somehow got hurt, that I'd have to stay at camp for at least a short while. I decided to run as fast as I could. If I kept on a straight path, I wouldn't hit any of the trees which were on each side of the path. I ran as fast as I could hoping that I'd run into a tree. Instead I ran in a perfectly straight line. It's almost impossible for a blind person to keep on a line, but I did it, and there I was—right at the bus. Eilene was there to see me off. She had a pretty fair amount of vision so she saw me try to run into a tree. She knew what I was trying to do. She calmed me down and helped me onto the bus. Then she quietly slipped away.

After I got home some of us went to Grandma's house. Grandma had gotten there to open up the house just a couple of days before we arrived. Aunt Avis was already there. She had arrived to help her mother get things ready for her summer's stay. I had gotten myself under control by then and was glad to see everyone. I don't know who was there. I know Uncle Art and Aunt Kitty were there at various times. Uncle Art still had that car with the wonderful rumble seat, and I got to ride in it with Aunt Avis next to me. She was there in so many ways. The ride was great. She knew I liked mysteries so she brought some books just so she could read them to me. That's how I became acquainted with some of the great mystery writers of the day, such as Dorothy Sayers. "Science Forum" was still on the radio, and my aunt was pleased that I continued my interest in science and music. We talked a lot that summer. She stayed for just two weeks because she had to return to her work as a records librarian at a leading hospital in Buffalo, New York.

During that visit Eilene and I kept up a correspondence in Braille. I could hardly wait for her letters!

Mom and Dad came for a week while they were on their vacations. When they went back to Brooklyn, I went with them because it was almost time for school. Mom was not happy with my school grades because she was sure that the only way for me to make a mark in the world was by going to college and getting at least a bachelor's degree. She asked me to bear down and improve my grades so I might obtain a New York State scholarship. If I didn't get that scholarship, there wouldn't be money enough to send me. I can't say that I cared about college, but I did tell her that I would try.

Chapter 12

So back to school I went. It was September, 1946, and I was a junior. I moved into a dorm for older boys. That meant something to me. I have to tell you that I was on top of the world! The effects of both Eilene and my aunt were such that I never felt such contentment. Class work was a snap! I began studying Spanish. My sister was beginning to be an expert in the language, and she passed on her knowledge to me, not that I wanted her to.

In the past two years I studied General Science and Biology. This year I studied Basic Chemistry. It was a tough course. I knew that I would complete it because Eilene was there during almost every Social Hour. This was the first time since enrolling in the Institute that I had real peace. I ignored any attempts by others to bully me, and they left me alone. Why couldn't I have done that earlier? I guess it was because my peace was dependent on external things rather than from within.

Monthly report cards looked good. Mom couldn't believe it. I never shared the facts about Eilene with her. Eventually my folks would meet her. Father Martin started something called The Catholic Guild for the Blind. It was a place in which blind people of all ages could meet one Sunday afternoon per month to socialize. This organization grew to where it had more than one, central meeting place. It also had social workers and other staff members who offered services to meet the special needs of blind people: aiding in finding employment, clothes for impoverished blind people and more.

Eilene began coming to the meetings which were held at our church. Because they were held I made some new friends there. One person I met was Lester Friel. He had attended Public School 93, and he also came to the New York Institute for the Education of the Blind. I seldom ran into him there. On Sundays, Eilene would come home with me and would stay with my family until it was time to go back to school, so she would join us on the subway ride. Eilene had fairly good vision so it worked out that she would take me to school and nobody in the family needed to go with us. You know how great that was!

I learned more and more about music. When Eilene was with me some Sundays, I experimented with playing piano as she sang. Those early attempts, although not great, permitted my family to hear her great voice. She encouraged me to work at becoming a good accompanist, and that made me practice and develop some skill. Some of my musical ideas came as a result of listening to singers and the orchestras which "backed them up". My collection of phonograph records was increasing so I had a variety of artists to listen to.

Meanwhile I was learning more and more about radio and electronics. Perhaps it was because many folks in the apartment building knew I was a radio ham, but in any event people were bringing me radios to be repaired. I was actually making money doing something I loved. Sometimes I got stuck on a repair job which I couldn't handle. We now had our own telephone. I could now call Mr. Gun who was always available to bail me out. He was glad to see that I was showing initiative.

Things were going so well. The school year was flying by. It was February, 1947. In three months I could take the test which would permit me to talk to other hams rather than using Morse. I should have known that it couldn't last.

It was a Social Hour, and I was with Eilene as usual. I was holding both her hands, and the magic was there. All of a sudden a proctor came up to us and demanded that we stop holding hands and never do it again. If anyone was gonna cause trouble, it had to be the proctor who was also the Dean of Boys. He ranted on about how he ought to report us. I didn't even have a chance to think this over. What I knew was that this guy was taking away something so very important! I reacted by bending my knees and then rising up and hitting him hard enough that he went down and stayed there. I don't know how long he was down and I didn't care. Actually my memory of the whole business was very sketchy. All I can remember was running as fast as I could to my dorm. I do remember one of the guys coming up to me and telling me that I really decked the proctor and he didn't think I had it in me. Others were also shocked by my actions, as was I.

I was in big trouble. I knew I'd get a call to the principal's office and be either expelled or at the least suspended. This was bad, and I knew I deserved whatever happened. But what about Eilene? Would she be punished to the same degree as I would? So many bad memories of those earlier years in that school flooded back. I could hardly sleep that night.

The next morning went as usual. I had a study hall period, and Eilene also had one. We both awaited our calls to the office. We weren't supposed to talk in study periods so as not to disturb other students. Someone came into the room to say that I had to report to the office of the Assistant Principal. That was a good thing because the Principal had no understanding of students' problems and that had to mean disaster. I didn't know much about the Assistant Principal. As I left, I quietly told Eilene that I'd tell him the truth, that she wasn't to blame for anything.

When I got to the office, I was physically shaking with fear and sadness for what I did. Mr. Mitchell, the Assistant Principal, was very calm, only asking if I understood why I was in his office. I told him I did. He invited me to take a seat, and asked me to tell him what happened as I understood it. My mind raced. How much could I or should I tell him? Mr. Mitchell was so calm and easy-going that I made a decision to tell my whole story of my problems at school and how important it was to Hold Eilene's hands. He let me tell my story in my own way and never interrupted. When I was done, I told him that it was wrong to hit a proctor and I was sorry for having hurt him and that I would never do something like that again. It was just that he was taking away something of such great importance that I reacted without thinking.

Well, there it was. All the cards were on the table. Was the top card the Joker? Mr. Mitchell was quiet for what seemed like an hour, but it was probably for less than a minute. I can't remember any of his exact words. He said that he understood I had a problem and somehow he found an answer to it. He said that other proctors saw us holding hands and were not concerned about it. It was just this one proctor who decided to come down on us. He told me that various proctors rotated so what he wanted me to do was not to come to Social Hour when he was on duty. He gave me the schedule so I'd know when to stay away. He also said that I absolutely must go to that proctor and apologize to him. Mr. Mitchell believed that the man would forgive me.

Mr. Mitchell said that he couldn't let this go without some consequences, so he gave me nine demerits—one less than what would be needed before I'd either be suspended from school or be called before the Student Government. It meant that for the remainder of the school year I'd have to behave perfectly so I wouldn't get that demerit. He said that Eilene would also get five demerits, and that I should tell her so she would not have to come to his office. I couldn't believe he really seemed to understand what it meant to hold her hands.

I usually got a few demerits for one infraction or another, but you better believe that I was a model of propriety for the rest of that year! As soon as I found an opportunity, I apologized to that proctor. He believed I was sincere, so it was over! I dreaded that encounter, but it worked out fine.

One morning during recess I ran into Witty. He was doing so many things and earning money for some of his efforts. I asked him how he managed that. Was he a teacher's pet?

"Joe, you could do even more than I do. You're smarter than I am, but you don't try." I didn't believe I could do what he did.

I continued going to Mass each Sunday even though I really didn't understand the meaning of the various elements of a mass. The fact that the Mass was in Latin didn't help. My most important problem was with God. Nothing I ever heard led me to an understanding of His ways. He seemed remote, and I began doubting His very existence. Eilene was as available as possible and was always encouraging me. She had a strong faith in God, but no matter what she tried to impart, I didn't get it.

Dad didn't always go to church; so if he didn't go, neither did I. One Sunday when I attended Mass, Father Martin preached a very interesting sermon on the book of Revelations. He described the panic which overtook the entire world. He noted that many people wanted to run from the madhouse, but stressed the point that there was no place to run to! That's how I felt for much of my life in school.

After the Mass ended, Father Martin wanted to see me. I thanked him for making Revelations feel so real. After thanking me, he took me into a part of the church which I had not seen. He handed me a large, wood cabinet. He told me it was a phonograph which could transmit whatever recording was playing to nearby radios. He said that if I could repair it, I could keep it. I thanked him and was excited to get home and check it out.

In the first place, the turntable ran very slowly. A bit of lubrication fixed that. The remaining problem was that the transmitter didn't work. I wondered how serious a problem this might be. There was a single tube which tested well, but it didn't get hot the way vacuum tubes should. I couldn't find the reason why. A new record store and radio repair shop had opened nearby. On the next day I went there, figuring that someone there could fix it. Immediately upon opening the door I was greeted by a most pleasant woman. After telling her what the problem was, she brought her husband from the back of the store. He was a vet from World War II—a great guy.

I told him about all the tests I made; he said that I missed the most obvious check. The cord used to power the unit had a third wire which was special. The power line voltage was higher than what the tube was made to withstand, and that portion of the line cord failed. He reminded me that this was a resistor. When I asked what its value was, he wouldn't say. "If you studied radio," he said, "you should know Ohm's Law which can be used to calculate that value". I was so annoyed with myself for missing the obvious.

He made me figure out the proper value, he then sold me the part. What amazed me was that he could have accepted the equipment as a repair job, but he didn't. I never saw such kindness from a stranger. I bought quite a few phonograph records from his shop even when I knew they were more expensive than they would be if I bought them in one of the many discount houses in New York.

After installing the new part, I turned on the transmitter. There it was, coming from the radio. I played a record and heard it clearly. That was exciting; it reminded me of Mr. Schmidt's transmitter which he used to send Hitler's speeches to neighboring homes several years earlier.

I continued to get good grades, raising my average ever closer to what it needed to be if I was to be granted a New York State college scholarship.

The month was April, just about a year since I was licensed as a radio amateur operator. It was time to take the exam which, if I passed it, would grant me the privilege of being able to talk to others. I took and passed the exam with ease.

Many others were applying for their ham licenses so it would take time before I received mine. I had to bide my time till I could go on the air. I had the extra equipment needed to make that possible, and I admit I was tempted to use it before I had the license in hand. I never did.

The license came in the mail while I was away at Camp Wapanacki. That was a pretty good camp season, partly because Eilene was there. I didn't go to Mass that summer, but I learned some hymns and played piano for the camp's nondenominational services. Eilene was disappointed that I didn't attend Mass, but she remained a faithful friend.

It was announced that there would be another talent show, so Eilene found the time to practice with the hope we could win the grand prize, whatever it was. I remember the song we worked on, "Let's Take the Long Way Home". I didn't own the recording, but I heard it on the radio often enough that I knew the song.

The singer was Jo Stafford—with Paul Weston's rather large orchestra. I loved his work and bought a few of his albums along with other recordings in which his orchestra was used. He was one of my early music heroes.

I wanted to use some of the orchestral phrases heard on that recording, and I eventually learned to play them. I don't think we won, but we received "honorable mention".

As in other years we hiked into town each week. My friend from past camping seasons, Nario, was with me on this hike. I told him that if we could get back to camp early enough, I could spend a bit more time with Eilene. Would he help me get back to camp? With his good vision, he could guide me while we ran. That run would include West Hill, a rather long and steep climb. He agreed to the plan. I think that he believed I wouldn't have the stamina to get through the run.

We checked our watches so we'd know our starting time. We knew we wouldn't break the all-time record for completing that trip, but it must have been at the back of our minds that it was a possibility. The run was brutal! I wish I could remember the time that run took, but we did break the record! The problem was that we weren't supposed to be back that soon because we'd be UN supervised. Darn it! We couldn't tell anyone what we'd done. I consoled myself with the thought that nobody would believe us anyway.

There was a new camper that year, Alex by name. He had a rather horrible voice as a result of some physical problem. He so much wanted to sing an operatic aria in that talent show. He asked me to accompany him on the piano. He sang the aria over and over again so I could learn enough of the music to do at least a credible job with it. I felt bad for him because his singing voice was really unpleasant. Well, at least he sang on pitch, but he didn't win any prize.

Alex was interested in good audio quality just as I was. I thought I could design a system for him, and he said that his Dad would gladly pay me if I could come up with something. I got his mailing address so we could keep in touch during the design work. What had I taken on? I questioned whether I could actually do it.

The month of camping was just about over, but something happened which was at once funny, frightening and awesome. We were to go on a lantern hike, which is just what it sounds like. The hike was taken after dark, with nothing more than the stars and the light of a few lanterns to guide us.

As always, I didn't want to be on it, but as always, I had no choice. The hike to our destination was rather long and arduous. We were at a "haunted house," so we were told. Perhaps the little kids believed that but most of us didn't. We still entered into the spirit of the occasion.

We were about to explore the abandoned house when our leader told us that the sky looked ominous and that we had to get back to camp immediately.

We rushed back. I couldn't believe how quickly we arrived. Apparently while getting there our leader walked us through rough terrain for the experience and for a good hike. I can't image how the smaller guys kept up!

Shortly before we got to the porch of the main building we heard thunder and rain fell. We picked up the pace.

There was a flight of perhaps six steps leading to the porch. For reasons which I never figured out, there was a boulder blocking the start of the steps. We had to keep to one side to avoid it. A few paces behind me was another camper, Pierre Jacko. He was not quite to the first step. I sqeezed over and climbed the first three steps. There was a huge thunder clap! For a second or two I couldn't move! Pierre did! He began to run, passing me. All the while he was yelling, "Lawd, Lawd, the devil's after me!" He ran onto the porch, continued around the building onto the dock and into the lake. No harm done; he was fine.

I was on my way to breakfast the next morning. I began to squeeze to the right as usual but stopped in my tracks! The boulder was gone; the ground was absolutely flat! That rock had been there since the camp opened many years ago because nobody could remove it. One lightning strike took care of it! The bolt struck between Pierre and me.

After camp was over, I again visited my Grandma. At various times all the members of my immediate family were there, including Aunt Kitty and Uncle Art. They brought baby Alice with them. I learned that Aunt Kitty experienced a major depression after Alice was born and had electroshock treatments which did bring her out of her gloom.

There is little else to say about that summer, except for one evening. Aunt Avis and I were in the living room. I don't know where the others were. I had the radio on, listening to a somewhat distant station in Delaware. Aunt Avis was reading and probably was smoking a cigarette. The announcer was talking about a just-released album called "Music Out of the Moon". This was a Capitol recording as were most of those I owned. Each of the six selections in this incredible album featured an instrument known as a theremin, which is played without touching it. It sounds like something between a musical saw and a human voice. There was a small chorus plus a handful of musical instruments. A chorus yes, but it sang no words, just "oohs" and "ahs". The DJ didn't play the entire album, just one piece, "Celestial Nocturne". Almost from the first note I was struck speechless. I was so excited. A few tears of joy fell as I listened with absolute rapture. No music up to that time captured my imagination so completely. I got my aunt to listen, but she didn't react very much to what she heard. She saw my reaction, however. It was just about all I could think about. A couple of evenings later the station played another selection from the album. I sure wanted to own it.

When I got home from Grandma's I was ready to make my first ham radio contact using voice. I remember it because it turned out to be that he was just a couple of blocks away from my house. His ham call was W2pwJ. He said his name was Ralph and then he gave me the business. He said that my signal was about the worst one he'd heard and wondered if I even had a license. I didn't know what to say to him. I finally said words to the effect that if the signal was really bad, could he come over and help me make it better. He immediately came over and tinkered a bit but, given what equipment I was using, he could only make slight improvements. He saw the piano and he started playing. He was a superb musician. He knew and loved good jazz. We became good friends.

The summer ended.

Chapter 13

It was September of 1947, and I was beginning my senior year in high school. Eilene was still in school, taking a year of post-graduate courses in business and some other subjects. I don't think she planned to go to college. I didn't want to go either, but my folks insisted, so I tried harder to keep up my grades. They continued to improve.

I had one more year to study radio and electronics. Even though I passed the Amateur Radio Exams, there was more to be learned, and I kept wanting to suck it all up. Mr. Gun had me work on the design of the sound system I had promised Alex as a part of the course. John Wahlen knew what I was planning and he knew of a good radio store which could supply me with all of the parts for the project. I made a complete list of what I needed, including the wood to be used for the cabinet.

I wrote to Alex with the cost of all the parts plus my time and labor. I think it came to $200. Alex answered my letter with an immediate go-ahead, plus a good chunk of the money so I could buy the parts and start building the system. It took a rather long time to get the work done. Dad was glad to build the cabinet which would house the electronics, loudspeaker and two turntables. He was a pretty good carpenter and the finished system looked professional.

When I heard the unit, I was really pleased with the sound it made, except for a small amount of hum. I asked Mr. Gun to look at the amplifier portion to see what could be done about the hum. He examined it critically and told me in no uncertain terms that most of the soldering looked good but the layout was all wrong. He did his best to get rid of the hum, but it was not possible. I'd have to accept the results or build it again from scratch. I didn't dare ask Alex for more money for parts so I had to settle for what I had done.

I phoned Alex and told him the equipment was ready, and he and his Dad came to my place, a drive of more than a hundred miles, to pick it up. Meanwhile I wrote a full instruction manual. I think I called the unit a Giotone, after the first three letters of my last name. I was pretty proud of what I did, even though it wasn't quite perfect. I only hoped the hum wouldn't mean that his Dad would reject the product and ask for his money back. Alex and his father came to our apartment and when I demonstrated the unit for them, they were ecstatic! What a relief that was. It was the most difficult electronics project I had undertaken up to that time.

I learned that radio stations used two turntables in order to play records continuously. My design therefore used two turntables rather than a record changer. I didn't like those changers because they were rough on those shellac disks and could break them. I heard about a few, commercially-designed audio systems but mine was the only one which solved the problem of continuous playing of recordings. Alex knew his music and his record collection; so, I was sure he could play a symphony continuously despite the number of 78 RPM disks which were what was available at that time. I learned some important lessons developing that system.

It was an exciting time in my life. I spent as much time as possible talking to other hams. My Aunt Avis sent me money to buy "Music Out of the Moon". The radio receiver I was using was rather crude. I wanted something better and had enough money to buy it. I told Dad about that and through some contacts he had, found someone who was an official in the company which made the radio receiver I wanted. He said he'd try to get me the set at a good discount. I was anxious. I told Mr. Gun about it, and he was happy for me. One day he handed me a little gadget. I recognized it as an adapter which would allow a pair of headphones to be plugged into a special "jack". I wondered why he handed that to me. Then he wished me a great weekend. I didn't know why. He never did that before.

When I got home the following Friday, I found a large carton. My new radio had arrived! It turned out that Mr. Gun knew that the radio would be at my home when I got there. He knew that I would need that adapter. He realized I'd stay up late listening to the new set which meant I'd need headphones because a speaker would wake up the family.

Lots of good things were happening, but something was terribly wrong in my dorm. John Wahlen was one of my dorm mates at that time. He came to me with a problem that almost reduced him to tears. "Joe, Gene T. insists on having sex with me. He told me that if I say no, he'll tell the principal what he has on me. I don't want that, but what choice do I have?"

I thought about that for a second. This particular Gene was a rather nasty character. He sure wasn't like my musician friend, Gene. "John, what does Gene have on you?"

"I don't know."

"Hey, this creep's bluffing. Don't go for it. Let's stop this now. When does he wanna try this?"

"Tomorrow an hour before we're supposed to wake up"."

"Okay. Tell him you're all set; agree to what he wants. You're in the next bed from me. When he comes in, tap me awake. Leave the rest to me, and don't worry. I'm gonna bring down the curtain on this bird."

When I went to bed that night, I was prepared for Gene's big scene. I was sort of awake when John tapped me. Gene went to John's bed; I waited till he was gonna try his little plan. I raised my heavy shoe and came down with all the force I had and conked him on the head. He was shaken up and tried to run out of the dorm. I told him that he had a date with the principal the next day.

The little creep said to me, "Don't you dare send me to the principal or I'll tell him all I know about you." I thought real fast. He couldn't know about Marjorie or Eilene, and even if he did, it would be embarrassing but that's about all.

"Gene, you don't know a thing about me and you don't know a thing about John. You play rough, but you've met your match. See you in the morning. Now get the hell out of here or I'll give you a better going over than you already got!"

Even with his slippers on, I heard him run out of the dorm.

I ran into Gene on the line as we marched to morning assembly. Gene was a scared kid. He said he'd do anything for me, but don't tell the principal. I just said that he made a messy bed and that he was gonna lie in it. After assembly I asked another guy in the dorm who witnessed the event to go with me to the principal as a witness of what I had to say. We went into his office and I explained what went on. He asked me to describe what I meant by sex. While I was telling him about it in as clinical a manner as possible, I thought of that subway scene of years ago when I asked Mom what fuck meant. I suddenly was in a pretty grown-up situation.

The principal was all for immediate expulsion. I was almost all for it, but I didn't have the heart. Gene lived with his grandmother who had a very bad heart. I said so to the principal, wondering if it might kill her. I suggested that the Student Government be called into session and have Gene explain his actions. He'd be shunned by everyone. His life would be a worse hell than mine had been. That was the end of the matter. I was no longer an easy pushover but I hadn't figured that out even then.

I wasn't done with odd problems. I was in History class. A few kids were assigned to give oral reports about various aspects of modern Russian life. My assignment was to give a brief history of the evolution of the Russian Secret Police. I had read the lesson and I thought I could give a quick report and get it over with. Marjorie whispered that she hadn't done the lesson, so could I make my report long enough so the period would end. She knew that she'd have to give her report right after mine. I reluctantly agreed, even though I no longer needed her help. Never the less for past favors, I agreed to try. How much of this boring stuff did I remember?

Our desks had a shelf under them in which we could keep our books. I usually had my hands on that shelf. When I was called on, I gave my report slowly, spelling the various Russian words and the abbreviations for the various evolutions of the Russia's secret police and what that goon squad meant to the people. I concluded what I knew was a better report than I intended to give.

Mr. Sayer, the history teacher, immediately yelled: "That report earned you a big, fat zero! I said it should be an oral report and you were reading it. I saw your hands on that shelf."

I got really upset and started crying. I turned the desk over and said that I wasn't reading. "Do you see any Braille paper?" I left the room. Marjorie never thanked me.

When I came to the next History class, Mr. Sayer apologized and said that was the best report he heard and I got a hundred! We got to be really good friends from then until I left the school.

Other than these two unpleasant events I was glad to be alive. We had some very good singers and musicians in my school. When I think about this, it was amazing that a school with a small number of students (perhaps 150), would be so endowed. I decided to enlist three of these folks plus Eilene and form a singing quintet. I chose my old friend, Robert Graves, Tony (Kwong) Lee and Sam Pugh. Because I listened to small vocal groups such as The Pied Pipers and the Modernaires, I thought I could write in that style. I would sing bass—something not usually done with this kind of group. The song I chose was "Among My Souvenirs".

Meanwhile, Gene, whose arrangement of "Dream" started me on my way to playing better piano, formed a similar group. One of the teachers worried that our two groups would feud. I knew this wouldn't happen. I only wanted a bit of fun; Gene was a better arranger than I was! I heard Gene's group rehearse. They were good!

My group gradually learned most of the song, and I couldn't believe how well our voices blended and the arrangement was better than I expected it to be. That was my high point as a choral arranger at that time. A couple of the guys didn't like it that I assumed leadership. I said that maybe we didn't need a real leader. If a member of the group arranged a piece he wanted us to sing, he would lead during its practice. Well, the idea seemed fine, but the guys weren't satisfied so the group broke up before it ever really got started. My only consolation was that Eilene stuck by me and loved my arrangement, and the sound was such that, if the chance ever came along again, I could write a choral arrangement which would be at least as good as "Among My Souvenirs".

Another thing which made me feel good despite the loss of my singing group was the start of an organization called the Concordia Club formed by some young, blind people. One of them had contacts with local off Broadway theaters so could get seats for little or no cost. I think it met once a month. I heard about it and joined as did Eilene. Some of the other guys and gals from my school joined as well. It was a wonderful experience to attend plays which were good even if they did not quite make it to Broadway. There were some wonderful musicians who were really friendly and loved talking about music from the standpoint of people earning their livings as musicians. What a time!

There were some sighted volunteers with vans who would pick us up, take us to the theaters and drop us off right to our front doors. One of those long rides would have a profound impact on me. As we were riding along talking to one another, Eilene suddenly put her arms around me and pressed me against her! I have no words to tell you what that was like. It was like holding her hands but ten times more powerful. There should be tons of words to express my feelings but none come to mind. I couldn't even adequately communicate the power this had, but I think Eilene sensed it. In fact, knowing her, she knew that what she was doing would be of great aid. She wanted the best for me and would do anything to help me get along in school and get the highest possible grades.

There were other van rides and she was always ready to hold me. Naturally it was something we couldn't try during Social Hours at school. The school was operated with State and private money. The administrators were always on the watch for anything which might result in a scandal that could result in money sources drying up. Like holding hands, this was not in any way sexual. It was a highly charged emotional experience.

I wondered quite often why this hit me so hard. I thought back to my earliest recollections and recalled the last time Mom held me. She said I was too old for that. Deep inside I wanted, no, needed more of it. It's something not quite recalled but repressed, awaiting something to trigger that need.

School work was never so easy. Besides radio, my best grades were in Spanish.

At home Dad was after me to design something which would allow my phonograph to play with more volume than it did at that time. I agreed with him but hadn't put thought into the idea. I finally did and came up with a relatively simple way to get the job done. It would slightly compromise the radio's performance but the phonograph would, if I was right, play louder. I assembled all the parts and enlisted Dad's help so it would get done quickly. I was always astounded by the things Dad could do, including soldering.

There are very few dates which stick in my mind, but Friday, December 26, 1947 is one I won't forget. The next day there would be a meeting of the Concordia Club, and that meant seeing Eilene.

Mom and Mary were out so Dad and I had the place to ourselves. We got an early start. We had the phonograph almost ready to try, but we both were hungry and decided to take a lunch break. I mentioned in passing that I'd be going to the Concordia Club the next day. He was always negative about that, and I never knew why. He was about to say something, but he stopped talking. He said that nobody was going any place. He had looked out the window and saw two feet of snow blanketing Brooklyn. He was right. No way would the streets be clear. For good measure three more inches fell. The local weather forecast called for light flurries!

I forced myself to put disappointment out of my mind and get back to our project. It was ready to be tested and Dad selected a recording he'd like to hear. The project worked perfectly. We added a switch to the radio cabinet which would select either the radio or the phonograph. Given that this radio had been made some time in the 1920's, it sounded wonderful now, because of my improvements, and also because of the work Mr. Schmidt did before the beginning of the War.

We had a New Year's Eve party with lots of Dad's relatives there. We demonstrated the new phonograph to the amazement of the guests. One "cousin-in-law" had too much to drink as usual and that could have ruined the evening, but we got through it. Now it was the start of 1948. I had just one more term before my graduation.

I wanted to study piano tuning if for no other reason that I wanted to know how to tune my piano. Who could tell? If I was good at that, maybe it could be my future career. In order to be able to take the course, I'd have to drop English. That was almost my worst subject. In order to drop the class early, I had to take a special State test and needed a rather high mark to pass it. I took it and got a somewhat higher grade than was needed. Thus, I then could drop English and use the remaining part of the school year to study piano tuning.

The instructor, Karl Rice, was an experienced tuner, having worked with many piano manufacturers. I wondered how he'd accept me. I knew my reputation in school was not particularly good. The first thing he said was something like this.. "Joe, you don't have a good reputation here; you know that. From what I hear, you have a good sense of music and are pretty handy with mechanical things. Piano tuning has a little bit to do with a sense of music; there's lots of mechanical work, and there's lots of common sense needed. I don't care what some people around here have said. I know and expect you will succeed."

Mr. Rice was a pretty strict person, so he immediately started teaching me, no, cramming the basics into me. He wasn't interested in anything I might say by way of thanks for his encouragement. I had only a half a year to work so work it was gonna be! I was really excelling in the course.

Meanwhile there were Social Hours. Eventually there would be another Concordia Club get-together; I was feeling good.

One day when some of us guys were in the dorm's living room listening to some new recordings, one came along which hit me with incredible power. It was "California Suite" by Mel Torme. Yes, this was another Capitol Record. Mel was a composer, an arranger as well as a fine singer. The lyrics were rather trite, telling of the glories of California life and a bit about New York City life. The music! That was the thing. It was performed with a rather large orchestra and chorus, along with solos by Mel and some small group sections featuring the Meltones, his singing group.

If you add this experience to "Music Out of the Moon", you have the two single recordings which shaped my musical thought and how I play piano right to this day. Not that I didn't have other heroes in jazz and "bop". There was George Shearing just emerging as a jazz luminary. His specialty was unusual chord progressions. I could hear them and for the most part, I could imitate them.

This was an amazing time for me. I was learning new things about radio and music. I had Eilene's constant encouragement, but also her constructive criticism if she thought I was getting too cocky.

There came a weekend when one of the girls in school invited Eilene and me to her house for some good food and talk. I'll say there was talk! Somehow it happened that Eilene and I were by ourselves. As I think about it, I think she arranged for us to be alone.

"Joe, I've really tried to help you, but do you love me?" I was really taken aback. I didn't know what love was; I didn't know what to say to her as an appropriate reply. I knew she was a great person, and it was wonderful just being around her. Well, maybe I was in love with her, so maybe I better say that I was.

"Yes, Eilene. Of course I do." Was I lying? I don't recollect anything else about that day. It would be a year or so before I found out why she asked that question. Indeed, circumstances in her life were such that it was important for her to have my reassurance.

Love! What was it really? Would I ever truly know? The question haunted me for many years.

Meanwhile Mom and I were studying college catalogs and recognized that after graduating, I still would lack some necessary credits. I would need another year of Spanish and a year of Intermediate Algebra. My real fear was algebra because, despite my technical abilities, math was not my strong suit. The school offered a post graduate program for those of us who needed additional training.

After enrolling in the program, I had time to learn more about piano tuning because there was room in my schedule for it. There was nothing more that Mr. Gun could teach me. What was still permitted was that I could continue to keep my key to the Radio Room. I could continue to experiment with recording. I could use his powerful ham station. It was so much better than my poor transmitter. I had, however, that good receiver that I got a few months earlier.

Speaking of receivers, I came home one weekend to find two bulky pieces of equipment in my bedroom. It was a radio receiver with a separate power supply. When Dad came home from work, I asked what he knew about this unit. He said that it was a gift from his boss to me. He told me to be sure to write a thank you note. I was glad he told me about that and how to show appreciation for something very special. It was something that I might not have thought about. Nobody had ever given me anything like that radio receiver.

Dad said he didn't know anything about how the thing worked, leaving me to figure it out for myself. This was a really complicated unit, much more sophisticated than the one I bought only a few months back. Like the radio I bought, it was designed for communications. It also had really good audio quality. No communications receiver that I owned or examined had ever had such superb quality. It was set up so that a recorder could be connected to it.

That unit was much better in all respects than the one I bought. With that said, there's something about earning money to buy something which is more exciting than receiving a gift, regardless of how great it might be.

I also had time to learn how to play the organ. One of my growing number of pretty good friends was Herb Severtsen, an excellent organ student. He could really play that wonderful organ which was in our assembly hall. From time to time he'd show me some of the layout of the organ. I had to learn about Stops, Combinations and Generals. He showed me why the organ had three rows of keys (known as "manuals").

Because I had some time in my schedule, I asked the organ teacher for permission to have practice time on the organ even though I wouldn't take lessons. He agreed to this because he knew of my growing interest in music.

But Eilene had taken all the courses she required. She was not coming back!

Some of my school work that term was rather easy for me, but Intermediate Algebra was a challenge. There was no way that I could earn that scholarship unless I excelled in that course. I asked the math teacher for extra help and he only said that I'd just have to keep up with the rest of the class. Well, that was no help. Normally I would have sassed him and gotten into trouble; it was always what I had done before. This time I stayed calm, but I just had to do better in that class.

Throughout my time at this school we had foreign exchange teachers who came to observe our teaching methods. At this juncture there was a brilliant man from India, Mr. Natesh. It seemed that he knew something about just everything. I had gotten to know and respect him. I asked if he knew Algebra. He did. I asked if he could take time to help me with it. He agreed to do so. He could give 15 minutes to 30 minutes most days of the week. He asked me what we were studying so he could know where and how to help. That first lesson taught me more than just Algebra. He began explaining a difficult concept. I told him that I didn't know the Braille notation for Algebra so wouldn't be able to write the information down.

He got very, very excited. "Joe, we won't write things down. Writing is for peasants! You have to think and nothing less will do!"

In a way I sort of knew about that because of my working out radio problems. But this became almost a credo. Don't talk, don't write; just think!

While he was a task master and a hard driver, because of him my grade in Intermediate Algebra steadily rose. Some of it almost read like a story.

It was getting near the end of another school year. There was a tradition in our school that near the close of the year, seniors would have a special experience. One day we could take over classes and teach. Because students could get out of hand when a senior was teaching, we were given temporary permission to issue demerits. When that day came, I taught a history class. Some guys and girls tried to give me a hard time. I reminded them that I could issue demerits, and the class calmed down. I don't remember what other classes I taught.

One day we had a class picnic. It was pleasant in the park, really beautiful weather. One of the seniors was Esther. She knew Eilene and also knew that Eilene held my hand. Esther offered to do that during the picnic. With the stress of getting ready for final exams, I was glad for her help. She did that on some other occasions and it was fine with Eilene. I only mention this to show that the proctors who chaperoned us were not as strict. It was, in general, a relaxing week.

There were other events during that week. Someone wrote a play to be presented on Senior Night. I found time to write another choral arrangement of "My Romance," a great tune by Rodgers and Hart. Fortunately the singers I chose stuck it out. Eilene was not eligible to sing with us, but I chose a girl who sang with Gene and her voice blended very well with the rest of us.

Senior Night came. The only things I remember about that night was a performance of the play I mentioned, a comedy version of Washington Irving's book about Icabod Crane and the headless horseman. There was my choral arrangement as the final presentation of the night. The play came first. I was "the headless horseman". I don't have a good sense of direction so, when I jumped onto the horse, I rode him backwards! That got a laugh which was not planned but it looked to the audience as if it was. The next line was spoken by another actor: "There goes the horseless Headman!" That really brought down the house. I didn't have time to be embarrassed because there was so much laughter. We were a hit!

As our quintet was being announced, I was painfully aware that rehearsal time was woefully inadequate. The very last few notes were never really rehearsed. Remember, we couldn't read music! What would happen? We began well enough. We sounded really good! I might have been excited except for my concerns about the ending. I never should have worried. Most of these singers were also musicians who understood jazz. I knew my part. The lead singer only had to sing the melody or so I thought. The last notes were terrific even though I didn't write them. Nobody in the audience could have guessed that we dodged the bullet. The arrangement was a hit. People were surprised that I could have written it. After the program was over I found my singers and thanked each one for making the song sound wonderful.

Near the end of the year I took whatever exams which were needed to complete most of my credits toward entering college.

It was Graduation Day. Mom, Dad, and Mary were all there. Dad had his trusty camera and took pictures of me as I stood on the front steps of the school building. Then we moved into the auditorium. The Senior Chorus performed (it included me). Awards were presented to those who accomplished extra things. Witty got a ton of those. He did many jobs in the school, such as locking each classroom door every night. He earned money as a result of running the candy stand. Other guys and gals were also given awards. I didn't get one.

Of course diplomas were handed out. I did get one of those. The ceremony closed with the singing of the school's Alma Mater, led by our chorus. This was written many years earlier by the director of our music department. As far as I was concerned, it was a cut above most high school songs. Despite all the bitter years which were behind me, I nevertheless was moved by that ceremony.

After a week off, I'd be back at Camp Wapanacki for the last time. I made up my mind that regardless of what the schedule called for, I would do what I damn well pleased. What could they do? They could tell me I couldn't come back to camp. I wasn't gonna be back in any case.

It would be a different camp season, partly because Eilene would not be there. I figured I'd probably get by though because I wasn't going to get myself stressed out doing anything I didn't want to do. I meant it, and it's what I did.

My friend, Nario, was there as he had been every year since we had that silly fight and then became close friends. He knew all about Eilene and what she meant to me. He could see the changes which she made possible.

I decided to join him and others for an overnight hike, something we had to do each year. I had never hiked with Nario so thought we could have some fun. We did, all right! We had our supplies ready to go, our canteens, mess kits, and ponchos. But Whitty was a counselor that year. The camp director was experimenting by having the best campers become counselors even though they were totally blind. My friend, Gene, was a counselor. At any rate, Bob was our counselor on the hike. The weather was ominous. There was dampness and a slight mist. Would it rain on our parade?

Bob (or "Witty") was amazing. He knew his way around the local trails so had a very good idea where to find our camp site. Nario and a few others had pretty good sight and they could help locate it when we got close. We were out in the field near a farm. I don't know if the farm was in use but Nario and I explored and found a barn in which there was a tractor and some tools. We had a vague idea that these new-found items would come in handy. Witty was really good so he stacked some wood which was conveniently in the vicinity. He had some kindling made of twisted newspaper which he brought along. In spite of his best efforts and those of a couple of other guys, the fire would not burn.

Nario and I volunteered to get it going. Witty wondered how we thought we could do that when nobody else could. We quietly went into the barn. Our idea was to drain some crankcase oil from the tractor and use it to start the fire. I knew what to look for so I got under the tractor. Nario found a suitable wrench to loosen the drain cock. We found some kind of container to hold the oil. I had Nario get ready to hold the container under the cock when I got ready to remove the nut which kept the oil from running out. I loosened the nut and just as it was about to fall out, Nario got the container under where the nut would come loose. I got it out and oil ran right into the container. It filled so fast! I got Nario to get out of there so I could put the nut back. We lost some oil, but I don't think it was enough to cause damage to the tractor.

We got back, poured some of our precious booty on the kindling and used Witty's cigarette lighter to get the oil to catch. Oil won't burn the way gasoline does, but it did get the kindling going, and eventually we had a nice fire for cooking our cans of pork and beans and brew coffee. Witty was a bit suspicious of us. He asked us how we could start a fire when he knew we didn't have the experience he did. I remember asking him if he was happy with the fire. When he said he was, I said that we had a magic power which was limited to only a precious few people. Witty decided it was best that he not know what magic we had. HMMM! I wonder why he didn't smell the burning oil.

A day or two later after dinner I was walking up the cabin line toward my tent when I ran into a little kid. He seemed to be doing nothing except standing around.

"You know," I said to him, "you're standing on a path which lots of guys use. I wasn't moving all that fast or you'd have been really banged up.

"I'm sorry. Oh, are you Joe, the radio guy?"

"Guilty as charged. I don't remember your being around here. What's your name?"

"Rod," he said. "How did you get into radio and that stuff? I sure would like to get into that, but I can't."

"Why not," I asked?

"Everybody says I can't because you have to have sight."

"Rod, if I ever listened to all the folks who said that I couldn't do anything, I wouldn't have been in that field. I love it; it's such great fun."

"I don't think I can do it."

"Hey, Rod! Don't ever let me hear you tell me that! Stop that idea right now, unless you don't really have a burning desire to do this stuff."

"Oh Joe, I really want it!"

"Yeah, I'll just say one thing: Don't let anybody steal your dreams. Dream big and find a way to make it happen."

I walked away and never saw the kid again. I wondered if he had the guts to try, really try. It was perhaps 40 years later when I was running a newsletter for blind computer users. He was one of the subscribers. I didn't notice his name on the subscribers' list because the incident was all but forgotten. I got a letter from him, telling me that he earned a PH d. in physics. He said that it was because of what I told him so many years ago that he had the courage to pursue his dream. I was so happy for him.

I digress. Back to that camping season. Some of us older guys graduated from a cabin to large tents. Each tent could sleep four with plenty of room for luggage and odds and ends. One day Nario and I were outside our tent and heard something odd. We went to the tent and found that the center pole of the tent was collapsing. We managed to keep it from completely falling but we were not able to raise it either. If we walked away, the entire tent would collapse. We were supposed to be in the mess hall, and fortunately a couple of people came looking for us. We were about to be called down for being late, but we showed them what was happening. When they figured it out, they helped and we were able to get that pole centered just the way it was supposed to be and there was no more trouble with the tent. We were heroes!! Campers and staffers alike couldn't believe what we had done.

I really loved boating on the camp's lake. The oars were designed to be held in place in their locks so they would maintain their positions. Of course we couldn't feather them but at least we could count on their being at a good angle. I hung out on the dock teaching boating safety to some of the younger campers.

One day many of the campers took a bus ride as a kind of field trip. Those of us who couldn't go because the bus was full had to take boats out on the water as a kind of "moonlight row". My favorite boat was an aluminum racer which could probably hold four or five people. I hoped I could take it out with no passengers because I just wanted a quiet row. One of the counselors would let me take that boat out but with the proviso that I had to take two passengers. I asked for the lightest kids so I could row the boat at a good speed.

It was easy for a blind oarsman to row on the lake and return to the dock safely. The camp had a PA system which was near the dock. Music would play through it during the boating time. The oarsman could use the sound as a guide and come right back close to the dock so that a counselor could guide the oarsman back and tie up.

One of the passengers was a young kid of perhaps nine or ten years old. This kid, John P., had a sad history. He lived in Italy during the war and his town was heavily bombed. He was an orphan. He also had lost his eyesight. I have no idea how he ended up at our camp. I do know that he could be very tough to handle if provoked.

The other boy, Henry, was the son of the school's grounds keeper. I knew he was sighted so that would give me the opportunity to row in a part of the lake which was hard to navigate because of numerous lily pads. I started off and all was well. The kids didn't talk. I got the boat moving pretty well, considering the extra weight I was hauling. I got to the point which I thought was near to my destination, so I asked Henry if he could guide me into that area. He said he could and began giving me very good directions.

John got violent. He tried to turn us over. The boat was very narrow and I thought he had a good chance to succeed. I lost an oar! He yelled that he hated sighted people and that we all had to die. I kept my cool. I yelled to Henry to duck, and I took my remaining oar and swung it with all my force and conked John on the head. He fell unconscious into the bottom of the boat. I asked Henry if he saw the lost oar. He said it was close enough so he could grab it. He did, and I jammed it into the lock and rowed as fast as I could go until I docked the boat. I found out that John threw all the life jackets overboard, so it could have been a catastrophe. I do not know to this day why I hadn't insisted we put them on before we started out. It was probably because of my mood as a result of my being stuck with a couple of kids I didn't want in the first place.

The counselors on shore could see the whole scene and were horror struck because all the other boats were out so they couldn't do a thing but watch in fear. I was asked to help John out of the boat. I refused. They said that I could take the boat out alone, just the way I wanted. I wasn't interested. The evening was spoiled. The incident went through the camp and, I was a hero again.

The school Principal's daughter was doing quite a bit with music. I don't remember what she was doing, but it was more than she could handle so she asked me to take on some of her tasks. I accepted. I also played for the nondenominational service as I had done last year.

I noticed that some of the younger kids were learning the game of baseball. We had a nice diamond so I joined one of the teams as a player/coach. The counselor in charge was glad because he had nobody to spare to do that job. I explained how to hold a bat. I had the pitcher bounce a few balls two feet in front of the plate the way it was done in gym class. Then we played our first game. The first batter on my team struck out. I asked the counselor how he swung the bat. He told me that the kid never took the bat off his shoulder.

I called the team together for a conference and said, "Guys, I can understand that you want to get the sense of the ball and maybe feel the slight breeze as the ball crosses the plate. When I come to bat, I may do that too. What I won't do is take that third strike without swinging the bat. I don't mind if you swing and miss. I will mind big time if you take that strike and not swing. You'll hear from me and you won't like it. Now don't let me bench you for this because I will if I have to. Got it?"

All the kids yelled that they understood. Sure, there were strikeouts; but I don't remember even one time that the batter took that third strike. I didn't either. I told you earlier that I could seldom hit the ball in gym class. Well, I'm here to tell you that I batted .500 that season and my team won most of its games! Gee, those kids thought I was Babe Ruth. Can you believe it? What was different now?

The last night of camp came—Awards Night. I got just about all the awards there were, including the coveted "W" patch which stood for Wapanacki. It was the highest award there was. Of course, there were lots of deserving kids and they got awards as well, but yours truly got more than anyone else!

I came home with pride I had not known—not the pride of arrogance but the pride of achievement that comes with some hard work, which I thought was just having fun for once.

As always, I went to Grandma's house with the usual assortment of visitors. Aunt Avis was there, complete with mysteries and some books devoted to funny historical events which I looked forward to hearing as she read them to me. Uncle Art and Aunt Kitty were there with their 3 or 4 year old daughter, Alice. One day Alice was riding with me in the rumble seat of Uncle Art's old car. We were going along and Alice was determined to stand up on the seat. If there was a sudden stop, she'd go flying and likely be killed. No matter how nicely I told her or how I yelled at her, she was determined to stand up. I had to grab her and hold her down. That was the worst ride I had in that rumble seat. I was ready to let her fall out. She reminded me of all the problems I had with kids when I was small and they wouldn't play with me, and those who bullied me at school. Truly, I just plain disliked kids, any kids.

One day I was in the shed playing that old parlor organ. One of the straps used to pull the bellows broke. More notes quit working. It was time to repair the instrument, but would Grandma let me? I asked her and she gave me the go-ahead. I asked her if she'd help if I needed her, and she consented.

Grandma trusted me with the organ, but once I started, I wasn't at all sure she should have. The entire mechanism had to be lifted from the bellows (wind chest) in one piece. Once I removed the many screws which secured the mechanism, I found that I almost had no room to lift it away because I was wedged in between the organ and one of the shed's walls. Grandma lifted one end, and I had the other and together we moved it to a table where I could check it out.

One of the stops was called "Vox Humana". It never worked when I pulled it. It was just that the bearing which was in a little hole was about to fall out. Once I hammered it into place, the bearing was straight and the device could freely rotate. There was a series of blades which, when turning, would partly open or partially close the airway which forced the notes to sound.

Next, I had Grandma vacuum the inside of the wind chest. Lots of dust had accumulated over who knows how many years. She vacuumed the underside of the mechanism where the reeds were. These reeds were very much like what you would find in a harmonica.

Grandma even had the exact kind of cloth needed to operate the bellows. We measured the proper length. I had her sew a kind of rolled seam along each side of the cloth. Then I attached it to the bellows and the pedal; the work was complete. In short, when the organ was reassembled, everything worked. The Vox Humana now worked. Its effect was to add a bit of tremolo or vibrato to the overall organ sound—adding a beautiful texture. Grandma was overjoyed. I was sure glad about that because it looked at first as though I was in over my head.

The visit ended soon after that. I was about to return to school for my last year. I spent my last week of the summer at home experimenting with my ham radio gear and helping Mom with odd jobs.

Chapter 14

I couldn't believe it! It was September, 1948, my last year in that school. While I had accomplished so many things, I really didn't know them for what they were and later for what they would mean. All I understood was what happened during those earlier years. I wasn't able to put all that behind me. It was extra baggage that I didn't need or want, but those bad times continued to be in the background—haunting me and taunting me! Well, it was a relief to know that I would soon be done with that place after what seemed like a lifetime!

I was certain that this year would drag by, but, in fact, it was perhaps the most challenging and busiest year of all up to that time. There was no Eilene; there were no radio classes. I had two major subjects in which I had to excel if I wanted to obtain that scholarship, or really my parents who wanted and which I definitely did not.

Now and then I went to a Social Hour just to hang out. Most of the girls ignored me, but there was Esther. While I attended lots of classes with her, I didn't pay her any serious attention. She knew Marjorie and Eilene and had heard about my need to hold hands. In fact, that was all over the girls' dorms.

So Esther offered to help me during Social Hours. Indeed, I knew Eilene would be happy that I would get that help. Even with my strong need, I do not think I'd have accepted it had I known that Esther had her own, personal agenda. She had decided that I would marry her. She told a few students that it was almost a "done deal". It became apparent that Esther needed to be the center of attention. She'd tell stories about how mistreated she was and how people were against her. I always treated her nicely but gradually withdrew from our friendship. Just a few years later I'd have a similar pattern repeated.

Dad was going to church much less than he had been. He loved to play golf, and Sunday was a golf day. Dad didn't begin playing the game until he was forty years old. Dad was a natural athlete. In time he could shoot in the high 70's on a good day. When we were at Grandma's, Dad would have his golf bag with him. Uncle Art also started learning the game, and he and Dad would play a round whenever they had a chance. I began going with them and caddied for Dad. Well, I couldn't do everything a caddy could because I couldn't locate balls for him. It amounted just to my carrying his clubs. Some of the courses they played were long, championship-style courses—so, I got a lot of exercise. Even when we weren't at Grandma's, I'd sometimes would go with him when he played golf and carry his bag.

I was beginning to question God's very existence. He never answered my prayers. I stumbled on a book by H. L. Menken which might put light on the matter, titled "A Treatise on the Gods". It was well written. He made point after point which demonstrated that there was indeed no God. The Church was designed as a way to rob people of their money. However, I wondered if it really could be that bad.

As usual I went to Mass one Sunday and spent time after the mass ended, with Father Martin. I didn't have the nerve to bring up what I read and question him. I wanted to learn how wrong Menken was. As I was talking to the priest, I heard some noise behind me. Something was being dragged along the floor. I asked what it was. Father Martin seemed as though he was about to dance. He rubbed his hands with glee.

"Look at those burlap bags of money! The armored truck will have a good load this time."

I excused myself and went home. "Yes," I thought. "Menken was "right on target." I saw it for myself.

I resolved not to go to church because it really was a place whose sole purpose was to steal from us. Father Joe was serving in the church along with Father Martin. After some Masses he would play baseball with some of the children from the church. He helped to set up a little league where children from other churches would compete. He was so approachable. Everybody loved him, but all thoughts of him vanished after this encounter.

I was still in the Senior Chorus. We learned "Die Almacht," by

Franz Schubert. What a soaring tune—that was mixed with a quiet, beautiful solo voice. I should have thought about the fact that this piece was deeply religious—a deeply worshipful piece of music, dedicated to Almighty God. I did not, however, think about that. We were told that we were to sing in New York's Town Hall with the New York Philharmonic Symphony Orchestra! I was not much of a singer, but I could blend well, and was so proud to be singing among the other basses. It was the sort of moment that only a musician or true music lover can experience—a high that cannot be had with alcohol or drugs!

Meanwhile, I had to bear down with Spanish. Because there weren't many students taking the course, it was not scheduled as a formal class. I talked to the Spanish teacher, Mr. Rodriguez, who said he'd occasionally tutor us. Those of us who were taking that informal Spanish class got together during some study halls to compare notes. Somehow I became the leader, explaining all the vagaries of Spanish grammar and translating some hard passages for them. I can't remember who the other students were; well, I think there was Lorraine, a great singer who Gene used when he ran a quartet. She played it "cool" with me, but underneath I think she understood me. I never tried to find out though.

In addition, I was doing very well with Piano Tuning. I was getting quite proficient and gaining speed. I was almost as good as the teacher. He could tune a good piano in a bit less than 40 minutes; I could tune one in a bit less than 50 minutes. Eventually the teacher thought I was good enough to tune most of the pianos in the school, and there were a lot of them in dorms, classrooms, and practice rooms.

One problem I did run into when I was assigned to tune the piano in a classroom. Everything went well until a bass string broke. I had some training in replacing broken strings, but I don't think the teacher had any of the special strings which I needed. All I could do was finish the tuning and report what happened. Mr. Rice was furious. "I thought you were better than that," he said. "You must have been careless and tuned the piano's pitch too high! I told him that I didn't do that. That made him all the more angry. This happened on a Friday, so all I could think about that weekend was the broken string and dreading the next tuning class.

On Monday when I went into the classroom, the teacher came to me and apologized. He said that my tuning was perfect and that he found there was a weakness in the design of the piano which led to the string's breaking. He was able to splice in a bit of piano wire and all was fine. Was I relieved or what?

After that, tuning was fine. Mr. Rice was a fine and honorable man. He expected much from me—maybe a bit more. He called me into his room and told me that our school was beginning an experimental project of teaching veterans who were blinded in World War II—and he wanted me to teach a few of them about piano tuning. Whether they learned it so it could be a career for them wasn't the point. The skills they would learn by using tools and thinking about music and what constitutes good sounding instruments would train both their hands and their minds. This was a real challenge and I wondered if I could be of real help. Because Mr. Rice was my teacher, I knew I would try. It made me think about how a sighted man must have handled his environment before and then after his loss of sight.

I don't have a clue about what I taught those three guys. They were not with us very long; so, I don't know how much of what I taught had any lasting benefits. I do recall one of them. I'll call him Frank because I don't remember his name. It was our second day together. We were climbing the stairs to the 4th floor where the tuning rooms were located. Apparently Frank had "seen" windows on the flight between the 3rd and 4th floors. Suddenly he let go of my arm and moved with surprising speed to the nearest one.

"I've had it with life. Blindness is a living hell, and there's no escaping it. I'm going to jump through this window and don't try to stop me!" He was a big guy over 6 feet. My mind raced to find something to do or say. I thought about all my troubles in school.

"Frank," I said. "I've had a bad time in this school. I've almost been expelled, and I don't think it would take much more before that's gonna happen. Hey, do me a favor. Please don't jump on my watch." He didn't. I don't know what happened to him after that. He and some other vets left the school's experimental classes soon after this scary experience. I hope and pray that he found the courage to go on.

One day Mr. Gun called on me to help him with a special project. He was developing a remote controlled camera for the Government, and he needed someone to handle the remote control unit so he could check the camera's actions. That was exciting.

While I was still in his class, he told us about designing what was then a rather small portable radio which could almost fit into a shirt pocket. Now a year later, he gave me one of the prototypes to test for him. I only had an evening to play with it, and after spending time with it, I returned the radio to him with a report of my findings. Eventually the radio was marketed as "The Minitron".

The Concordia Club still met each month, which always meant that I'd see Eilene. She knew that Esther was helping me as best she could, and Eilene was glad. I wasn't at all certain whether she would be jealous or not.

There was one particular meeting which stood out. John Wahlen had joined the group, and he was a fearless subway traveler. He told me that he was able to do it by using a white cane in a special way. He became more and more insistent that I learn to use a cane so I'd be able to move around New York City independently. At that same session a woman named Cecilia was there. She was a certified teacher of mobility for the blind. People at my school talked about a need for this training, but it wasn't being taught. John asked Cecilia if she'd be willing to show me a little about using a cane. She was not in the group as a teacher, but she said she'd be glad to show me how to use a cane. As usual, I was afraid, but I made myself try it. I won't go into detail, but what she showed me essentially was that the cane is held in front of me one step ahead of where my feet are. When I stepped out with my left foot, I'd move the cane to my right. If I stepped with my right foot, I'd move the cane to the left. The cane would touch the ground where my next step will be. This protects me or anyone using a cane for that matter against inadvertently falling down stairs or showing where the edge of a subway platform was. I had one or two lessons, and I then understood the principles. However, I didn't want to use the technique because Mr. Gun managed to go wherever he wanted without the aid of a cane, a dog, or any travel aid. And I wanted to be like him.

Another one of those meetings I recall was when some of us were seated in a room. I don't remember why we were there. While we waited for whatever was supposed to happen, a recording of "South Pacific" was playing. The odd thing was the songs flowed seamlessly from one to the next. There wasn't time to change from one 78 RPM disk to the next. Not only that, there was no background hiss as would be expected when playing 78's. I discovered that I was hearing music recorded in a new way on what was called "microgroove" recordings. Columbia called them "long playing" records which was its trademark. Eventually everyone called them LP's. Dad had also discovered these new recordings, and he knew enough to make small changes to our phonograph so that we could play them.

I thought about Alex and his sound system. I included turntables which could turn at the speed needed to play LP's, so I knew that with a very small change, he could play these new recordings. It wasn't that I was ahead of my time, but by including that speed, Alex could play "Talking Books" for the blind. That was probably the last time I thought about that sound system for some years. I lost track of Alex.

On some weekends I'd use the wireless phonograph, which Father Martin gave me, to play recordings for as many people in the apartment house who might care to listen. I got a bit more elaborate by adding a microphone so I could talk as well as play records. We had some golfers in the building, and I would sometimes interview one of them, and, of course, those interviews were broadcast to my rather small audience.

I continued to repair radios for some folks in the apartment house. I'd occasionally repair a radio for others in the neighborhood who heard about me from satisfied apartment house dwellers. Radio experiments cost money, and this work supplied me with the money I needed. I wouldn't get it from my folks because they were saving for my education. Even if I got a scholarship, it would not cover all the expenses. Did I really need college?

Maybe I'd make a career of servicing radios. I didn't know what lay ahead and about how the design of radios would change. Radios were made by running wires from one point to another and I could follow those wires and trace out a circuit. Within perhaps five years, the wires would be replaced by lines of thin foil which meant blind people would be unable to trace radio circuits nor could we solder connections. This would be the end of most repairs, except for older radios.

The school year moved on. My advisor told me that it was time to select the college I would attend. I wrote for catalogs for several colleges which had courses in various aspects of radio, not so much about repair as how to work in commercial radio stations. I was thinking about becoming a "radio engineer". This didn't mean designing radio equipment. Rather, it had to do with being "the guy behind the mike". It would take only a few years and there would be very few people who did engineering exclusively. An engineer would have to announce, pick out records to play, read the latest news, and more. Before I completed college, these changes would begin to take place. This was something which was totally unexpected.

Getting back to schoolwork, I was raising my grades to the point where I was told that I had to take some tests which would demonstrate whether I was or was not college material. That meant that my teachers considered me likely to pass such tests. I was told that I did well on them.

I sent in applications for entrance into several colleges. I had to specify whether there were any physical problems or special housing needs. I was rejected by a few schools because "blind" was on my applications. I remember being rejected by one school because its location was such that it was very cold, and there'd be lots of snow. The officials decided that I could not handle those harsh conditions. This is so typical of how people decide what a blind person can or cannot handle based on nothing! It was their inability to put themselves in my shoes. In fact, most people have so little experience with blind people that they cannot imagine how a blind person can handle even small tasks. I would find this situation hounding me in so many endeavors over the years.

The school year was winding down. One day I got a real surprise. Syracuse University accepted my application! The faculty and Deans bent over backwards to find out what I needed in order for me to matriculate successfully. The University had every radio course I wished to take.

However, it didn't automatically get me into that college. There was a special department for the Blind in New York State called Vocational Rehabilitation Service (VRS). This organization sponsors vocational training of blind people on many different levels. I had to make an appointment to speak with one of its counselors who would have to pass on my credentials for the scholarship. I found out that I was going to be under the direction and guidance of the toughest person in that department. He didn't let people get by with much. At that time very few blind students were accepted for a college education.

When the time came for that all-important interview, I was intimidated but glad at the same time. If I didn't qualify, it would mean that I didn't have to go to college. I was tired of school and the thought of four more years of boring study. When I sat with the interviewer, he said that I might qualify, but he planned to make it hard for me. He wanted to know with reasonable certainty that any guy who passed his tests would stand a good chance of handling college. He said that it was no picnic. I do not remember what questions he asked. What I do know is that what he asked were reasoned questions and that I had answers for them. He told me that he gave me his fullest endorsement and believed that I was sufficiently mature because I answered all his hard questions with comments based on the fact that I truly understood what I was getting into.

There was one thing I absolutely had to do sometime after school closed, and that was to go to at least six radio stations and talk to their chief engineers and ask them if they believed I was capable of working in commercial radio.

It seemed like forever, but I knew the school year would end. We were going to have the final dance of the year. In this one there would be a dinner in which the boys and girls would sit with each other rather than on their respective sides of the dining room. Well, I had to eat so would sit at a table with girls. I do remember that Marie was sitting with us. We were carrying on a brisk conversation—exchanging jokes.

About the time the dinner was over, Marie said to me, "Joe, I never knew you could be fun!"

"You never gave me a chance."

I was upset and ran out of the dining room and would have loved to skip the dance. But because Mr. Mitchell asked me some time before this if I would spin records so the dancers would have music, I stayed in the radio room for a time and calmed down. I got the equipment set up for the dance.

I thought I'd have a bit of fun. I had two turntables to work with so I could play music continuously. It was along the lines of that sound system I designed for Alex a couple of years before. I played music as I was supposed to, but I had one disk which was not music. I planned that one near the end of the evening. It was the sounds of an air raid which was recorded in London during World War II. I thought I'd mix it in with music and see if I could generate a bit of excitement. The time came and there were the sounds of planes and the screech of bombs on their way to targets below. Then there were the booms as they exploded. There was a sudden scream. There was confusion enough. I wondered if my silly prank was as funny as I thought it would be. I found out that one of the girls, Winifred, had fainted. She suffered through many German raids over London during her younger years. My recording was too real. She was all right, but I wasn't. How could an apology ever sound sincere? I had to try. She explained how it hit her. She understood what I wanted to do and was even sorry that she ruined my stunt. I never tried anything like that again!

It was down to my last two months of school, and I'd be off that campus for good! Something which seemed unrelated to the rest of the year actually had a profound meaning for many of us. One of the girls wanted to sing in the auditorium and asked one of the piano teachers to accompany her songs. I think it was Miss Thode, my old nemesis. At any rate, the girl, Mary Duffy, ran out of her classroom crying, which was noticed by a few of us who were around the area of that classroom. I'm pretty sure Bob Whitstock was one of them. I figured that was how the school always did things so that would be the end of the story.

Whitty was really annoyed and talked about this to quite a few of us. We all believed that the school's staff didn't appreciate what talent there was in the school, and it was decided to show all of them once and for all what we could do. But it was just a bit less than two months before school would be closed. How could we mount anything which could showcase our abilities? Whitty talked to more than thirty people whom he thought were not given due credit for what they could do. Everybody was highly motivated to do a show and do it to the best of our abilities. We wanted to leave a mark of absolute excellence which would be remembered long after we left that school!

Assignments were handed out to everybody who had a serious interest in mounting what would end up being a spectacular talent show. Whitty assigned himself to write two short playlets. Mr. Mitchell (the one who got me out of trouble) heard about our plans and showed one of the musicians, Herb Severtsen, a kind of xylophone which had little cranks that when rotated, would play a note. Herb said he could master it. He would use it as a part of a pseudo country band. There were two girls who could play guitar and sing country songs, so they would be a part of the band. They needed a bass player. My friend, Herman Foster, could play the bass, but he was needed to play piano and sax in a jazz combo so he couldn't handle the bass. In fact, his jazz combo also needed a bass player. It happened that the school owned a really good full-size, upright bass. Herb and Herman elected me to play it. I had never, ever seen a bass, but because of my personal study of music, I was acquainted with the bass lines needed for various musical styles. I had to learn how to play it and play the notes exactly on pitch! It should take years to learn that, and I had to learn it in six weeks!

Along with all this, Herb assigned me to write two choral arrangements. Herb would also write one. Whitty assigned me to play small parts in his playlets. How could I do all of these things and still do my homework and pass the final Regents exams? I knew the only time I'd have to write the two choral arrangements would be during Easter vacation. I wrote the two choral arrangements, but Herb and I decided that with rehearsal time at a premium, that we could only do one song. I converted one of my songs to an organ and piano transcription. The piano part was beyond me. There was a really nice Cuban girl named Irma Maso who was an accomplished pianist. I gave her the Braille score, and she learned it almost immediately. We only had time for two run-throughs. And we sounded really good. I was the organist. I wrote the music and called it "Love Moods". I borrowed a few phrases from "Music Out of the Moon" for thematic material.

Then there was the choral arrangement. The song I selected was "Blue Room", a tune by Rodgers and Hart. I had 24 voices to work with, and Herman Foster to sing solo in some places. I knew he had the perfect voice for this. In one section there were eight separate parts, which seemed as though it would be too "busy," but it worked out to be seamless and beautiful. There was a problem, however. The girls didn't like me, at least most of them didn't. They said that if I wrote anything, they wouldn't sing it. We had to tell them that Herb wrote it.

One of the girls who was to sing in the chorus was Mary O. I didn't know her very well, but I remembered her from that Eurhythmics class of many years past. She was a good music student. When she understood how the girls felt about me, she said that she would teach the girls' parts and would keep my secret that I wrote the arrangement. The guys knew that I was the arranger and had no problem with it. I taught them their parts which they learned quickly. They were all in the Senior Chorus; so, learning choral parts was nothing new to them.

The song required a combo consisting of piano, drums, and bass. I had to play the bass and thus I couldn't sing in my own arrangement. I couldn't play the piano part, of course. It occurred to me that Albert Peroni was not doing anything in the show and could play a somewhat mechanical-sounding piano. He agreed to learn the piano part so he'd play the correct chords. It took a bit of time, but he did get it. Someone told me about Vera Bishop. I asked if she was willing to play the drums for my choral arrangement as well as for the jazz group. Vera was, well, an underachiever, so was glad for the chance to show the world what she could do.

The rehearsals for both the girls' and boys' choral parts were almost complete. The girls were having their final rehearsal before the whole chorus was to do the full arrangement. I was quietly listening to them as they sang. They sounded so great that I had to applaud despite my not wanting them to know I was listening. Some of them figured out that I was the likely writer of the arrangement. They liked it and since it was too late for them to quit, they would sing my choral arrangement despite themselves.

One of those rehearsals was with the country group. I was not yet solid with the bass. I was working with the two girls who were singing a Cajun song, which I never heard until that moment. I got the hang of the tune all right, but my pitch was a bit off. You know what almost happened. They didn't want me to play along with their singing because I was ruining it. I knew my notes were just a bit off and my hope was that I'd get it right before we were to perform. With practice I did become quite proficient with the instrument, which amazed some people who knew that it should take years to learn to play accurately.

To say the least, it was perhaps the most hectic time in my life thus far. I had to learn my two, small parts in Witty's playlets, and I had to play the bass in several songs. Added to all this was that I had to keep up with schoolwork. Could I do this?

Let me tell you, rehearsals were taxing. One minute I had to go up to the organ loft so I could sound like the angel Gabriel calling down from Heaven. I hardly had time to run down a couple of flights of stairs and grab the bass for the next number. Even though I got things right in the dress rehearsal, I had no confidence that I could do all the many things when the night of the performance came.

A few days before the performance I asked Mr. Gun if he'd record the show for me. He refused, saying something to the effect that this show wouldn't be worth recording. This was the only time in all the years that I knew Bob Gunderson that I was really angry with him.

Witty persuaded the principal to invite our friends and families. I was able to ask Eilene to be there. I wanted her to witness the culmination of our efforts. It would be wonderful for her to hear my bass playing, organ playing, and what I knew was the best music I'd done. She would hear the culmination of many hours of hard work done by so many people! My family would be there. I never told them that I learned to play the bass and the organ or that I did some choral writing. I wanted them to be surprised at all the people and their various talents.

The night was here. I was really nervous and I needed to calm down so I could get things right! Esther was somewhere, and I found her. I asked her to hold me for just a few minutes. I knew Eilene would understand, and truly I really wished it could be Eilene and not Esther. I knew a rather private place where we could be alone for fifteen minutes or so. It was a bit risky. We'd both be in trouble if we were seen. We were not discovered, and I had the time I needed to calm down.

It was time. The curtains were closed. I stood center stage, about three feet from the apron. Just as the curtains parted, I started to play a "line" of a few notes. Then the audience saw Tony Lee entering from stage left and begin to sing the opening notes of "It's a Pity to Say Goodnight". They saw Tony walking confidently toward me until we met. Then a small jazz combo filled in, giving a full background to Tony's singing. We sounded great! What a beginning! The curtains closed so the next act would have time to set up. I wondered if the show could sustain its momentum.

We never got around to printing a programme, so I can't give you a blow-by-blow commentary. I can say that, as each act set up, our MC, Betty, smoothly made transitions between the acts. She carefully named the performers. I do remember the last part of the evening. Everything was going unbelievably well. The final skit was ending. I was in the organ loft about to be Gabriel, shouting my final line from Heaven.

I ran down the stairs to the auditorium level. I was all sweated up. My hands were wet, and I had to play the organ. I splashed water on my face and rinsed my hands and got to the organ bench in time for Betty to introduce Irma and me when we were to play "Love Moods". It went perfectly, just the way the previous acts had done. It was time for the last act, the big choral number. The singers took their places. Albert was at the piano; Vera was at the drums and I had the bass. A few notes of introduction and the arrangement rolled out like liquid. When it ended, there was thunderous applause. We bowed to the audience and the applause continued for a considerable time.

The principal then stepped to the podium. "During my many years as principal, I didn't believe the student body had any special talents. Our chorus had some successes, but what I saw and heard tonight made me very proud to be your principal. This was absolutely professional in every way. I hope this night can be repeated every year. Thank you for what you taught me. Good night."

I left the building as quickly as I could. I couldn't talk to anyone. All this work, cramming it in while studying, and it was over. I doubted that I could ever be a part of anything so special. And since Mr. Gun didn't record it, it was gone.

However, as I recalled some of what that evening produced, I also remembered that I had heard Betty announce my last two pieces without mentioning my name. Was it just the nerves of the moment or did she purposely not mention me. How many would have known that I put those two pieces together and composed one of them or did they see me as only the organist and bass player. I'll never know. I saw Betty one day but decided that it was best to leave it alone.

Three surprising things happened the next day. One of the school's piano teachers stopped me as I walked down the school building corridor. "I know you wrote those last two arrangements, and they were really good." I thanked her. She always was annoyed when she heard a student playing jazz. There couldn't have been a higher compliment.

The next surprise was at once gratifying and sad. I ran into Mr. Gun, and he was chagrined as he told me what a big mistake he made by not recording our show. He hated to back down on an opinion once it was openly expressed, but this time he sure changed his mind.

Regardless, what counted for me was that there was no trace of all our work except in memory.

The next surprise was not good, not at all. I knew that Marjorie was paying special attention to Tommy. Before that Tommy was with Esther, which caused some conflicts. I was a friend of Tommy's, but he resented that I sometimes spent time with Esther. He wouldn't have believed me even if I told him that I needed Esther's help, but I was not interested in her in any other way. Suddenly, it made no difference. He now was interested in Marjorie, and I seldom ever saw her.

One of the guys said that on the night of the show the two of them were in the middle of a little sex and were caught by a teacher. From that time until the close of the year they would be isolated from the rest of the students. They would be permitted to graduate but could not even stay to receive their diplomas. Actually Marjorie was in her post graduate year just as I was. Just before I was to take my last exam, I found Marjorie in Study Hall crying. I went over to her and I softly spoke her name.

"Get away from me. I'm not supposed to talk to anyone. You'll get into trouble just the way I have."

"Marjorie, I frankly don't care. For all those years in this school, trouble was my middle name. What can they do to me now? So, well, I have to talk to you this last time. Marge, I'm sorry for doubtless annoying you all too often. In spite of it, you came through when I needed you. Maybe you didn't want to do it, but I just have to thank you for being there for me even when you might not have wanted to. I can never say enough to show my real appreciation."

I don't think she was gonna say anything, but I went back to my seat because I thought I heard the Study Hall proctor walking down the hall.

Later I heard that Marjorie went home to face her parents. Tommy was a coward. He went uninvited to one of the students he knew. That student didn't appreciate Tommy's coming to him without so much as a phone call. I think Tommy did stay with him for a couple of days, and I heard nothing more until the grapevine told some of us the news that Tommy did marry Marjorie after she graduated college.

It was time for my Regents exams. There was a conflict. The Algebra and the Spanish exams were scheduled for the same time. That meant that a proctor would stay with me to be sure I didn't talk with any student about the exam. I don't remember which exam came first, Spanish or Algebra. Let's say it was Spanish. For some people, they took Algebra. The proctor had to make sure I was isolated from all students until my special exam would be held later in the afternoon.

Eilene gave me a ring some time ago, and I always wore it. It gave me comfort. I forgot to put it on that morning. It took a bit of convincing, but the proctor let me make a trip to my dorm to pick it up. My nervousness about the Algebra test calmed down almost immediately. I went into the exam room, and my old history teacher, Mr. Sayer, was the one who administered the exam. We got along very well. He would often make me laugh when things were tense. I remember that he read a very difficult question involving a polynomial equation. I was struggling with it for too long, and time was moving on. The exam had to be completed within a specified time. While I was stewing, I kept touching the ring. Mr. Sayer said: "Joe, if you don't get this, I'm gonna give you a job mopping floors!" I laughed like heck, and immediately solved the problem. The exam was over. I scored in the high 90's! Who would believe it?

Tragically, the story was not over. I met Al Peroni the next afternoon, and he was extremely downcast. I wondered why. He had been accepted to matriculate at a very prestigious college where he would study high-level physics. So what was the problem? He said that he intended to die. Why? It was because he expected to get the highest mark in Intermediate Algebra, and I beat his mark by two points. I was just happy to get a good mark. To Al, being the best in that subject was a driving ambition and he saw himself as a failure. I'd have been happy to get the mark he got. I thought about that vet who wanted to kill himself. Why me? I already had that problem earlier this year. I saved that vet, but what can I say to Al?

"Al," I said, "the only reason I passed the Regents was because I asked for and got extra help from Mr. Natesh. Without him, I'd have failed. If you don't believe, me, ask our math teacher. You got a great mark, and you did it by yourself. You're outright better than I'll ever be in any math subject. I needed that high mark, or I wouldn't go to college. You're already there. You're so smart that you breezed through your scholarship. Without that good mark, I wouldn't have mine. In fact, I still have to do some things successfully, or I might not get the scholarship. So let's forget about suicide. You have great things to do, so get out of here and do 'em!"

AL walked away without a word, but it was clear that I said the right things. I hoped I'd never have to go through that again. A few years later, however, I'd face a very desperate man who owned a gun collection and was bent on suicide. I'm glad I can't know the future.

It was my final day on campus as a student. I was still singing in the Senior Chorus, and we sang our hearts out for the last time, accompanied on the piano by Miss Thode and the organ teacher.

Diplomas were handed out to graduates. I already had my diploma from last year. I received no awards. Witty sure did, and I was glad for him. I never saw him again. My family was there. When we walked out of the building, we stopped only to go to the switchboard operator so I could hand in the key to the radio room that I had carried for so long. It was the end of something—a special privilege. It was the end of an era; it was the beginning of an uncertain future. All the problems and triumphs I experienced in that school were at last behind me. But I was afraid of what was to come next.

Chapter 15

It was the end of June, 1949. There were many things to do. Our old radio which had provided so much pleasure both for me and for the rest of the family was beginning to show its age. I doubted that it would last past summer. I had planned for this during my final days at school. Mr. Gun told me where I could buy a high quality AM tuner and an FM tuner. I got the circuit for a new kind of phonograph system, something which would radically improve the playing of phonograph records. Along with all this I needed to design another amplifier which I determined to be better built than the one I made for Alex. For one thing, I finally learned the secret behind the improvements Mr. Schmidt made to our old radio. It is known as "negative feedback". In a year or so it would be a part of every commercial sound system. This, along with the improvements in phonographs, would bring about an entirely new industry, that of mass-produced, quality audio systems.

Yes, I was free from "that school!" I wasn't exactly free yet to tackle the construction of my latest audio project or to enjoy the summer. I still didn't have the college scholarship. In order to complete the requirements, as I mentioned earlier, I had to go to six radio stations and interview their chief engineers in order to get their thoughts and opinions as to whether I could compete on equal terms with sighted radio engineers.

I called various radio stations and made appointments to speak with their chief engineers. Fortunately Dad had time to take me to each appointment. This was important because, even though I had training to use a white cane, I had yet to learn enough to navigate the New York subway system. In each appointment I discussed what I knew about radio stations and asked each man about aspects of the subject with which I was not familiar. It became apparent that I would need specialized equipment which would then make it possible for me to work in smaller radio markets where the pace was less hectic than in large markets such as New York City. In every session I was encouraged to give it a try.

At that point I hoped that I was free to do nothing if I wanted to, but alas! Mom reminded me more than once that I had to write a report to be sent to The Vocational Rehabilitation people about my six interviews, but I kept putting it off. You can guess that I was anxious to finish the audio system before the summer ended. I guess that in the back of my mind was the idea that if I put that report off long enough, I'd miss the deadline and not have to go to college. I usually procrastinated in any case.

Dad was on his vacation about this time; so, I asked him to help me wire the system. He could do it faster than I could. We were making good progress on the project.

There was a gathering of the Concordia Club, and by now you know how important that was. Esther and Eilene were there and Esther told me about a two-week camp for adult blind men and women. It was run by The Jewish Guild for the Blind, but it was open to everyone without regard to religious affiliation. I decided to try it. As I recall, it was held during the last two weeks of July. There were many details to work through when going to a college which was more than three hundred miles from my home. I went to that camp anyhow.

As the time drew near to when I'd go, Mom "got on my case" to write my report. I did it on the night before I was to leave. I hated writing it because it was too much like being in school. Even so I completed it and left for camp. All that remained between me and Syracuse University was whether the report was satisfactory.

I enjoyed this new camping experience. The majority of the attendees were Jewish adults ranging from folks my age to rather old people. I learned to appreciate Jewish culture and learned quite a lot about Jewish cooking. Esther was there and she walked me through a considerable amount of what Jewish life was all about. Esther was also preparing to go to college. We talked together quite a bit about what was needed in order to be ready for the changes which college life would bring.

Music was a large part of what people wanted to do, and as usual, I was right in the middle of it. I was the only one with some experience playing piano; so I was recruited to help with talent shows. Naturally, I played pop songs of the day, but I had to learn songs from many lands, including Russian peasant songs and others of Czech origin.

I don't have much more to tell you about going to a camp of this kind. I went to it a few more times, but as I did so, I found that I was tiring of it. Eventually I stopped going.

When I came home from camp, I had to get back to the audio system. We lived in a three-room apartment and my project was making already crowded conditions worse. Partly because of that and partly because our old radio was getting ready to die. It was important to complete this work before I left for Syracuse. As for the old radio, I knew that I couldn't obtain the parts which were needed in order to fix it. Of course I wanted an excuse to replace it.

There were other important matters. I kept up with some of my friends I made during my time in The New York Institute for the Education of the Blind. Quite a few of them were also going to various colleges. At that time there was just a handful of blind college students. I could perceive that we would be watched very closely to see if we could handle all aspects of college life. We were almost pioneers hopefully blazing trails for other blind students.

I learned that I was accepted for a New York State scholarship. There was no turning back. There now was even more work to be done. I doubted that I would even have time to see Grandma that summer. I wondered, too, if summer vacations were things of the past. All of my preparations for college life put such pressure on me to the point where building the sound system was less enjoyable.

I had to think about how I could take notes in my classes. A Braille writer would be nice but it was a noisy contraption which would disturb others. I thought about the electronic gadgets which were available at that time. Mr. Gun had a couple of wire recorders which were more or less compact. Perhaps I could use one to record my classroom lectures and summarize them in any spare time I might have. I checked with the Dean of Students as to whether doing that would be permitted, and received permission. Although I figured that the wire recorder was a way to temporarily store lectures, it would be a good plan to use phonograph records for permanent storage of notes. I bought a wire recorder and spools of wire and worked with it so I became fluent using it.

And then one of those things happened which would help me in so many ways. Dad found out that his boss had a disk recorder that he was getting bored with and offered to sell it to him at a very good price. He brought the instruction manual home so I could study it and see if it would help me. Mom read it to me, and right away I knew it would be exactly what I needed. It had to record at a lower speed than 78 RPM so I could use less blank disks. This recorder could indeed play and record at this lower speed. Coincidentally, its turntable speed was such that I could play LP's. I wondered if I could adapt this unit to record them as well. If so, I could use even fewer disks. Anything I could do to make storage easier was important.

My folks bought the recorder for me so I could learn how to use it before I got to Syracuse. It was great fun, but I couldn't just mess around; I needed to know how to use as many tools as possible if I was to succeed in college. Summer was almost gone, and I'd soon leave to begin a different life, which I could only dimly imagine.

My final meeting of the Concordia group was to feature a boat ride up to a park where we would disembark and have a picnic and be picked up by another boat which would take us back to the city. Both Eilene and Esther were there so I thought it would be a great time. But it wasn't what I hoped it would be. Eilene was different somehow. I wondered if she was becoming jealous of Esther. Eilene could not know that she had nothing to fear. In any case she was there, doing whatever she could to help me. She knew I was nervous about the changes which would take place in just a few days. She said very little. I couldn't imagine what her problem was and she would not tell me. It wouldn't be too long before I'd find out!

Al Peroni was going to R. P. I, a college which was on the way to Syracuse. I made arrangements to spend a day with Grandma and go straight to school from there. I arranged that when the time came, Al would meet me at the Albany railroad station and we would go to Grandma's and leave the next day for our respective schools.

Meanwhile, I had to finish the audio system. I'd hardly have time to test it before I left. I had a short time to listen to it, but it was everything I hoped it would be, and there was none of the hum which was in Alex's system. The negative feedback which Mr. Schmidt put into that old radio worked even better in my system than it had in that old radio. A funny thing—when Mom turned the old radio on, there was a considerable noise and then heavy smoke came from the old set! It ran just long enough for me to get the new system going.

Everything was about set for me to go. Dad told me that his golfing buddy, Jim Murphy, had a good friend at Syracuse University. He was the priest in charge of the Catholic students' religious affair. Jim wanted me to be sure to look him up. I didn't want to do it, but I didn't want to hurt dad's feelings; so, I'd look him up. I knew Jim because I caddied for Dad and sometimes would be a part of a foursome which included Jim. I have to say that I never liked Jim much so, in a way, I hoped to forget about the whole thing. Hadn't I already had my fill of priests?

I was ready to leave for Grandma's with all of my clothes and equipment. The night before I was to leave, Dad's family threw a send-off party for me and brought me many presents, including a terrific leather war surplus flying jacket which would stand me in good stead during the cold winters in Syracuse. My cousin, Joe T., taught me a couple of country songs and I accompanied him on the piano as he sang them. That might have been the night when he introduced me to Jack Daniels, his favorite liquor. I don't drink often but when I do, I think about Joe T.

Early the next morning Mom, Mary, and I got into a taxi to Grand Central Station to board a train for Albany. At that time many of the trains had a passenger representative aboard, whose job it was to help passengers in any way that was needed. In my case she arranged for all my luggage to be put on the train. Then we would be met by another representative who would get all our "stuff" off the train. We had to take a bus to Grandma's.

We had to meet Al's train and had to add his luggage to mine. I don't think Mom was overjoyed about all this but she liked Al and felt sorry for him. Otherwise she'd never have put up with this added burden. I introduced Al to Grandma and they got along famously. I showed him the restored parlor organ and Grandma's old 1928 Temple radio.

Morning came fast. We got to the train station, got Al on to his train and got all my luggage on ours. My new life was about to begin!

Chapter 16

When we arrived in Syracuse, the day was quite advanced. Mom decided that, rather than going directly to my dorm, it was a better idea to check into a hotel and go to the dorm in the morning. I didn't know that Mom made reservations earlier. It wasn't a fancy place, but the rooms were clean, and it was near the university campus. I had not been in a hotel before—so it was an adventure. I had my own room and Mary and Mom shared another.

I unpacked the few items I'd need for this brief stay, and then explored the room. It was a rather large one with a dresser and a desk. I saw what I later found was The Holy Bible. There was hotel stationery, a pitcher of ice and some glasses. I found a radio on the dresser but could not figure how to use it. Of course it needed a quarter; it was the first time that I had to pay to use a radio. There was a radio station on the top floor of the building. Eventually I'd visit the station and that visit helped me to make an important choice.

I wondered where we'd eat supper and just about then, Mom phoned to tell me to get ready to eat; there was a restaurant right in the building. I knocked on their door and Mary and Mom came out and we trekked to the restaurant. After dining we went back to our rooms. It had been a long day and I worried about the next day when I would set foot on to the campus of SU. I took a long shower. I remember that the water pressure was very high. When I got out of the shower stall, the floor was quite wet. Fortunately there were a lot of towels available and hence I managed to mop up the excess water.

When morning came, I was already awake. I dressed, met Mom and Mary and had a good meal in the restaurant. And off we went—straight into my new life!

We went to my dorm to register. It was located on Marshall Street, 106 Marshall Street to be precise. We were met by the Robinsons. They were graduate (grad) students who lived in the dorm and earned extra money by being in charge of the dorm and helping us new-comers. They explained that this was "orientation week," which meant that classes would not start right then. We would use that week to acclimate ourselves to the campus and register for each of the classes we would take that semester. We were then on our own.

As usual, Mom knew exactly what I should do. She acquired a map of the campus and we went out to see my new world. I made up my mind that I wouldn't use a white cane or a cane of any kind. I didn't want to stand out any more than I had to. BESIDES, Bob Gunderson never used one and I wanted to be just like him. I had no problem with that during my four-year stay.

Marshall Street was where many small shops and restaurants were located. The dorm was on a corner, facing both Marshall Street and South Crouse Avenues. If I faced South Crouse and crossed it, I'd be at a store which sold phonograph records and did radio repairs. If I went to the door of that store and turned left, I would be at The Varsity Restaurant which was diagonally at the corner of South Crouse and Marshall. We walked on South Crouse until we crossed Waverly Avenue and finally arrived at University Place. I learned that once we crossed it, we'd be on the campus proper.

It was obvious to me from the get-go that I'd need to take notes, which I was prepared to do. There were no recorders available in those days which could fit into a shirt pocket. I had to lug a Braille slate which is nothing more than a flat board sized to hold a sheet of 8" and a half by 11" Braille paper. There is an arrangement on these slates to hold the paper in place. There's a "guide" which is composed of a top piece and a lower piece. It's hinged at the left end so that it can be opened before the page is mounted on the slate. The guide is closed and the paper is sandwiched between the top and bottom parts of it. The guide is set up so that each Braille cell can easily be located. The dots are punched by means of what is called a stylus. This rudimentary system is still used today for some purposes. (For further details about Braille writing, see Appendix A.)

I can still picture my surroundings clearly. I can see myself crossing

University Place and walking on the right side of South Crouse Ave. I'm walking on the right side of the side walk so I can find the steps which, when climbed, will take me to the massive Hall of Languages building. As I climb the steps I feel each step and notice that they are badly worn because so many feet have trod them over many, many years. HL is the oldest building in the University and still is one of the most important buildings for Liberal Arts students.

And so it went. I learned how to identify my location by land marks: a tree here, a lamp post there, a corner where a sidewalk turned. I learned the names of other streets. If I turned right on Marshall, I learned the names of each shop and restaurant. The next crossing was University Ave. If I continued along Marshall, I'd learn other streets: Comstock Ave., Walnut St., Walnut Place and a couple more. On these streets were other dorms, some for ladies and some for men. I'm actually a bit hazy about some streets.

There was no trouble crossing these streets by myself because there was very little traffic on most of them. University Ave. was a rather important thoroughfare, but if I waited at a corner, there would be a pause in traffic and I could easily determine if I had time to cross safely.

This orientation took more than one day to complete. Mary and Mom brought me a really good sandwich that I ate in my room. It was time to say our good byes, and I was alone. Good as my sandwich was, it was difficult for me to eat it. This was the first time that I was really on my own, and I felt the weight of the world pressing down on my shoulders! What should I do? How do I start this new life? There was no Eilene. Who could guide me? Who could comfort me?

I said to myself that I must get going. Maybe I was procrastinating because that's what I often did when there was no "light at the end of the tunnel". I had a state scholarship which allowed me to be here. What if I failed? Who would I blame? I was on my own and there was nobody to blame but me!

I did some rearranging of baggage and equipment. Then it was near supper time. I had to eat in the college dining room for my freshman year. Where was the dining room? I remembered where it was. Would I find it? I felt swallowed in the vastness that was this huge campus. I didn't know anyone. Everyone needs friends, don't they? How will I meet anyone?

I heard a door closing somewhere in the building. Because I was shy, I felt that I just couldn't knock on any door! It was time to move! An idea came to me, as though someone planted it into my mind. I'd go downstairs to the living room and try to find the piano. I never had learned where it was. When I got there, the room was empty—at least I thought it was. I found the piano, sat on its bench and I began playing. Several folks came into the room and introduced themselves. I remember Arthur Yun because he was from another country, Korea. I never met anyone from there. He would often help me during that "frosh" year. I didn't think about it at the time but later I wondered if he was lonely, too. After all, he was much farther from his home than I was from mine.

The next day dawned. There was more learning to do. Off I went to begin my exploration. Taking my trusty notes, I started walking on campus. I was completely absorbed in what I was doing so I didn't hear a student coming the other way. We crashed together.

"I'm so sorry," I said. "I was reading my notes which tell me how to locate various buildings on campus and just plain didn't hear you."

"No problem," she said". I'm a music major and was looking at a score and didn't pay attention to what I was doing."

"My name is Joe. I am a freshman, majoring in radio.

"I'm Joanne Parker. I'm a senior, majoring in music as I said and live in Haven Hall".

We shook hands. Wow! She had the kind of hands which make me excited and calm at the same time!

"Is everything all right? I saw a look on your face and thought there was something wrong."

"No, nothing at all. Guess I'd better get moving. I wanted to check to see if I can find Smith Hall because I'll be taking some classes there."

"I have to move along, too. If you ever need a friend, stop in at Haven Hall."

"I might just drop in on you some day." Would I ever have the nerve? I knew it was a sure bet that I'd need her friendship and her help, but how will she react if I try to take her hand? No, this was not a good plan.

A few days passed, and it was Sunday morning. I would try to find the Crouse Auditorium, attend Catholic Mass and meet the priest that Dad's golf friend, Jim Murphy, told me to get to know. After Mass ended, somebody helped me find this priest, Father Ryan. He assigned one of the guys to take me to and from Mass each week. He seemed very nice, and I liked his sermon. Perhaps this would ultimately lead me back to God; that is if there was one.

Classes commenced the next day. It was time to try the wire recorder which I wanted to use to record lectures in my first class. I made my first lecture recording. I had an arrangement which would let me change wire spools quickly, but it was a lot more difficult to do than I thought. No, it wasn't realistic for me to use this machine in the way I'd planned.

When I got back to my room, I played the recording and summarized the lecture on a phonograph record just as I planned. What would I do for other classes? I had no way to take notes. I made the only practical decision: to listen very carefully and summarize what I learned as soon as I could get into my dorm room.

After a couple of classes the next day, I got to my room; I tried to sum up my recollections of the first class. I could not record anything. The mike cord had pulled loose from the little plug which connects the mike to the recorder. I went to the radio repair shop which was right across the street. I met the proprietor and his wife. He was a cold sort of guy, but his wife was very sweet. He introduced me to Dave Eller who was in charge of all repairs. I explained what I needed and he said he'd take care of the connector while I waited. When he came out of the repair area of the shop, he asked what I was doing with the mike. After explaining the way I was going to record summaries of my class lectures, Dave became fascinated with the idea of my having a disk recorder. He lived in town and was about my age. He didn't attend S. U. but worked full time in the store. He said he'd love to see my dorm setup, and we eventually got together. It was the start of a friendship which lasted until his death in 1988.

Chapter 17

At that time freshmen lived at Skytop, which was a group of prefabricated buildings. These were just a bit off campus. Buses ran between Skytop and the campus buildings. Only because of the foresight of the Dean of Men was I allowed to live in that old, ramshackle hotel at 106 Marshall Street. His decision was of tremendous value and importance.

Even after two weeks of classes, there were still a couple of empty rooms in the building, but they soon filled. I remember a great number of those men: Al Beheller, Bill Lapel, Bob Damburg and so many more. They were special men and, as it turned out, special friends. Most of the men in my dorm were veterans of World War II. The GI bill enabled most of these folks to obtain their education. They had seen much; they had done much. These were men in every sense of the word. I was a kid and a confused one to boot. Because I was surrounded by these guys, I grew to understand life and becoming a man in ways which could not have been possible had I lived at Skytop.

They took me under their wing. I wasn't shielded from life; they showed me life. I couldn't be arrogant as I might have become because one or another of those vets knew much more than I did about almost anything. I recall an incident just a few weeks into my first semester. I was taking a beginner's class in philosophy and learned about a man named John Stewart Mill. I tried to show off my "great" knowledge of Mill to Al Beheller. He ripped into me. He was an ardent student of Mill as well as many of the world's great philosophers. After showing me the errors and incorrect assumptions I had made, he continued by giving me a severe lecture about not trying to be a "know-it-all".

I slunk into my room. For that one thing alone I owe him my

deepest gratitude. I never tried anything like that again. What I learned was that, rather than trying to act like a "smarty pants," that I shuld hang around those who know more than I and learn from them. It's a practice I maintain even now. I left my room and looked for him. His room was two doors from mine. I had to tell him what a fool I was, and I wasn't yet a sophomore. It was a hard thing to do but it was a hard and good lesson for me.

After such a great lesson, I observed people, not to judge but just to get an idea of their backgrounds. I was surprised to notice that I had a better grounding in general education than so many others. "That school" gave me a first-class education, but, of course, I hated to give the school any credit.

As a part of some classes, it was necessary to attend a special lecture at some other place than the regular classroom. What I'm thinking about is a Citizenship lecture held in the nondenominational, Protestant chapel. What is memorable about this lecture was that it was given by a world-class historian. I won't mention his name because it was such a disaster. Those attending watched and listened to a brilliant person who said very little that was coherent. Plainly he no longer grasped concepts for which he was justly famous. Occasionally his brilliance shown like jewels, but mostly the man was just babbling.

As the lecture ended, I found that I was sitting next to a very nice young lady named Stella M. As we were walking out together, she asked where I lived and if I needed help getting back to the dorm. I was about to accept her kind offer, but she said that she lived in Haven Hall. I asked if she knew Joanne Parker (the one who I accidentally bumped into). She did and told me what I already knew—that she was a very sweet person. I said that I had been thinking about visiting her but didn't have the nerve. Stella insisted that if that was the case, do it. She walked me to Haven Hall. She found Joanne and brought her to where I was standing.

Life in girls' dorms was very strict back then. Unless a man had a definite reason for being in a girls' dorm, the visitor would have to leave. Joanne welcomed me and we went into the living room. We sat and talked. She played a bit of Rhapsody in Blue on the piano which she did extremely well. She asked me to play, which I reluctantly did. I don't know what I played, and it wasn't much, but Joanne seemed to enjoy it. When we were again seated, I moved my hand slightly closer to her, and she immediately took it. I could hardly say anything because of the power in that hand.

"Now I know what that look on your face was when we first met. Holding hands must be special for you."

"Yes, but only if the person's hand is right. It has to have a special quality which I can't explain."

We sat talking for some time, not about personal things but about college life, music and small talk. For much of that time I wanted to hold both her hands but didn't dare ask for that. I didn't move my hand toward her. That's what I did the first time, hoping she would notice it and take my hand. I thought it would be a bad idea to do that again. She said, "I see! You want my other one," and gave it to me with no hesitation. Once again I couldn't speak, but now she understood. It was approaching the time that any male visitors had to leave the dorm. She said that she'd walk me home. I was glad of that because I wasn't positive that I could find my way back. I asked Joanne how she knew that I wanted her hand.

"Well, Joe, sometimes I know things like that. I can't explain how I know things but I do."

"Can I ever come to see you again?"

"Yes, but you should call to be sure that I'm in."

We said our goodnights, and that was that. I had work to do in connection with some of my classes, but that work seemed effortless as a result of seeing Joanne.

I suppose that a week or so went by before I called her. It was a Sunday afternoon. I called, she was in; so, I went to her dorm. I had no problem locating it. After she let me in, we went into the living room again. "Joe, meet my boyfriend, Ray Myrick."

"Hi, Ray. I'm Joe. I live on Marshall Street, about three or four blocks from here."

Then Joanne asked, "Would you please play for us. That will give us time for a dance or two?"

I did and figured it was no place for me there. Ray wouldn't likely understand about my needing Joanne's help. I said my good byes and went back home. A few of us were going out to dinner. It was the one night when the dining room was closed.

I thought about Eilene and wondered how she'd take it if she knew about Joanne. Joanne was a wonderful gal, no doubt, but she's taken. And Eilene was so special!

Nothing came from that Sunday visit, so I called the following Thursday to see if that was a good time to visit. I didn't talk to her. Another girl picked up the phone and said that I definitely should see Joanne. That sounded very odd. Why didn't Joanne talk to me herself? I was uneasy when I got to Haven Hall. The girl I'd talked to on the phone took me into the living room. There was Joanne.

"Hi, Joanne."

"Go away from here."

"What's wrong?"

She really started yelling and screaming! I got out of there real quick. When I got back to my room, I wrote her a note. I called Stella and asked her to take the letter to Joanne. In the letter I just said that if I could do anything to let me know, and I'd try. A day or so later Stella told me that Joanne dropped out of school and had already left the University. Stella said that what I witnessed was Joanne having a nervous breakdown.

I had to put all thoughts of these ladies out of my head if I was to get class work done.

Later I went out with my new friends to a restaurant called Pop Welch's which was owned by the biggest gambler in town, who also owned a big league basketball team which was well known at the time. The place had some truly excellent Italian food which was just like the food which my family was used to eating. It's occasions like this which often help to cement friendships. Having a combination of good food, and a glass of red wine always ends up that virtual strangers become good pals.

Speaking of friends, I wondered how I might meet more girls. Most of those in classes didn't appear to notice that I was there. I heard about something called "rushing". Many guys were "rushing" fraternities to select one which suited their life styles. I had absolutely no interest in them. A flash bulb went off in my head. Of course, there was no light, but I knew I was on the right track. There was sorority rushing. I would rush those. When I learned that a sorority was having an open house, I went there. I'd ring the bell and when the door opened, I told the surprised girl that I wanted to rush the sorority to see if it suited me. The reactions were usually spectacular. I remember one such time when the person in charge sat me down and filled out an application for membership. She was trying not to laugh. I was introduced to many coeds, and it was fun for all of us. It didn't end up with lots of close friends, but I did meet people who I would see quite often during my four-year stay in Syracuse.

Days moved on. The wire recorder lay unused, but I figured that it was small enough and light enough that I could take it around to record events. I began thinking about recording a recital and offering a phonograph record of it for sale to the performer. I could transfer the wire recording to a phonograph record. I put out a few feelers, and the first thing I knew, I was doing just that and making a little money.

Wire recordings were rather poor sounding so I didn't want to offer them to musicians who wouldn't like what they heard and then wouldn't want other recordings from me. I heard about something called a "tape recorder" but had not seen one. They were supposed to be quite good. I had no money for one. By that time I began to view life as having more than a past and more than a "now".

I corresponded with a few friends from my previous school. One was John Wahlen. Time passed. It was getting close to the Thanksgiving week. I got a letter from him, giving me the gist of what he was doing and what he knew about some of the other students. I got to a paragraph which, to say the least, kicked me in the face:

"Joe, you'll want to know this. Rumors are going around that Eilene is engaged." I tried to dismiss the possibility of such a thing. Well, I knew that when I got home, I'd call her; and we'd have a few chuckles over that one! Even so, I had to admit that I was disquieted. I suppose that it was the Wednesday before Thanksgiving when I boarded the train for Grand Central Station. I took a taxi and arrived home at about 4 o'clock that afternoon. I unpacked my stuff and called Eilene.

"Hello," she said.

"I'm so glad to hear your voice. I hope you're sitting down because you'll crack up over this. I got a letter from John Wahlen and he told me about a dumb rumor that you got engaged. How about that for laughs?"

After a long silence: "The rumors are true."

It was Eilene talking, but her tone was so cold that I figured she swallowed a couple of ice cubes! What should I say? What could I say?

"When, I mean—I mean to whom?"

"Lester Friel."

"Eilene, he, he, I don't know what to say!" Lester was a student in my old school who wasn't too sharp. He wasn't even a particularly nice guy. I wanted to ask her how in hell did she pick him, but I didn't.

"Well, that's just the way it is. Don't call or try to see me again. Well, maybe I'll try to help you some day, but don't hold your breath!"

She hung up.

What was there to say? Eilene was more than the sum of all she had done for me. I thought she'd wait until I graduated and maybe we'd marry. No words! I broke down. I didn't want Mom and Dad to see me that way. I couldn't have said anything to them. Aunt Avis was gonna visit us for a couple of days. As a matter of fact she was due any second. The bell rang, and there she was. When I opened the door, I couldn't speak to her. She took off her coat and sat me down. She gave me her hands and waited till I quieted a bit and asked me to tell her what was wrong.

I did, and she had to wait until I regained control of my emotions. Then she said, "It's bad now, and you won't believe it now; but this will pass away and better things await you. You just have to believe and wait. There's lots to do in Syracuse, and you have to finish what you've begun. You have your whole life ahead of you. I won't even ask you if that sounds good. It probably doesn't, but you absolutely must trust me."

When my folks came home from their jobs, they greeted me as though I'd returned from the dead. I was glad to see them as well. I remained calm outwardly. They had no inkling that anything was wrong. The next day, before we sat down for a fabulous Thanksgiving dinner, Aunt Avis asked if I wanted to go for a walk. Of course I did. It was a cold, crisp day and the air felt bracing. The walk helped me to burn excess energy.

The weekend was very pleasant. It was wonderful seeing some of Dad's family. I didn't have classes on Monday so I could stay home an extra day. Knowing I would miss dinner, Mom filled a thermos with hot chocolate and packed some of the Italian cold cuts I loved and which would keep without refrigeration. When I got to my dorm I had some of those goodies and went to bed. My first class was at 8 AM and I woke up so late that I thought I'd miss the start of the class. No time for breakfast. I opened the thermos and drank Mom's hot chocolate and I do mean hot!

I settled into the school routine, but every once in a while I would lose my control.

Bill Lapel, one of my dorm mates, had a good friend who after graduating from the Syracuse Business School got a job with the 3M company selling tape recorders. He came to visit Bill and brought a tape recorder with him. Bill knew I'd be interested in this new technology and invited me to his room so I could see the machine. Andy showed me how to use it and how to thread the tape between the two reels. There was a big football game that night and that's why Andy came all the way from Minnesota. I wasn't interested in the game so I asked Andy if I could play with the recorder while Bill and he were at the game. He didn't mind so when they went off to the game, I worked with that machine.

I didn't think about Eilene at all.

The recorder was connected to Andy's radio which he brought so he could show Bill how to record. I started the recorder just in time to record a pianist whose name I didn't know, but the music was excellent. His virtuosity was astounding, but I thought a bit overdone. The musician was Oscar Pederson. He played backup piano in a few gigs, but this was his first album. I played that tape over and over and continued to be impressed. Perhaps best of all was that the recording sounded just great—far surpassing what a wire recorder could do. I hoped I could get one soon. Andy's machine was quite light, weighing about 15 pounds. If I had one I could record recitals and who knows what. And if my phonograph disks sounded as good as the taped sound, I knew I could sell many recordings. I remembered with sadness the loss of the talent show because it had not been recorded. I could use that as a sales pitch. "Keep your precious memories of your singing." Of course, I was day dreaming; I didn't have a tape recorder!

Syracuse U. had a small low-power FM station, and I would study there at the start of my sophomore year. I occasionally visited there to see how it was set up. I was dumbfounded to see that the station had a terrific disk recording system much better than what I owned. I wanted to learn how to run it. The chief engineer at the time discouraged me. He said it was necessary to use a microscope to check the depth of the grooves; I almost was discouraged. Wasn't I already making good recordings on my above-average home recorder? I didn't need a microscope. In fact, none was provided. Didn't that mean that its use wasn't absolutely necessary?

I got to know some of the announcers including a fellow named Al. He asked if I was willing to be a guest on a show he had which talked about various outstanding students. He heard that I played piano and thought I'd be a good candidate for his show. I asked the chief engineer of the station if he'd record the show for me. He hesitated but eventually said he would if I didn't tell anyone about it. After the show he handed me the recording. When I got back to my room, I played it immediately. The sound was marvelous, a bit better than my machine could produce, but my recorder already did sound very good. I don't know if anybody heard Al's show but it was interesting that I was becoming noticed around campus.

A girl in one of my classes, Ellen Franko, invited me to her dorm to play for some of her dorm mates. I liked Ellen so I went. People loved what I played and they all liked me! Memories of life in "that school" came back to me when I could not get along with the girls. Now I didn't know how to deal with popularity. I don't know what I said, but I do know that Ellen took whatever I said in a way I hadn't intended. I never found out what I said but Ellen was a little cooler after that. Later I could have fixed things up, but when that chance came, I didn't take it.

Ellen was a bright, perhaps brilliant girl. When she rushed sororities she was never accepted. Why? Because she was a Jew! It reminded me of Herman Foster and how his blackness resulted in his not being permitted into my home. Ellen tried to hang herself but fortunately that attempt failed. I always thought I should have at least tried to befriend her but somehow I didn't. Ultimately she received justice. She was granted various scholarships to study abroad.

Meanwhile, losing Eilene and Joanne's dropping out of school were always lurking somewhere in my mind.

Christmas was coming, and I loved it even though I didn't

understand its reason for being. It was great to come home for a couple of weeks. Mary and I bought Christmas presents for our folks as usual. Soon would come the time to set up and decorate the tree. Even if I couldn't see the beauty of the lights reflecting from many, multicolored ornaments, there was still something special about doing it.

I needed a few radio parts so asked Dad if he had time to go with me. He agreed. Mom and Mary went too. When we got on the subway it was a 45-minute ride to what was then known as "Radio Row". It was odd that Mom and Mary came long, but I didn't think about it beyond that moment.

It was a Saturday, and when we got to Hudson Radio and Electronics, there was Bob Gunderson. That wasn't surprising because he was there every Saturday, being paid to answer technical questions from customers. After greeting us, he put something heavy on the counter and asked me to examine it. It took me a short while to know what I was seeing because it was different from the appearance of Andy's recorder. It was a tape recorder with a reel of tape mounted and ready to run. Then they all yelled "Merry Christmas." I had my very own tape recorder, a Masco 375! I remember talking to Bob about it and he must have told my folks that it would help me in school. And it certainly did in so many ways.

When Mary and I decorated our Christmas tree, I recorded the event, including when Mary dropped a bulb. It smashed, and she gasped in surprise. She wasn't overjoyed when I played that part of the tape—which is why I played it. We always kidded one another, so I thought this was a trump card. It was a truly wonderful Christmas. Soon the time came to leave and return to finish out my first college semester by taking final exams.

Chapter 18

It was the day after New Year's when I got back on campus. It was winter, but you'd never know it. The temperature was near 80 degrees, and that wasn't a typo! I had some business at the Office of the Bursar. I couldn't believe I was walking with wearing just a shirt!

My reason for going to the Bursar's office was because of a new program which New York State offered. The State recognized that blind students needed many books to be read. Under this program other students would be paid to read them. I learned how to keep records of the time each reader worked and then submit the information monthly to the Bursar. What a nice person she was. Her name was Miss Weed, and I've never forgotten her kindness in helping with the numerous details of such a program.

I walked back to my dorm with a spring in my step. I certainly needed readers and it was always hard to find them. Many students needed extra money to help defray expenses. I knew that if I posted a need for readers, I'd have them.

Classes started the next morning with my first one at 8 o'clock. Believe it or not, I didn't own a radio to hear weather forecasts. Again, believe it or not, the overnight temperature dipped well into the teens, and I started out to breakfast with just a shirt. I turned back to my dorm to bundle up, which almost made me late for class.

It depended on the teacher, but most had a zero tolerance for lateness. I just got to the class under the gun.

It was an interesting math class which dealt with number theory. We are used to thinking that after we write "9", the next number is "10." "Tain't necessarily so". It wasn't well understood in those days, but now it's commonplace to note that we often need to write up to fifteen single digits before we write the number 10. Considering all my trouble with math in high school, I loved that course and easily sailed through it. This was the final week of that class before the final exam. Actually this was true for all my classes.

It was cram time for every student, and on top of this, we had to plan what our next courses should be. Luckily we had advisers to help us in our early college days. Later some advisers were millstones, dragging us down because many of them knew less than we did as to what we needed. Plus, I had problems which other students didn't have. I had to find out what teachers I'd have and what textbooks each one would use so I could buy them early. I had to find readers who could start putting these books on phonograph records. All of this had to be done so I'd be ready when my next classes began. Finding readers at that time was not simple because those potential readers were also cramming for their own finals.

And there was this other problem—one which other students did not have—the crushing loss of Eilene and then that of Joanne. Even as difficult as this pressure was, I knew I must suppress those needs and move on.

During "finals week" all went really well. I know I got a decent grade in the Number Theory class as well as in Spanish. And I got a solid A in General Philosophy. I'll never forget that teacher, Dr. Ethel Albert. She was as concerned and kind as anyone I'd seen, and, for the sake of telling you the full story, she had incredible hands! It was so hard not to say anything, and I didn't.

My exams were about over when I received a letter from Joanne. She invited me to come to Pennsylvania to spend a long weekend with her and her family. "Be sure to come because I have a surprise which you'll want." The guy who read her letter was one of the vets I mentioned earlier, and he laughed about my secret girl friend. He helped me write my answer to her invitation and aided me in selecting a suitable gift to bring with me. I never got an "invite" to anywhere and knew nothing about how to respond to one. Those men were always there whenever they were needed. They were so different from childhood friends.

A day or so later I took a cab to the Syracuse bus station and climbed on the bus headed for Allentown, Pennsylvania. I remember that it was about a three-hour trip, and the closer I got to Allentown, the more nervous I got. Joanne's family didn't know me. Maybe they wouldn't like it if I took her hands, and I had to do that!

When the bus pulled into the Allentown depot, I climbed off and there she was! I could hardly have said hello when she threw her arms around me. What a surprise her actions proved to be! She knew I wanted that and showed me as quickly as she could that she understood and would even try to help me with that.

"How did you know?"

"I just know these things. I think the Lord gave me a gift which lets me see things that other people miss."

Her older brother drove us back to her family's home. We were in the back seat, and she held my hands for the whole trip to the house. What a relief that was. As you read this, you doubtless can't feel what I felt at that moment. Mere words won't describe or explain it. It was a relief and I could just relax, far from wondering if I could keep up my grades so I could hang on to the scholarship. My life had felt empty and college work was tough. I could choose to do my studies or not and nobody watched. The teachers didn't seem to care if I studied for midterms and finals or whether I would fail or make the grade. All that faded as Joanne was there.

During that weekend she asked about Eilene and all that happened. After I finished that story which had such a strange ending, Joanne just said that it was part of God's plan for me. I asked what that plan was, and she said she didn't know, that I'd find out when God's timetable said I'd know.

"There's no God. If he was real, how come my prayers were never answered at the time I thought that I was praying to a real God?"

She was very quiet for a bit. "Joe, there's a God all right. Tomorrow's Sunday. Will you go to church with me?"

"Do you really want me to do that when I know there's no God?"

"Yes, I really do. Who knows how you'll feel after the service."

"Okay then, I'll go with you."

And so I did. There was something different, so relaxing in the small, Methodist church Joanne attended. I met the Pastor and his wife, and he said there'd be an evening supper that night and would I come with Joanne and talk to those at the gathering about me and about blindness? I reluctantly said I'd go, even though I hated speaking in public.

After the service, I went home with Joanne and ate a delicious meal. I heard a really nice hymn, and I sat down at the piano to really learn the tune. Many years later while visiting a friend, he got a phone call asking him to get his worship team together to perform at some kind of naval memorial. He was supposed to play The Navy Hymn, which he didn't know. I knew it because it was the hymn tune I learned at Joanne's church. My wife had a friend who knew the words of the hymn. At the close of the memorial service he was told that his rendition of the hymn was one of the best he'd ever heard.

It was a warm day in Allentown and Joanne took me for a walk through a beautiful campus of a local college. A slight mist began. We sat on a bench and Joanne told me that I'd never forget this moment. Here we were sitting on a bench with an umbrella perched on her head and her arms around me while the mist increased. I'll never forget that moment: There was Joanne's kindness, that umbrella resting on her head to keep us dry, and her warm arms around me. As you read this, can you somehow feel the moment?

And then it was evening in the Fellowship Hall of Joanne's church. The people were so caring and interested in me, really interested! It was nothing like anything I'd known. Of course there was no God, but the people were special. We ate and I was asked to talk to the group. I wasn't a bit nervous; I spoke with assurance, and then the evening was over, and people applauded whatever I said. Joanne was pleased as we left the little church. My time with her and her family was just about over and while going to bed I started crying. The weekend was so extraordinarily wonderful and now I was going back to emptiness and hard work!

Joanne's brother drove me to the bus station. It was her first day at a new job so she couldn't see me off. I decided that it was probably much better that way. When I got back to the dorm, the guys kidded me about that weekend. They had ideas about what must have gone on, and I just laughed along with them. I knew what they were thinking, but my weekend was so very much different from what my friends imagined.

As classes began I was buoyed up on the wings of that wonderful weekend and Joanne's strong faith. I'm sure that I disappointed her about that, but she never said a word about my lack of religious faith. There were new teachers, but Dr. Albert was there for my second term of Philosophy. I was still going to the Catholic Church but the services just didn't compare to what I experienced in Joanne's church.

My expenses I found were a bit more than the family could send me so I wondered how I could earn a little extra money. I started phoning fraternities and sororities to see if their glee clubs and choruses wanted to be recorded. I got a few responses but I was spending quite a bit of money on phone calls.

Among some of my new friends were some who volunteered to work in the Protestant, nondenominational chapel. They thought I'd enjoy the camaraderie, so I often visited there. I got to know the Chaplain, Dean Noble. Something about that chapel and its dean was such that I ended up revealing quite a bit about myself to him. I complimented him on his kindly manner. I told him that I wanted to play music for pay and do some recording for the students. He invited me to use his office for all my phone calls. I even told Dean Noble that I really didn't believe in God, and he wasn't fazed. It was little short of a miracle that some of God's people I met were UN fazed by my attitude.

One day while at the Chapel, I heard a girl crying. She was in the Dean's office and the door was open. I couldn't help hearing their conversation.

"Dean Noble, I love volunteering here, but this is the last time I can come."

"What's wrong," he asked.

"I'm Catholic and Father Ryan said that if he ever finds out that I came here, he'd ex-communicate me from the church!"

Dean Noble said that he understood and not to be concerned. He told her to do what Father Ryan wanted, and not to let this incident affect her faith. I don't remember the girl's name, but right then I swore never to go back to Father Ryan's church. Once again a priest proved to me that there couldn't be a God. The next Sunday, when the student came to pick me up for church, I thanked him for his faithfulness, but I decided that I wouldn't be back to a church which had no room for people who didn't tow the Catholic line.

It wasn't long before Dad phoned me to ask what happened. Father Ryan told Jim Murphy about my dropping out of his church. I told Dad the exact truth. He didn't like it much, but I could tell that, in his heart,

Dad didn't like Father Ryan's handling of the girl. Sadly for Dad, his golfing buddy wanted nothing more to do with him.

At that time in my life I knew only Father Ryan and Father Martin. As time went on, I met many truly humble and dedicated Catholic priests who served God as representatives of Jesus Christ. Pope John XXIII brought many changes to the church. Pope John desired that all people should be brothers.

I sometimes attended Services at the Chapel. Although I met many wonderful people, there was no convincing me that God was real.

I was becoming known for my recordings. At that time there was no recording studio in Syracuse—so the city and the University were wide open for anyone to set up shop. I was often seen carrying my relatively new 40 pound tape recorder around the campus to tape a professor of music or a sorority sing.

At this time, too, LP phonograph recordings were becoming popular and many students wanted to play them but not spend too much money. Small players were produced and sold for very little money so that people would have a way to play these new kinds of disks. People, however, had no way to use these players unless they could attach them to existing sound systems. Not many people had those, but just about everybody had a radio. I made considerable money wiring these players to students' radios. With the flip of a switch they could hear their favorite radio stations. With the flip of that same switch, they could use their new disk players.

With all this added workload, I still had to study. Fortunately, I had a pretty good memory which helped me learn with less effort than other students had to put in. It still was not easy no matter how you slice it. I had to prepare my monthly reports to the good people at VRS who gave me the scholarship. There was little to discuss from month to month, so I learned a little bit of the art of saying almost nothing in lots of words.

While I was fortunate to find people to read to me for pay, I was amazed at how poorly some people read which forced me to dismiss them. One person who offered her service was Stella—the young lady who encouraged me to visit Joanne early in my first term. Stella came to my dorm and did quite a bit of reading for me, and I couldn't have asked for a better reader. One day I got a call from the Dean of men to explain that Stella should not have come to a men's dorm, and she was in trouble. I was warned not to bring any girl to my dorm for any reason.

I wasn't sure whom to talk with. I went to the bursar and poured out my tale. Stella was only trying to help me, and I didn't want her to face suspension or worse for her unintended infraction of the school's rules. Mrs. Weed sincerely cared and pulled strings somewhere so that Stella only had to face a reprimand. Arrangements were made that I could bring my tape recorder to the reader's dorm. This wasn't a good plan because my presence would tie up the living room when I needed to be read to. But it was the best that could be done and I got few complaints from other girls who might want to use their living rooms at the time I needed reading done. I looked for as many guys to read for me as possible, but it was hard because so few guys were good readers. Reading textbooks would plague me many times during my four-year stint at SU.

Class work was going quite well except for Calculus. At that time there was no Braille notation for the various calculus symbols. It was almost impossible to solve calc problems in my head. I was not keeping up and knew that I never would. I was forced to ask the calc teacher to let me take an "incomplete"" which meant that there would be no record of my having ever taken the course. I required three more credits in a math course as part of my Bachelor's degree. My advisor enrolled me in Analytic Geometry. Because of the time lost while attempting Calculus, I was way behind. I did my absolute best to catch up, but it was a losing battle because I needed the basic information which I missed because of joining the class late.

When I got to my dorm after dinner one night, I heard a guy playing part of Rachmaninoff's Second Piano Concerto on the living room piano. He was good and I was spellbound. I couldn't wait to meet him. He said his name was Roland. As I found out along the way, he was related to the Nigerian Ambassador to the United States. He was more educated than most of us and was so approachable.

I mentioned my need for textbook readers, and he eagerly said he wanted to do that for me. When I asked if he could read my Analytic Geometry book, he said he knew the subject and began to read. As he read, he'd break off and explained all the fine points of the course. It was solely because of his patience with me that I got a decent grade in that subject. Roland was a faithful reader and friend during my stay at Syracuse University.

Roland seldom ever played piano in the dorm. I might never have met him except for that one time when he did.

I did well in Spanish. I had three years of that language in high school and was in my fourth year of study in college. One day after the Spanish class was dismissed, the prof asked me to stay so he could talk to me. So many memories of times in high school came upon me—memories of my doing something wrong and forced to stay in a classroom waiting for the axe to fall. This was different. This prof had a few things for me to consider. His name was Professor Rutti, who was the advisor to the Italian Club which was on campus. First he told me of a concern about a man coming on campus from Chile. He knew no English.

"Would you mind staying with him for a few hours. He's an important man, and there was nobody around I can trust to keep him occupied than you. I'll take him off your hands as soon as I can."

"Well, I'm not sure. What can I do with him? I never had spoken Spanish with a non-English speaking person. What can I do to entertain him?"

"I heard you play piano quite well and that you like electronics. You two will have lots to talk about. Just take him to your dorm and let things happen."

"I'll try this, but please know that I'll probably embarrass you."

"No, you won't do that or I wouldn't have picked you. By the way, there's something else I wanted to talk to you about. The Italian Club is putting on a show and we need an accompanist to play with a couple of singers. The show's in a couple of weeks. Would you be willing to work with these singers and be ready to perform for the show?"

I had a lot more confidence in my ability to do that than I had in my ability to entertain a guy from Chile. A couple of days later I met this South American gentleman and it was as though we were long-lost friends. Our talk flowed effortlessly. When I didn't know a word for an object, I'd point to it and he would tell me the Spanish equivalent. It seemed like only a few minutes went by before Professor Rutti picked him up.

Then I began rehearsals with the Italian Club singers. I had to learn a couple of Italian songs which I still remember and play sometimes. The show was a big success and I loved the part I played.

All of this extra work was added to an already busy schedule, and it was getting a bit taxing. I carried on, fighting to suppress thoughts of Eilene and Joanne. This was especially true in Dr. Albert's Philosophy class because I had that same teacher who had those incredible hands. No way was I gonna tell her about that, no sir!

After one of those classes a girl went to her in tears.

"You destroyed my faith! All these books you had us read demonstrate that there's no God!

"There are always two sides to just about everything. I want you to read these books and we'll talk about that later. Remember that we are studying the thoughts of many men. You've jumped to conclusions without waiting for the whole story to be told."

Then she wrote the names of a few books on the blackboard.

I'd stayed in the room only because I had a question about an assignment. I never intended to get into a discussion about that sad student; it wasn't my business, and besides, there was no God.

"Joe," Dr. Albert began: "It's sad that this girl has such weak faith. A person well-grounded in her beliefs should not have been shaken by what she read. I just hope I can restore her faith after she studies what I assigned her to read."

"Dr. Albert, didn't you tell me one time that you didn't believe in God?"

"Yes, I may have said that, and it's true. I personally do not believe, but I know enough philosophy so that I can present to her what she should have already known."

"Well, I'm on your side. There sure is no God."

Dr. Albert said nothing more. I got my question answered and left her classroom.

The term ground on. I was getting pretty good grades so I had good things to say in my monthly reports to VRS. The University was about to have a fund raiser and one day I got a call from the man who was going to be the MC. There'd be lots of alums present as well as some specially chosen students. It was a big deal, and I was asked to play piano! Was I willing to participate? I decided I'd do it so the MC asked me what I would play and how I should be introduced.

"Well, I'm not a fancy kind of performer, so I can't play anything that's real fast."

"Would you say that your music is slow and dreamy?"

"Well, yes, more or less."

"Okay, Joe. How about my introducing you as a talented gentleman who doesn't play slow or fast? He just plays sort of half assed!"

And that's just how I was introduced, and everyone cracked up. We talked this over ahead of time, so the MC told the audience that I could take any phone number and play a piece based on that number. The idea here was that I'd assign a note to any number from 0 to 9 and play someone's phone number on the spot. People would shout out numbers and I would play their phone numbers as songs. That was a hit. It was a good show. Even the Chancellor of the University played jazz sax along with a band composed of a few teachers.

All these things were a strain and I needed Joanne! Just about that time she called and said she'd be coming to Syracuse to see some of her friends, including me. She came, and I'll say that she was nothing less than resourceful. She knew I played the organ in high school so she suggested that we go to a practice studio that she knew about. She said she wanted to hear me. I hadn't played since the high school talent show, but it was great to play a Hammond organ. But Joanne had something else in mind. She knew that the studio was never busy on a Saturday so there wouldn't be anyone around. She used the practice room to hold me for quite a long time!

Then she went off to see her other friends and she was gone, but that visit sustained me for quite some time. I thought about how strange it was that I had so many things work out for me and for no understandable reasons. This was sure different from how life was in that school I hated.

The term was near its end and I couldn't wait to have a whole summer to rest and mess with electronics. Once again it was cramming time. My dorm mates could hear sounds from my room while I was reviewing my lecture summaries. They'd often bring me coffee to keep me going. I hated the stuff, but I never told them because it was kind of them to think about me. I drank it. However, as semesters rolled by, I found myself liking it more and more.

I only remember what happened during one particular exam,

philosophy. Dr. Albert said before we started: "I noticed that your friend, Stan Kagan, took almost the full, allotted time before he turned in his answers, and how he'd change his answers quite often. He'd get an A. I notice that you finished in half the time and if you changed an answer, it was wrong. You got an A last term." She wondered how it would work this time.

I couldn't take my exams with the other students. The prof would give me an oral test. He'd read the questions and I'd answer them. If there was an essay question, I was permitted to bring my typewriter so I could write the essay. You can see why it had to be done that way. It was extra work for the prof, but none of them seemed to mind.

Then came the philosophy test itself. Most of the questions were multiple choice, and I was charging through them with confidence. For some reason I became uncertain and changed two or three answers in a row.

Dr. Albert said, "Joe, we're getting out of here for a little while. I could use a lemonade, so I'm taking you to the Dutch Haven, and we'll get fresh air while we walk there."

"What about the test?"

"Never mind that. Let's go."

This was my last exam, and I just couldn't handle it, but I didn't tell Dr. Albert.

She took my hand, and we ambled to the restaurant. After she ordered, we waited to be served. She kept my hand. What a relief that was. I wondered what other folks in the restaurant would say if they noticed us, but if Dr. Albert didn't care, I sure didn't.

Our drinks came, I nursed mine. While we were still at our table, one of the guys from our college radio station, WAER, came over to us.

"Hey, Joe, I'm sure glad you're here. I know you have some kind of recording setup and we have a problem with the recording system at WAER. Let me pick your brains because we're all stumped."

I said it was fine and he explained the problem. After asking a few questions I think I figured out what was up and explained what I thought they should do. He left, and there I was, still sitting and holding her two hands. After the guy left, Dr. Albert suggested that we walk back to the classroom and finish the exam. I'd almost forgotten about that! We walked slowly and when we were again in the classroom, we got down to business. She repeated the last three questions and I unhesitatingly answered them and the rest of the questions. She dismissed me, saying that she'd send me a postcard with my grade.

Did she know that my physical contact with her was important? Well, of course she didn't! I never ran into her again.

A day or two after the exam while packing to leave for the summer, one of the guys gave me a postcard. I asked who it was from and would he please read it to me. The only thing the card said was: "A, of course. Stan got an A also."

I didn't get straight A's but I did well enough that I would keep my scholarship. I was free and went home. Yeah, this year was sure different from any high school year!

Chapter 19

No question about it; I was glad to come home. By now I had so many items to transport that it was not practical to carry them on the train. I started using Railway Express to handle most of my belongings. I was very eager to get my disk recorder home because there was a letter waiting for me that said the maker of my recorder had designed a new set of gears which would permit the machine to record LP's. It meant that I could record textbooks on to phonograph records rather than on reels of tape. Some blank disks were much cheaper than tapes, so this was a definite advantage.

Once home I had more room for my extra gear because my sister, Mary, had moved out and gotten her own apartment. She was not able to get along with either parent. She did come back on weekends.

There are few things about that summer which stood out. Certainly the conversion of the recorder so it could record LP's was a highlight. Once I had the machine ready to use, it required time to master what was involved in this new way of making records. The machine came equipped with something called an "advance ball" which was supposed to help keep the finer grooves to be more evenly spaced. I found that it made recordings too noisy so I removed it. Many years later I'd have to reckon with the advance ball again, but for now I happily avoided using it. A sighted recording engineer determined the groove width and depth by using a microscope. I certainly couldn't do that and as a matter of fact, the revised recorder didn't come with one. I found a way to make those determinations by touch, which worked well for a while.

Much of the summer involved working with recordings in another new way. I found that many books for the blind were recorded on very thin sheets of plastic. In my sister's office such disks were being used for dictation and transcribing correspondence. Could I use these? I got a few of these thin sheets but found that the stylus used to cut grooves onto regular recording blanks would not work with these sheets. When recording a phonograph record, the sharp stylus produced the grooves by removing some of the blank's coating to produce them. Care had to be taken to remove the resultant "hair" (actually called "chip") so that it wouldn't get caught under the stylus; that would ruin the recording. If that material was not disposed of carefully, there was a chance that it could burn so rapidly that it was nearly explosive. Mr. Gun told me that carelessness could be costly; I never failed to keep this in mind.

Recording on these thin sheets didn't require that any material be removed. The pressure of the stylus on the plastic was sufficient to deform the surface of the sheet in such a way that the grooves were molded rather than cut. This process is referred to as "cold flow". After obtaining the correct stylus, I mastered the technique. Mary talked to a person who made the sheets, so I was able to have lots of them to experiment with. That led the company to ask me to compare their sheets with those of other manufacturers to determine if the sheets Mary used were better than the competition. After lots of experimenting, I found that the sheets which Mary was using in her office were indeed superior to all others. I found this work was interesting, and it never occurred to me that I could have charged the maker of those sheets for all the time I spent. I loved playing with sound recording, so who cared if I got paid for my work?

I realize much of this is technical, but it's too difficult for me to omit such discussions from this book as it was such a very important part of my life. Even so, I have tried to boil it down to as low a technical level as possible.

Dad thought I was wasting too much time with those sheets because he wanted to be sure I really mastered the art of making LP's. (Maybe I really wasted time on that!) He sort of hinted that I could make money with that newly-acquired skill. I was thinking along those same lines but never told him so. I should have, but I never told either of my parents what I was planning in most instances. This would have made them much happier with me, but at that time I was not able to think about family relationships. Because of the technical nature of what I was doing or thinking about doing was impossible to translate to my folks, there was always a gap among us. If either of them offered valid suggestions, I hated to acknowledge they were right.

I wanted to visit Grandma, Uncle Art, Aunt Kitty, and Aunt Avis. I was glad when that time came. I truly needed that peaceful atmosphere. Mary had her vacation coming up, and so we went to Grandma's together. She had a good friend who she knew from her early childhood so she would be coming with us.

I fell into the routines I had become so used to: filling the wash tubs, playing the organ, doing the dishes with Mary. As was so often true, Grandma would need something from the General Store. Some of those walks were special. Mary's friend, Bea, was one of those few people with beautiful hands, and I was able to walk with her despite Mary's objections. Bea was intuitive and knew it was important for me to have her hands. She'd tell Mary that she wanted to walk with me because she never got to do it in Brooklyn. Just as I hoped, Mom's family came to Grandma's at one time or another. Aunt Avis came for a short time and was her wonderful self, always finding funny or interesting things to read to me and finding time to hold my hands.

Time flew by, and there I was—back in my dorm. I actually looked forward to classes which now included my introduction to radio. Along with those classes, there would be lab work at the University's radio station. I wondered how long it would take before I would do engineering for real shows. WAER stands for Alpha Epsilon Rho. That's the name of the nation radio students' honorary. Our university station was Chapter 1. What an honor it would be for me to learn radio there!

Also, I was planning how to sell recordings. The fact that I was able to make LP's brought me quite a few new customers because an LP record can play for more than 20 minutes and the 78 RPM records could play only 5 minutes.

Sometimes one of the girls would ask me to her dorm to play piano for her dorm mates. It was terrific because I was discovering that I was accepted and blindness wasn't the barrier I was sure would show itself. Talk about knowing girls. We had a highly ranked football team and a few other good varsity teams. When there are teams, there are cheer leaders. The most popular cheer lady was Dotty Grover. I didn't know her, but after my last morning class, a very nice girl happened to be at a somewhat dangerous street crossing waiting to help me across. I could, and did, cross that street by being attentive to traffic sounds, but it was nice for her to be there. We had short conversations whenever we met, but it took quite a few street crossings before I introduced myself and asked who she was. When I found out that it was Dotty, I was almost tongue-tied! I was walking with the most popular girl in the school! Yes, she even had great hands.

The radio lab work was very difficult. It wasn't so much that I couldn't understand what was taught; some of what was required was to jump quickly from one section on the large control room console to another. It wasn't a question of whether I could master this but doing so would require time. Sighted students could see the entire panorama of the equipment and locate a particular section. I had to memorize where everything was and practice moving around the myriad of knobs and buttons. Unfortunately, the student chief engineer didn't like me. He poked fun at me when I'd have problems and told me that I'd not master the system so refused to teach me the layout. I ran into this sort of treatment at the station from time to time. Eventually I figured out that some people were jealous of me because they knew that, in fact, I knew more than they did about the innards of the station's equipment. I wondered whether it was truly an honor to work there.

Although I was doing okay in the classroom, I was excluded from further lab work. Sometimes I'd go to one of the studios and practice some techniques on my own. Because I had no help, I had to learn by trial and error. It was a slow and tedious process.

What a relief it was when I got a phone call from Joanne that she would be coming to see me as well as many of her other friends! She would get to Syracuse around lunch time. When classes for the morning were done, I met Dotty as usual and we crossed the street. Immediately when we got to the other side of the street, there was Joanne. She hugged me and said hello. I went to introduce her to Dotty, but Dotty was not there. I don't think I ever saw Dotty again! I was disturbed about Dotty's hurrying away. I knew that it had to do with Joanne's being there. I knew I should try calling her, but I was uncertain about what I'd tell her. So I never made that call. I'm not saying that Dotty could have been a special friend, but she was a very nice girl. I figured that she would probably hang out with one of the players on our football or basketball teams. After all, she saw those guys lots more than she saw me. I didn't have confidence with handling personal situations nor did I understand that I probably could have made Dotty feel better about meeting Joanne.

Joanne and I had a pleasant lunch, and she went off to do whatever she had planned. I had a couple of afternoon classes. It was wonderful seeing her. One night she brought me to a dorm in which she had lots of friends. She played some great piano for them. I was anxious to leave there because I needed to spend more time with her. She was a bit distant or it seemed like that, but it was nonetheless a good evening.

The next evening I was in my dorm finishing an assignment when I got a phone call from Joanne. Could she come see me? I was nervous about it because I wasn't supposed to have a girl in the dorm, but I agreed to see her anyway. I met her in the hall which led from the front door to the various rooms. She asked me to sit on the steps leading to the second floor. She took my hands as usual, but nothing about that visit was usual.

She began speaking very quietly and yet with force. "I have to tell you some things, and you won't like them. My friends saw you with me, and they could tell you wanted me to leave them. I've seen that before, but I know now that I have to tell you that you just can't have all my attention. In fact, when you're around others, you mustn't make it obvious that you want to take them away from whatever they may be doing. You'll lose friends that way.

"Now don't interrupt. When I leave you tonight, I'll not come back. You will not see me again. I know you're usually sad when I go, but this time you will not be sad. You'll have lots of memories of our times together—like our visit to the little Park in Allentown with my umbrella resting on my head. You'll recall these memories. I don't know when it will be, but your life will change in a very dramatic way if you let it happen and not shut it out. I'll say good bye now and God bless you. Remember those words."

She sat there for just a minute, let go of my hands and quietly slipped out the door. I never saw her again. I tried writing to her, but she moved and her letters were returned with no forwarding address. I was dealt a crushing blow, but, just as she said, I was at peace and not sad. On the other hand, I lost two friends just a few days apart. Who could I blame? Only me! Nothing to do now. I'd just have to suck it up, suppress all thoughts of holding hands or being held. Those things just don't come along very often, and my luck ran out.

In addition, I was not doing well with the engineering part of radio and that made me feel worse than ever. The actual class work in radio had to do with advertising. I was doing all right, but there would be an unbridgeable problem unless something could be worked out. I had a year to solve this problem, because I knew that in my senior year, radio class work would deal with writing, producing scripts and having them acted just as though they actually were being broadcast. That meant that the producer, me, would have to present the script and have it run in the allotted time. I would need a clock which I could read (by feeling the hands) right to the second. I couldn't find any clock like that on the commercial market. I asked Dad to hunt around New York to see if he could locate anything. He couldn't, and the term was moving on.

What he found, however, was a clock maker who was up to the challenge. After considerable false starts, the man came up with essentially two clocks, one to read seconds and the other to mark minutes. The latter timepiece needed to buzz at one minute before each quarter hour. He built that one inside the case of an old ship's clock. The one reading seconds was installed into a round case about 4 inches in diameter. There was a single, second hand arranged with a buzzer which sounded each minute with a switch to shut this buzzer off if necessary. It was ingenious, and Dad was so excited that he sent it Special Delivery. I never heard of such service. He sent it out in early morning, and I received it in early evening of the same day! I never had service like that since then. It was amazing about Dad. He had no education beyond 8th grade, but he could solve practical problems very easily much of the time. I wish I had appreciated him more then than I did.

Mom certainly did her very best for me as well. Between semesters she'd record textbooks on LP disks. Best of all, she could be paid by the reader program provided by New York State. I was more fortunate than I knew. As my life moved on, I learned the value of taking more notice of what people did for me and to at least compliment them for what they did. I was beginning to glimpse these things—but not fully.

My dorm mates were quite interested in my recording projects. They were amazed at how I could carry close to 80 pounds of equipment all over the campus and with no white cane. As I think back to those times,

I wonder how I managed to do that. It was something which I had to do so I just did it.

The ability to make LP's brought me lots of work from quite a few professors in the music department and the drama department. All of that was important but maintaining my grades was just as important. Somehow I juggled both tasks. Expenses were a bit more than my folks could provide so I had to use some of that money for basic school essentials rather than on audio gear. I knew I had to save as much as I could if I was to buy a better recorder. The amount of time I was using that tape recorder which I received a Christmas earlier, showed me that it wouldn't hold up. I also knew that the disk recorder I had did a pretty fair job, but it lacked a feature which would allow my recordings to work well when played on record changers. I was surprised that I got very few complaints about that.

It was not yet a conscious thought, but somewhere in the recesses of my brain there lurked the idea that I liked working in radio less than in the recording field. It was becoming more and more apparent that some students were really jealous of my abilities so wouldn't let me work with the station's recording equipment. They did allow me to check it out, and I could see that disks which were made on this gear could indeed play on record changers.

It wasn't obvious immediately but a couple of guys at the station were taking notice of me in better ways. Norman Ross was an excellent writer and he was always interested in talking to me. Franz Hartman was a really good station engineer and we often got together. He was good enough so that he had a part-time job in one of Syracuse's commercial television stations. Franz would often come to my dorm and describe circuits of some of the equipment I owned so I would be able to more easily repair it if it broke down.

Franz was a master at turning these diagrams into word pictures which I'd copy into Braille notebooks. If I had an idea about building my own circuits, Franz would take my verbal descriptions of a circuit and convert them to print diagrams. He would occasionally take me to the school's station and show me some of its equipment in greater detail than anyone else. Franz knew that I understood what he showed me and that in time I'd know how to operate it with competence and confidence. Even the paid chief engineer of the station began to realize that I knew my way around radio equipment. I had no idea that I was impressing some of the most important people at WAER.

My sophomore year was just about completed. I was making good grades. I needed at least a B average if I was to continue receiving scholarship money. Even before the school year closed, I was contacting those who would teach me in my Junior year about textbooks I would need. When they understood why I needed my textbooks in advance, they were eager to help me. What a difference this was from my boarding school days when it seemed to me that nobody gave a damn about me.

I was coming home with all my clothes, equipment and the textbooks so Mom could read them in her spare time. It was going to be hours of reading and lots of blank recording disks so I'd have much less spare time than I used to have.

Once home I found time to go to at least one Concordia Club gathering. It was a boat ride like we had last summer. I always loved the sound of the water as the boat moved through it and to feel the sun and the breeze on my face. I saw some of my old schoolmates—some I didn't want to see but lots of those who I did. We caught up with what each of us was doing. I never failed to ask if anybody knew anything about Eilene and how she was doing and if anyone had any idea why she rushed into marriage. I didn't know it at first, but Eilene was on the boat ride but stayed away from the group I was with. I heard her voice once, and it was cold and nasty.

By fits and starts I pieced the story together. Eilene lived with her mother, who was a widow. The mother found a boyfriend who was interested in marrying her as long as Eilene wasn't living with them. This "wonderful" guy didn't care about Eilene, and it seems that her mother didn't care for her either. Her mother pushed Eilene at any boy who might want her. I had my chance, but that couldn't work because I was going away to college and her mom wanted immediate action. At various Catholic Guild for the Blind socials, her mother watched for possible marriage partners for Eilene and found Lester Friel as a great prospect. Even If I was at the Social, her mother would make sure that Eilene would see Lester. After I was gone, she pressured Eilene to marry him. As far as I'll ever know, those are the facts.

The summer went by so fast. I can't even remember if I got to see Grandma. Next thing I knew, I was starting my Junior year.

In addition to Radio classes and other B.A. requirements, I started taking psych courses. There were not enough radio credits, so I had to have a dual major in Psychology to fill the qualifications for a B.A. degree. I thought, too, that those courses would help me understand other people as well as myself. Although some of them were interesting, I didn't learn what I hoped I would. There was too much theory for me, and, as I learned, theories may not always prove to have meaning in the real world!

The first semester was well advanced. It was still important that I earn money so I could stay in school. I found that I could play piano in some of the city's local gin mills and that the tips were good. I could always find work because so many otherwise talented musicians would be too drunk to show up and the owners of these places found me to be reliable. I didn't drink on the job. I'd have a coke on the piano so that if a customer wanted to buy me a drink, the bartender knew to give me a coke. These were often three or four-hour gigs with very few breaks. They were hard work. The customers would ask for tunes I hated but I'd play them and, as they got drunker, the tips got bigger.

My recording work was increasing and that tape recorder was showing its age. I needed a new machine and soon. During a recording session of the University Concert Band I ran into Lyn Snyder, a local TV repair man and an audio enthusiast. He suggested that I buy a Webcore tape recorder, really nice but inexpensive. It had lots of features.

I asked Dad to locate a dealer who sold this machine so I could buy it during Thanksgiving break. Because that was just a short stay home, I decided I'd fly. That would be a "first".

I was beginning to have problems of another sort. I needed Joanne's kind of help, but that was gone. The pressure for those things was increasing, partly because I was working harder than I ever had. I remember that after lunch one day a student was waiting for me outside my class. (I'll call her Janice Evans.) She was studying Drama and Creative Writing and she wanted to know if I'd write music for a play she was working on. I played for her, and she thought I was just what she was looking for.

We started taking walks around the campus because we both liked to walk. I held her hand and that helped me. We'd sit, and she'd let me continue to hold her hand sometimes.

There was this particular day. I was in the living room of her dorm and for no reason that I know of, she put her arms around me. I had to react. "Don't stop," I said. She didn't for as long a time as she had and sometime later she asked for an explanation because my reactions were so strong. My explanation didn't faze her. Janice never finished her play and I never wrote any music for her. Time moved on as it always does and our friendship deepened.

In short, I went home for Thanksgiving and bought the Webcore recorder. It sounded incredibly better than the original machine so my services were in greater demand. Despite success, trying to do so many different things was dragging me down. I faced another challenge which I have not mentioned till now: Winter.

When I first applied to enter college, one college turned me down because of its "treacherous" winters. I'll never know how bad those winters were, but I do know about winters in Syracuse. It's in the "lake effect" snow belt. Sometimes there would be so much snow that it couldn't be cleared. The sidewalks were always well plowed, but what happened to the snow which was removed? Well, it's piled on either side of the walking path, in banks much taller than I am. In a way that was a help. I could never stray off the path. If there was a path at right angles to the one on which I walked, the pile on that side was removed. If I needed to walk that path, it was easy to follow the pile and turn with it.

When snow partially melts, it re freezes the next day and the paths will have a dangerous ice covering. There was a cure for that. Our local shoemaker had special cleats which were riveted to the underside of our boots. These were cleverly designed so that if I was indoors, the cleats were hinged so could fold back near the heels of the boots so they faced up and would cause no damage.

I had fun with my cleated boots. When I encountered one of those naysayers who'd tell me that I had no business trying to walk on the ice, I jogged merrily along as he slipped and slid. If he asked how I could walk so easily without seeing where I was going, I'd tell him that I had magical powers. Sometimes when I'd encounter someone who had trouble negotiating the ice, I'd ask if the person needed a hand. I'd take the person's arm and hold him up as we moved along, heedless of the apparent danger. Of course, there'd be people whom I told about the special cleats and where to get them.

No matter how you slice it, some of those winters were brutally cold. I remember walking back to WAER with my 40-pound tape recorder and other gear. The temp was 20 degrees below 0 and with a 40 mile an hour gale. As well dressed as I was, that kind of weather is just punishing! I remember one day where the temp went down to 40 degrees below 0, but it didn't feel as cold as when it was 20 degrees below but with no wind. That is as cold as it got during my four-year stay.

Tough winters, added to the many other pressures, well, life was getting to be too much. I told Mom that I wanted to quit. That was a long phone call, but in the end she convinced me that it would be better if I stuck with it. Janice was in her senior year, and she said that she had similar thoughts in her Junior year and that the Junior year was a problem for many students. Four years seemed to stretch to forever. I didn't want college in the first place. I had spent a hundred years in that boarding school and just couldn't face another hundred in college, but I made up my mind to hang in. If I make a decision, I stay with it.

Janice wanted to go with me on some of my music gigs. I told her that I didn't think it was safe doing that. I decided that I'd buy her the best-looking, fake wedding ring I could find and I insisted that she wear it prominently when we went to those gigs. That proved wise because Janice got some pretty strong looks till they saw her ring.

As time moved on, there were little highlights which stand out, and one occurred in my dorm. I don't know how it was arranged, but a prof, Dr. Hotchkiss, who teaches The History of Science, was going to give a lecture in the dorm's living room. Even girls were permitted to attend. The living room was jammed with people who wanted to hear this man speak. His chosen topic was "Today's Truths, Tomorrow's Errors". This man's words were so arresting that one could hear a pin drop. He received thunderous applause. I knew I'd have to study with him. I wouldn't mind even if I failed his course if I could just hear his lectures!

I spent time at the radio station and saw a professional tape machine, a Magnecord. In fact, there were two of these. The chief engineer was in the midst of building all the electronics for these machines rather than buying the ready-made ones. The sound produced by those two new machines was really terrific. I wondered how much such a recorder cost. It was $700. Maybe I'd have one someday.

The time for getting one of those machines was closer than I thought because my new machine was not very durable. I had to nurse the mechanism along. The two motors in the unit were badly designed. When the spring term was almost gone the recorder was failing. I had to replace both motors. One of my friends, George, was a good mechanic and he helped me keep the machine running. George was an incredible friend in so many ways. He was a serious student of anthropology and wanted to take equipment to Africa to record native rituals. I helped him plan what he'd need. There were no good portable recorders then so we had to plan for battery operation of a recorder which was not designed for that use. We managed something which was at least workable.

I had a decision to make about my senior year. If I was going to have enough money to buy all the gear I needed, for me to start my own recording business, I'd have to work harder with music and recording. There was no way I could handle a full course load load and do all this other work. I had to take at least six credits during the summer, and these would be accelerated courses. There'd be less class time and lots of study, but I knew I had to do this.

Finals were approaching and it was time for Janice to graduate. Her parents would be there, and she had previously told me they were both alcoholics. Now she asked me to do something for which I could never be prepared. She asked me to monitor them so they would be sober for her graduation. I said I'd try to help. I can't recall everything about that time; I do recall that her dad would get there on the actual day but her mom would arrive a day early to spend more time with Janice. There'd be times when Janice couldn't be with her mother and that's when she'd need me to be with her and keep her sober. I couldn't let Janice down, but I was really taking on something beyond my understanding of an alcoholic personality. All I could do was try.

Janice's mom arrived as scheduled. The one outstanding event I remember was showing her around the campus. She saw the line of restaurants on Marshall Street. When she spotted the Orange, she suggested we stop there to have lemonade. The Orange was the only gin mill on campus. I told her that the Orange had a bad reputation for its lemonade, and that The Dutch Haven was the best place in town for one. I almost had to drag her past the Orange, but I managed to get her to the Dutch Haven. There were similar situations, but I managed to keep her away from temptation—and Janice got through her graduation with sober parents. I was wiped out; however, Janice found the time to help me in the only way which could do me any good right then!

Her life as a student was over. During her last weeks on campus she found a job in town and got her own apartment. Meanwhile, I went home for a short stay and then started summer school.

Chapter 20

My return to school was really quite easy because I was able to leave most of my belongings in my dorm. I was able to stay in that same dorm room during my entire college career. The school planned to close the dorm for the summer, but there was a handful of other students who needed rooms so my dorm remained open to take care of us.

Because of the amount of somewhat expensive gear I had, I was permitted to have a key so I could lock my door when I was out. Syracuse University really bent over backwards to help me, for which I'll always be grateful.

Roland was one of those who stayed around for the summer, and I was glad he did. There was no time for anyone to read the textbooks I would be using. What with the accelerated study, I could not have kept up had Roland not been available.

My first course was The Psychology of Aging. It was taught by one of the authors of the textbook used for the class and I figured that this might be helpful should I need anything clarified. It didn't work out that way. This prof told our class that he encouraged discussion and disagreement with him about many points which would be covered. When he opened a discussion, I disagreed with a premise he proposed. I presented logical arguments against it. He thanked me for my excellent ideas.

After the class period ended, I met a guy who had already taken the course. "Well, you did it," he said. "You disagreed with him."

"Gee, he thought my points were well made."

"Yeah, but I found out that by disagreeing with him, I'd get an automatic C. From now on, no matter what you do, how hard you try, you've got a C.

"What if I didn't do any further studying? Would I get a D?"

"No. that C's locked in." He was right. I did get that C.

It wasn't fair, but it dawned on me that I could coast through that course and have Roland read the textbook for my next one. It was another psych course, but I don't remember the topic. This gave me time to hang around WAER and mess with the equipment if it wasn't used for on-the-air work or for script production. The recording system was off limits. Even Franz couldn't get me past that. It didn't matter that Franz saw me successfully operate my own system. Occasionally I had time to see Janice. I'd meet her after work. She introduced me to Summer Theater, and I got to see some interesting productions. I had to be careful about spending too much, but I did take her to a couple of famous restaurants in town, including Tubbard's. A few months later I took my folks there at the time of my graduation.

I practiced using that special clock which Dad had made for me. I'd try using it while reading a script. It was no good. When I checked the time, I couldn't find my place in the script. After all of Dad's trouble getting it, I found it better if I used someone in the control room to give me the time when I needed it. As you'll see, even that wasn't a good idea.

I had no trouble with my next psych class even though the material was quite advanced. The one C from my other class concerned me. I had to hope the C wouldn't drop my grade average too low when my case for the continuing of my scholarship came up. It didn't hurt me at all. I was still well above the B average required to keep the scholarship.

The prof was tough. I had less free time during that class. I'm tellin' you, that prof was a character! I'd invited my sister, Mary, to come up because the State Fair was being held near my school and I wanted to see it, and thought she'd be interested in seeing what one was like. We'd seen some great county fairs but we'd not seen a state fair.

She got there in time to audit that psych course. I wanted her to see that prof in action.

I'm not so sure whether I can paint a good enough word picture to do this justice. The prof started his lecture. It began with the motivations he thought were important when an organization pleaded its case for donating to its charity. ALL went well till that point. He started reminiscing about a time he had a problem about a particular charity drive. He became more and more agitated as he paced back and forth across the raised platform. He became very excited.

"What that group did was tell us to keep our porch lights on if we wished to contribute. Those guys held us for ransom. Sure, if we had our lights on, someone would come to our door and we'd contribute. But I didn't want to contribute so I didn't have my lights on! So I suppose all my neighbors thought I was cheap because they could see my lights weren't on. That's no way to collect money! There's no justice!" He then walked right off the platform. I guess he could have gotten hurt because it was a three-foot drop. He was a bit shaken up and quickly dismissed the class. When I told my sister that this prof was a real character, I didn't ever think that she'd get a ringside seat to his best demonstration!

I wish the rest of my time with my sister was as good, but it was the reverse. I had Janice with us as we toured the State Fair. She ignored my sister's trying to claim all of my attention. Mary could see the way Janice acted and was pretty upset. Janice ruined Mary's time with me. I didn't know what to say. What a bad impression Janice made! Later Mary told the rest of my family about my girlfriend. I was humiliated. I tried saying something to Janice, but she just said she had a right to my time. After all, weren't we thinking about getting married? Well, yes we were, but it didn't justify Janice's bad behavior. All signs pointed to Trouble, with a capital T. And I didn't know how to avoid it. I couldn't just drop her. She was all I had; I could never replace her!

I figured that I'd invite her to spend New Year's with us. I thought I'd have time to change her bad attitude by then.

It never occurred to me that the way Janice was acting was exactly the way I acted with Joanne!

Summer Session ended. There was a short time to go home, buy that professional recorder and get back to school. There would be no time for Grandma, Aunt Avis and the rest. That sure was a whirlwind trip! I bought the recorder, only to discover that it wouldn't work properly with the kind of mikes I owned. I tried using a step-up transformer with only limited results. Something needed to be done, but there was no time to do it. It was back to school work in earnest.

It was the beginning of my last year, my Senior year. I don't remember what my courses were except for The History of Science and

Radio Writing and Production. Here's where I'd have to write three scripts, line up the casts, rehearse them and then go into the studio to record them just as though they were live on the air. Much of my grade would depend upon how those scripts went.

Before actually taking my first class of the semester, it was of the utmost importance that I write a report to VRS to inform them, after three years of studying radio courses and doing lab work at our school station, that I was forced to conclude that I could not work in that field. Because of extracurricular work in the field of sound recording, I planned to spend my working life in that arena. Would VRS be sufficiently flexible to recognize that three years of immersion in radio showed me that the field was not going to lead to a fulfilling life? If they were inflexible, I'd kiss my scholarship good bye. Shortly after submitting my changed plans, I received a letter from them saying that my request was granted. My scholarship would continue as it was.

I don't think I'll ever forget my first class with Dr. Hotchkiss. He started off by saying, "You've been used to teachers taking attendance. I don't do that because I don't give a damn if you show up. There's a lot of reading if you expect to stay in this class." For the balance of the period, about 35 minutes, Dr. Hotchkiss did nothing but write the names of the books he expected us to read and master. When the class ended, I went to him and told him that I'd have to drop out of the class; there's just no way for me to read most of those books.

"Joe, now don't tell this to anyone, but I expect you to read just one book." He named it, and I bought it and then had it read to me on disk. I think it was my friend, George, who read it. He had taken the course. It was a very tough and exacting class, one of the most difficult I took during my four years, but I loved it. I got a C and felt lucky to get it. I hoped that C wouldn't wreck the rest of my scholarship, but it didn't.

People were calling me about my recording service. All I could do was ask them to wait because of being busy with prior work. Something had to be done about my microphones. Professional ones were expensive, and I didn't have the money to buy them. My only choice was to build a device which could be connected between the mikes and the recorder—and the problem would be solved. I had to sandwich time to buy the parts for this device and build it between classes. I didn't need the added aggravation.

Back to the Radio Writing and Production class. The first script was more of a run-through in preparation for the other two. Each of us had to explain our script, and the prof would critique it. His constructive comments were designed to help us write and produce the real scripts.

That first script was a nail-biter. After writing it, I read it at the speed I hoped my cast would read it, and then writing running times at each 30 second marks till we had all times noted. I think each script was to run for exactly 10 minutes. No radio station would tolerate a script running beyond its allotted time so that would count heavily when grading us. I remember that one of us, George Van Valkenburg, was the star of my play about a boy with multiple personalities. George and I would remain friends until he moved to Australia.

It was time to record our scripts. Because there were quite a few guys and gals in the class, several days were needed to record all of them. We were not told when our recording time would come, so we had to assume that we would be called next. There were last-minute changes in the cast, and I still had not asked someone to read the time prompts for me. Since Daisy always seemed reliable in class, I asked her to help me with that. She readily agreed. With her own script already recorded, I knew she'd be as conscious of passing time as I'd be.

Now it was my turn. The cast was assembled and we got our cue: "Tape rolling" George, playing the part of "The old French China Mender," began narrating this sad tale. I was reading the script. I'd ask Daisy for the time, and she'd tell me. I was running precisely on time. The last reading I had was 6 minutes 30 seconds. The cast was playing a bit too fast. I gave the hand signal to slow down. That sign was a widely spaced pair of hands which could be seen by the cast. A minute later I asked Daisy for another reading. Now the cast was reading too slowly. I gave the "speed-up" sign, a whirling finger. I didn't think we could make up the time. How could Daisy's times be so far off? The script ended. It was within 2 seconds of the 10 minute time limit. At least it didn't run over. I got a pretty good mark on that script, which would have been better had I gotten the time right on the money. It would have been even better if there was no slowing down and speeding up the reading. I tried to find Daisy to ask what happened, but she avoided me. It turned out that she tried to sabotage my work.

How I got through the second script I don't know, but it was not perfect. There was one, final assignment, to write a "singing commercial". I later understood that the prof expected we'd take a standard tune, write words to fit, advertising whatever it was and sing it.

With everything else on my mind, I forgot about it till about 20 minutes before the class. I ran to the piano, decided to write a little jazzy number about a soft drink called "Squirt". I think it was a lemon-flavored soda. I wrote the lyrics or actually committed them to memory. I figured out the tune and memorized it. I was almost late. I was the first one called. I went to the grand piano and performed. I was so afraid that I'd either forget the tune, the words or both, but it went off without a hitch.

The prof said, "Ya know that the music you wrote is too sophisticated to be used for a commercial, but the words were catchy—and I can't fault your performance. Just about everybody else in the class wanted my services as their accompanist.

One of the guys who ran a prestigious show featuring a piano and a string quartet complimented me on my work. It was a great day for me and that commercial raised my overall grade to something approaching an A!

There was a guy named Carl who wasn't liked by many. One day he came to my room with a recording he'd made at WAER. He had me play it on my equipment. He bragged about how great it was. It was quite good as a matter of fact. He made sure to tell me that I'd never have a chance to do what he could. Some of the guys overheard that and laced into him, but it didn't matter. I was shut out of recording at the station. Sometime later he came to us, bragging about a recording he just made for an important show. A guest poet was coming to WAER to read some of her poems with a harp playing in the background. Carl recorded that harp background.

The evening came when the show would air. The guys insisted that I listen with them. They seemed to have a premonition that this would be a very interesting experience. Carl was in the dorm with us, already bragging about his wonderful work and how important it was for the effect of the poetry reading. The program began. The guest poet was announced. Proper credit was given to the harpist, and the reading began. The music was great, just fitting in with the poet's words. Suddenly there was a horrible noise as the tone arm slid across the record. The engineer tried to restart the recording but it was no use. The grooves were not cut deeply enough into the disk so the stylus couldn't stay in those shallow grooves. Boy! Carl took a razzing. I have to confess that I felt a bit vindicated, and I don't mind saying that I was happy to see Carl being made a fool of. What would happen in Carl's next class? I never found out.

One day Norm Ross came to me to ask if I could record short wave broadcasts from various countries for a weekly radio show which he tentatively titled "International Listening Post". Once he knew I was interested in working on the project, he sought approval from the program director of WAER before any further work could be done. He got the approval. Franz let me borrow a short wave receiver owned by the station. I didn't like it very much, but it did work. My own receiver at home was better than what the station had. I hoped I could find someone to take it from my house to Syracuse during the Christmas break. I think Franz found the guy.

The show went well. I was pleased to hear my name crediting me the engineering! About the time I was to graduate, I understood that the show was submitted for a national journalism award. I don't think we got it, but never the less the fact that it was nominated gave our little radio station some prestige.

Then I had to find the time to design and build what's called a "mixer". It would both solve the problems with my microphones and have the added benefit of giving me the ability to use more than one mike at a time. I remember staying up half the night working on the project, which worked out well, fortunately.

It was Christmas vacation, and was I glad to come home and just rest—except, of course, to set up the tree, buy some gifts and help Mom shape cookies for her usual parties. What a great Christmas it was. With class work going well, I had no worries about approaching finals.

I had a bit of work because I had to record sufficient material for International Listening Post, but I called that fun more than work. I hoped I'd remember to pack the tapes for the shows in my suitcase.

New Year's came next, and Janice was coming to spend New Year's Eve with us. Lots of Dad's family was with us and that meant a terrific party. Janice arrived, and I introduced her to my folks. She got along with them, including Mary. After that, Dad's family straggled in, a few at a time. Janice appeared to behave until my cousin, Aldo, asked me to play piano while he sang. We did a couple of songs together. I thought things were all right. Later I was asked about what college life was like, and people were interested. I couldn't know that Janice was giving people dirty looks. She wasn't the focus she craved to be. To say the least, Janice did not make a hit with anyone.

Later Aldo took me aside and said, "Joe, take that broad behind the woodshed, fuck 'er and give 'er the heave ho!"

Dad hated her. Although he didn't verbalize the situation the way Aldo did, his feelings were more than clear. I told everybody how nice she really was, and with a little time, I'd be able to change her.

After that disaster it was time to head back to Syracuse. My receiver was picked up right on schedule so I would be able to record future programs with it instead of the one owned by WAEL.

During the long train ride back to college Janice kept popping into my mind. The way my relationship with her was going, I'd surely alienate my family. Yet how could I break IT off? I needed her. People who might understand me were difficult to find. No doubt about it, I was stuck in an untenable situation which would not allow me to shove it under the rug.

It was back to the few classes I had and all the music, recording, and radio repair work. I saw Janice occasionally and that still recharged me.

One of the psych teachers brought me a very fine radio to repair. I never saw one like it before. It had to be removed from a good-sized wooden cabinet. On the very front of the cabinet was a large dial. A pointer moved along the dial to show to what frequency the set was tuned. That pointer was attached to the cabinet, but I didn't notice that. When I removed the radio, the pointer remained with the cabinet, and the mechanism which moved the pointer stayed with the radio.

I repaired the radio all right but I couldn't figure out how to set up the mechanism so that the pointer could move. I had to call the customer and tell her what happened. She was happy that the radio played but was distinctly unhappy that the dial was inoperative. I couldn't charge her so my time and the money I paid for parts was lost. Worse, I lost that person as a customer. I'm sure she told others about her radio and that's bad advertising. I let someone down and that bothered me for a long, long time.

The term, my final one, moved on; and it was just about over. I started packing for my final trip home when I got a call from the program director of WAER. He practically commanded me to get to the station immediately. The King of England was on his death bed and the Program Director wanted our station to be the first one to announce HIS PASSING. That would be a feather in our caps if it could be done.

When I got to the station, there was a tape recorder waiting for me in one of the unused studios, along with the station's short wave receiver. I had to find some wire and throw an antenna out a window and connect it to the radio. Next I had to tune around with the hope that reception was good so I could get a good recording of the announcement of the King's passing right from the British Broadcasting CORPORATION. Luck was with me. The BBC was received loud and clear. I had the tape machine connected to the radio and waited for the impending announcement. Suddenly the on-going program was interrupted. Before anything was said, I had the recorder running. The English announcer gravely intoned that the King was dead.

I took the two reels holding the precious recording into Master Control, where another recorder was waiting to take it and play it on the air. We played the tape just the way we received it. Were we the first station to do so? I don't know but I think we were. It was about 30 seconds before the message showed on the United Press teletype machine. A loud cheer went up. We just were about certain that we were the first to air the news. There was no award for this: just the knowledge of what we accomplished.

Later that day I got another call from the station, this time telling me that, because of my hard work and mastering the complicated equipment at the station, I was voted into the Radio Honorary. One hurdle remained; I needed to demonstrate my understanding of the meaning of being voted into the Honorary. One of the guys came to my dorm to read the Honorary's constitution. I had a day or two to study it.

Because I was getting physically tired trying to take care of finals and other loose ends, I forgot to study for the exam. The time came to take it. All I could do was to listen to the reading of the Constitution of the honorary SOCIETY and hope that my hearing it would be enough.

I took the exam, and was even able to quote entire passages from the Constitution. I was told nobody ever did that before!

From then on life was a blur. I know I was busy but have no recollections of what I had to do. I know that I was still called upon to make recordings, which led to a small problem. I had quite a few on tape but didn't have the TIME to transfer them to disk. I had to make a list of names and addresses of those who hadn't received their recordings and mail them when I returned home.

There were a number of ceremonies to attend, visits to the office, and then the graduation itself. I told Dr. Hotchkiss about all the things which needed doing and how I didn't even know when or where some of these events were held. He assigned his secretary to be my personal guide through the maze and flurry of so many details.

Finally I was seated in our football stadium where the sun beat mercilessly on us. We had heavy robes on and the mortarboards sitting on our heads. It was a serious ceremony but it had its comedic side. I don't remember who the keynote speaker was, but I do remember the introduction to his speech. It listed the many jobs he held and his long list of achievements. I heard a guy behind me whisper: "Why couldn't this guy hold a job?" Later the awarding of diplomas began. As the valedictorian was announced, we were told that she had just under a straight A average. Another guy behind me said: "Who was the rat who gave her the B?" It's lucky that most people couldn't hear that or the solemnity of the moment would have been interrupted with raucous laughter.

She was, of course, Summa Cum Laud. Then those with Magna Cum Laud were announced. There were quite a few of these. Then the Cum Laud diplomas were awarded, and I got one. Here I was, a guy who didn't want to be here, getting a Cum Laud!

The graduation ceremony was over! There were so many of my Profs who came over to congratulate me—some who I thought didn't even like me. I was almost considered a hero because of all I had overcome. All I could do was to thank them all for their many good wishes.

Of course my folks and my sister were there, and Janice was there. I was the center of attention, and this time Janice didn't spoil the moment. My folks graciously invited her to have dinner with us. We dined in the most expensive restaurant in town, Lorenzo's. As we were being seated,

I heard some really great jazz played on a piano. I wondered who that could be. It was Paul, who I recognized from my Radio Writing and Production class. I never got to know him so didn't know he could play. When I think about that night, I wonder why he wasn't asked to play for some of those singing commercials.

After the meal, Janice and I walked around the campus for one last time. I was surprised at how sad I felt, knowing that I very well WOULD never set foot on those grounds again. Then it was time to go to a motel for the night. I wondered if I'd taken care of all the little details, like arranging for one of the guys to take my short wave set and bring it back to my house.

The next day there were a few more loose ends to tie up, and then, finally, I was on the train which would take me to Grandma's. When I arrived there, my sister wanted to watch the coronation of Queen Elizabeth on a neighbor's TV set. Dad and Mom stayed on the train and returned home. Me... I went to bed and slept 12 hours straight!

Chapter 21

I sure was glad to be with Grandma again. I wouldn't have very many more visits with her because it was getting hard for her to run her home even in summer. I'm not sure where she could go when she no longer could live alone. We wouldn't have room for her. We still lived in our three-room apartment and the equipment which I was using for my business took the space which Grandma would need. Uncle Art and Aunt Kitty couldn't handle another person. Little Alice required considerable energy and Aunt Kitty was very short on that because of an under-active thyroid. She also had a respiratory problem.

Aunt Avis was there for this discussion. Grandma's vote was to stay right where she was. Nothing was decided then. I hated to agree with everyone, but Grandma knew that the house should be sold and eventually would be and she would have to leave.

I couldn't stay with her too long. I had a life to start and knew I'd have to hop to it!

How will I start this new life? Life wouldn't come with teachers and grades, but that kind of life was all I knew. The new one, well ...

Once I was back home, I had some music on tape for which I was paid but had not yet delivered. The first thing I did in my "new life" was to finish those few records which I had not completed in my "previous life" and mail them out. I liked that because it would put off what I'd do next.

Dad's family was going to host a graduation party for me at the Bungalow, a place which held some nice childhood memories. There'd be lots of folks there—some I hadn't met. My cousin, Helen got married; thus she and her husband, Sam, would be there. I was in college then. Some of my cousins who were too young for me to really know while I was in school and they were growing up, and they'd be there. I had to meet a new family along with the folks I already knew. I heard that many planned to give me money to help start me out in my chosen field.

I knew a few things I wouldn't have figured out in past years. Not everyone would give me money; some might give me clothes. Some would probably give nothing because they couldn't afford to give. I thought about all this, and I didn't care what they gave or did not give nor care who gave me what. They were all going to be at my party to wish me well! It was gonna be a great party and I was ready to laugh and just have fun.

All was going great! Someone decided to start handing out gifts. It was a moving moment. Just about the time all the gifts were passed out, my Cousin Aldo showed signs that he had more than his share of fun. He became argumentative and violent. It took quite a few of the men to get him under control, but for all intents and purposes, the evening was ruined! I would see that scene repeated quite often. The party was over.

The next day I took time to look at all the presents I received. What a task it would be to send out "thank you's" to all. By then I knew about thank you notes. I knew there were commercial cards but Mom thought it was better if I typed thank you notes in person so I could acknowledge what each person did for me and thank each one in my own way. That was a real project. I had to Braille each name on paper along with the present, so I could refer to each one as I composed all those notes. I was amazed at their outpouring of—love? I wasn't sure about that because I didn't really know what love was. I completed the task of writing those notes over a several-day period.

I heard from VRS that in order to complete my training, I had to visit at least two recording studios run by blind people so I could learn their methods. It made sense to me. I knew that the organ teacher who I knew from high school had a disk recording setup which was relatively inexpensive but would do all of the things I required.

I called him and arranged a visit to his home studio. I was to get to his home in late morning shortly before lunch. By then I could handle subway travel to some extent. I discovered that his home was in a part of the city I knew nothing about, including the subway lines I'd have to use. Well, if Bob Gunderson could do that kind of traveling, so could I.

Off I went, just me, some money and the info I'd need in order to find his house. I was doing fine till I got onto a subway line with which I was not familiar. I knew at what stop I had to get off, but I had no idea how many stops were between me and my destination. I asked a passenger nearby if the next stop was the one I was looking for. I got off there. The station was really big! Which way do I go? The walk was on a double platform with tracks on both sides. I found a kind soul who walked with me to the street. I managed to find the house and was just a bit late. My host's wife was a clock watcher and made it plain that she wasn't happy about my tardiness. It felt like high school all over again. Before we could eat, there was grace to be said. I never heard of that being done in a house before. I didn't really want to say it or to even say "Amen," but I got by well enough.

I didn't feel too comfortable in that house. The teacher showed me his setup. He had not one but two Magnecords. His disk-cutting system wasn't the bulky arrangement we had at WAER, but it could easily fit on a sturdy table. It certainly would solve the record changer problem. He showed me the basics of using his system, so I could tell VRS that I had training in the use of the recording gear I hoped to own.

It was getting late in the afternoon when I started home. There were lots more people on the streets, and that subway station was crowded. I was sure that somebody would push me off the platform the way they were bustling around. I asked a man for help. It had been a long day and my mental stamina and courage to travel were failing fast.

"Don't you have a white cane," he asked.

"No sir. I never used one much."

"How did you get around here in New York?"

"Well, I managed fine for four years while I lived in Syracuse."

"Pal, this ain't Syracuse. I'm a cop, and I'm tellin' you to get a white cane before you attempt travelin' around here! Get it, Mac?"

I'll say I got it. I don't know how Bob Gunderson manages, but I just can't do that. I hated to admit it. I'd needed to have people see the cane so they would know that I might need aid. The cane, too, would let me safely walk on those double platforms and not fall onto the tracks. I was never so glad to get home in my life! All I could do was lie on my bed for an hour to calm down.

Although anxious to order the machine I just saw, I knew I had to report to VRS, the people who provided my college scholarship. I did so and they were satisfied, but they immediately assigned me for training at another studio operated by a blind technician.

Next, I took a subway to The American Foundation for the Blind, which, among many other things, sold white canes. It sure was easier once I started using the cane.

When I arrived at the studio, I was pleasantly surprised that the owner was one of the older guys at "that school". He showed me around the facility. He had a full-size studio which could easily accommodate a large orchestra if needed. His disk cutting system was impressive, a virtual duplicate of the gear WAER had. He had some terrific tape recorders which were lots better than my Magnecord.

All was not in what should have been a recording paradise. Just about all the chairs had "stuff" piled on them. I'm not the neatest person on the block, but I knew that all that junk haphazardly thrown around would make a very unfavorable impression on any potential client. His studio was in Manhattan so he had a high rent to pay. The way I saw it, he'd need a constant stream of customers if he was to keep his business. I told him what I thought, but I don't think he took me seriously. I played a tape on one of his recorders. It sounded just awful. He had never cleaned the oxide from the tape heads, which is mandatory if a tape machine was to perform optimally. I cleaned both tape heads on both machines and then the tapes he'd previously recorded sounded excellent. He showed me the basics of how to use his disk recorder. It sure was better than the one I'd soon order, but I knew I could get by without the absolute best. I learned about that machine so I guess I could say that I had some training. Truth be told, I spent more time getting his gear in proper running shape than I spent learning how to use his disk recorder.

I had enough money to order that new disk recorder and more. Dad's family was very generous. I telephoned my order for the machine. The company, Allied Recording, also made recording blanks so I had a one-stop place for all my disk recording supplies.

Then I went shopping for some specialized equipment which I needed in order to use the new disk recorder. Our family sound system was in another room, so I couldn't use it to play test recordings or other disk recordings. I needed a turntable and a decent loudspeaker. I found it all at Hudson Radio, where a few Christmases ago I received my first tape machine as a present. Dad helped me with all this because I couldn't carry it on a subway train and work with a cane at the same time. Dad built a cabinet to hold the turntable and loudspeaker. That cabinet was one of my worst designs.

After connecting everything and making a few checks to see how my disks sounded, my phone rang. It was my old friend, Louis Mitchel. He was living in the Bronx working and studying as a grad student at Fordham University. He had a couple of things on his mind. He knew a girl who was to play a short recital on Fordham's radio station. Could I record it for her? Well, yes, I could, and that was my first recording for pay since my graduation. Louis also wanted to know if he could buy my old disk system. He wanted to use it to record textbooks just the way I did. I was happy to do that. What a job it was to carry that heavy machine on the subway, but I managed. I spent the night with Louis, showing him the basics of disk recording. I got safely home the next morning.

Not much business was coming in. I wasn't sure how to proceed but began calling music teachers and dance schools, telling them about my service. One music teacher declined forcefully. "If the parents of some my students heard their little darlings play, they'd never bring them back to me for more lessons!"

While I was getting very little work, the owner of one of the dance studios I'd contacted called to offer me space to set up my studio in his building. In fact, he offered to finance a really big operation with the best equipment. I'm glad that, after thinking about this "too good to be true" deal, I turned it down. I eventually found that the financing would have come from the Mafia, and I wanted no part of that!

I wondered if maybe I could find work in someone else's studio. One of the guys in my dorm at Syracuse had the possible connection for me. His father was the manager of the RCA studio in New York. On the strength of this contact, I called and made an appointment to see him. First, he let me sit in the control room while a polka band was recording. Watching the ways the pros worked was a thrill in itself. Then the manager showed me around and was surprised to learn how much I knew about recording and the gear he showed me. I said, "I'm glad to know that you know I understand your studio. Just suppose I was looking for work here, would you hire me?"

He spluttered around and eventually said that he wouldn't hire me. That was disappointing. Well, I had planned to run my own studio. So that's what I'd do.

Just a day or two after that disappointment, I got a call from Lester Lewis of Lester Lewis and Associates, a small company which produced radio dramas. He told me that Bob Gunderson recommended me very highly. Would I be interested in recording a weekly show he produced called "Stroke of Fate". I would need to record it on the night it was aired and get the disk to him the next day. That's how I got my first steady work. I didn't know it then, but my new disk recording setup had a turntable 16 inches in diameter. I didn't think much about that when I bought it, but Mr. Lewis needed his recordings on 16-inch blanks.

I had that job for quite a while. Radio drama was rapidly being phased out by the new medium called television. "Stroke of Fate" was cancelled.

I called Bob Gunderson to tell him that the show was now off the air. All he said was: "If you didn't waste your time in college, I could have gotten you lots of work, but things are different now. I don't have any more contacts". Boy, that was a kick in the head. I never wanted to go in the first place and now I heard proof of my mistake.

I wondered if my recording future could lie with TV. I bought a small-screen set and wired it so I could record from it. I started recording quiz shows and wrote down the names of the contestants. Both NBC and CBS were airing such shows. After recording them, I'd write to the contestants care of the station which ran the shows.

I got results all right but not the kind I wanted. I received terse letters from the attorneys for the networks telling me to cease, desist, and halt my work because I had no legal rights to sell any recording unless authorized, and I would never be authorized. What could I do? I ceased, halted, desisted and even stopped making those recordings. Working in the "big city" didn't look too great right then.

Meanwhile my speaker arrangement with the turntable and the speaker in the same cabinet was a disaster. I had to redesign the speaker. I knew that anyone who came to hear any of my work would not like what they heard.

I remember what I noticed when I was in the 7th grade, about how a speaker cone might produce better bass if it could move more freely.

I got a rather inexpensive loudspeaker and cut slits into the outer edge of the cone. When I put it into a good-sized cabinet, the sound was markedly improved.

A few people from the photographic studio which my dad managed for a major magazine publisher, were impressed by what they heard and asked me to sell them loudspeakers. I refined them and I was selling quite a few of them. As usual, Dad did the cabinetry. I wondered if this was something in my future. Sales dried up so nothing came of the loudspeaker business for a couple of years.

Because of the loudspeaker work, The recording business was sidetracked for a bit. I had to get going with that again, and I got a flash. I called Steve Allen who had made a name for himself on radio and was now doing the same on television. I told his secretary about my little recording studio and did Mr. Allen have any need to have his shows taped or put onto disk? He didn't, but he had some tapes of past shows that he wished to have made into disks. He sent me a trial tape recording which, if he liked the results, he'd send more work my way. In short, he did and our working relationship kept going for a year or so until he moved his show to Hollywood.

Lots of people were in and out of the studio Dad managed, including lots of models and people who knew people. The result of this was that Guy Lombardo's brother, Liebert, wanted records of Bishop Sheen, a leading Catholic priest at that time who had a TV show. I recorded those shows for Liebert. Liebert told Guy about me and Guy had me record his TV shows. Of course I couldn't record the video.

Going back a way, I decided to write to Magnecord, Inc., the maker of the tape recorder I was using, to ask about any opportunities in the recording field which they might know about. I got a very nice letter from Magnecord suggesting that I talk to Harold Sherman who was doing pioneering work with stereophonic recordings. I called Mr. Sherman and found that he was in the hospital. I went to see him there and found he had serious complications from diabetes. I got the idea that he was unlikely to come home again. It turned out that I kept visiting him on a weekly basis, trying to cheer him up. I was learning about basic transistor circuits and built a simple device which I could show to Mr. Sherman. He hadn't seen such circuits but he knew of them. I learned about his many friends and how he did his recording work. It was a fascinating time as I learned about this sound pioneer.

During that time I joined the Audio Engineering Society, the professional group composed of men and women working in various fields of sound. I made friends with people doing advanced research at Bell Telephone Laboratories, and many of the people manufacturing sound equipment. Some of these people were great guys and fine friends.

There came a time when Mr. Sherman could no longer have visitors. It was just a question of time before he'd leave us. I found that he and his wife had virtually no money, not even enough to bury him. I started contacting some of his so-called friends and found that, now that Mr. Sherman was no longer of use to them, they just didn't give a damn whether he was dying! I can remember some of those names to this day, but won't waste print by naming them. I called a couple of my friends at Bell Labs, and they, who only knew a little bit about Mr. Sherman's pioneering work, raised money to bury him properly. I was getting exposed to the very good and the very bad of big city life. I couldn't help thinking what might have been had I stayed in Syracuse after graduation and continued my recording work there, where I was known and cared about.

Janice came to see me occasionally, but the family continued to dislike her. One time I borrowed money from my sister, Mary so I could go to see her. She lived more than 300 miles from my home. I figured to combine that trip with a visit to the Stromberg Carlson Company, the maker of the amplifier I was using in my recording setup. There I met the designer of the equipment who gave me a few ideas as to how I might improve its performance. Then I met Janice. She got me a room in a hotel which was near her home.

Her parents were drinking to excess. Her mother decided to take the two of us to a nice restaurant, which seemed as though it would be a marvelous evening. All went well; I didn't notice anything wrong, but there was. I do not know what got Janice's mother started, but suddenly she looked at someone and began yelling at her. "I see you, you filthy whore. I know what you're like and you're no damned good. Look at your friends there. They must work in the same whorehouse you do."

She then passed out. Janice was about to fall apart. I told her to get a cab while I paid the bill. I had to wait for Janice so we could take her mother out of there. We dragged her into a cab and got her home. Janice put her to bed and we went to my room. I needed her help before, but all this made it even more necessary. I know some of the busy bodies around the hotel thought Janice and I had other plans, but they were wrong.

Because Janice had to work the next day, she asked her younger sister, Jean, to take me to the train station. Jean had very little to say. Janice said that she was an impossible girl to control and was sorry to have to leave me with her. It turned out that I had no trouble with her. We talked about her hopes and aspirations. I don't remember what they were, but she was at an age in which she could have easily drifted into a gang which was starting up in town.

Jean was as nice as could be. If I asked her for anything, she'd do her best to be helpful. I never had the slightest trouble. I think that if I could have spent more time with her, I perhaps could have helped her a bit. At the same time I was beginning to know that nothing much could come from my relationship with Janice. She was all I had then so I put that thought out of my mind.

My old school friend, John Wahlen, had just been married and invited me to his new house, which was quite near my apartment, to meet some of his friends and to renew our friendship. I went there at the appointed time and met him, his new wife and two of their friends, Joel and Joan Shurgan. We shook hands! Joan had really incredible hands, and I needed them.

Joel was a chemist and very interested in electronics. Joan was a home-maker right then, and I think she had a very young son at that time. Both of these folks were extremely intelligent and could discuss just about any subject. I tried to figure how I could just touch Joan's hands. Our host, John, seemed to catch on to what I was doing, and he didn't like it. When the evening ended, Joan insisted that she walk with me to the bus stop. She wasted no time. "What were you trying to do by taking my hands? There's something more here than just flirting, so what's the deal. We don't have much time, so tell me, all of it!"

I told her about some people's hands being special and that hers could really help. I couldn't stop myself. I told her about needing to be held.

"Where do you live? I'll be over tomorrow, and we'll see about all this!"

True to her word, she came to my apartment and let me have her hands, and then asked about holding me. She did that, too. She invited me to her home, and told Joel about me and what I needed. He's one of these people who is quite solid about himself and with his marriage. He agreed to let her help me. That was the beginning of a friendship which lasted for 8 years utill they moved away.

It was obvious to me that I had to do something to bring in more money. If I was to live at home, I needed money for my expenses: food, telephone, etc. I called Bob Gunderson and told him things weren't good. He said that I really knew audio, so why not see if I could find work answering questions for one of the few magazines dealing with that subject. "Why not call your column "Audioclinic," he said.

What I did then was something uncharacteristic of me. I phoned Audio Magazine and asked to speak with the Editor. When he came on the line, he asked what I wanted. I told him what a great magazine he had, but one thing was missing. New-comers to the hobby would not understand the developing lingo, and that his magazine needed me to make a great magazine greater. I proposed that I write monthly column called "Audioclinic," which would answer questions of this sort. He asked how such a column could be run, and I suggested to him how it might be done. It became the system which he adopted and used with few changes for the more than 40 years.

He told me how to find his office and was willing to talk about my proposal. I didn't tell him I was blind. I figured if I did, I wouldn't be taken seriously and the interview wouldn't happen. I had to travel to Long Island, which I never did before. It involved riding on the Long Island Railroad. I managed to do that with no problem. I was wondering what he'd say when he met me and discovered I was blind. I needn't have worried. When I got to his office, he shook hands, sat me down and just talked. We talked about all sorts of things. I wondered when he'd get around to interviewing me for the job.

Then unexpectedly he asked, "Joe, what do you think of Magnecord?"

How should I answer him? This firm advertised in his magazine. I had a couple of years' experience with the equipment. Although it sounded good, if something went wrong, it was a real dog to open it up and make the repairs. The repairs were usually pretty easy, but reassembling the machine could take a couple of hours because of bad design. I decided to level with him. I told about my problems with the recorder and that, given a chance, I'd sell it and get something easier to fix. After all, if something fails in a studio, lost time is lost money.

"You're hired," he said. This editor, C. G. McProud, and I became good friends for some years before he sold the magazine.

My column, Audioclinic, would depend on letters written in by readers, but I knew that for the first column or two, there would be no letters. I'd have to make up questions and have them look as though they came from real people. I suddenly realized that I was never good in English composition. I turned to Joel's wife, Joan. It turned out that she had once been a tech writer for an oil company. Thus she knew how to write technical articles. I gave her the information about a few questions and she showed me how to turn my writing into readable prose.

It was a matter of waiting until July, 1955, when my first column would be published. When it was sent to me directly by Audio Magazine, I showed it to my parents and, of course, Joan. I hoped she'd like my final draft. She did.

Eventually letters poured into Audio Magazine. My column was a hit!

Chapter 22

1955. What a busy year this was! "Audioclinic" consumed quite a bit of time because I was still honing my skill as a writer. I continued to have ambitions as a recording engineer even though I was getting very few clients. I sold a loudspeaker here and there.

Along with these things, I was able to see Joel and Joan occasionally. Joan was a really good cook! Janice came to see me just after I had been invited to see Joel and Joan so I asked if I could bring her with me. They had heard all about Janice so they were interested in meeting her. After Janice left, both Joel and Joan said they believed that, in the long term, Janice and I never could be happy together. I listened carefully to what each friend said.

I had known Janice for a few years, and I knew we had some sort of bond, but I decided that this bond was not a healthy one. Therefore, after much soul searching, I reluctantly wrote Janice what I hoped would be a nice, but convincing letter explaining to her why I thought that our relationship should end. I said that I knew she would find happiness just as I hoped that I could. It was over! I told my folks and they were very much relieved. I had much to think about and so very many things to accomplish.

My old upright piano did not sound good; I definitely had to find another one. My customers would be playing it, and it had to be as good an instrument as possible. After shopping around, I found a Knabe spinet that at least had an action which was better than my old upright, except for some keys which would often stay down after they were pressed. I complained to the dealer who agreed to repair the instrument. I went with Dad to the shop to check it out. It was a good thing Dad was there because as I played it, all appeared fine. Dad stopped and yelled at the salesman to stop lifting a key when it stuck. That salesman was a very good musician, but he wasn't honest. He knew I wouldn't see that he was lifting stuck keys.

The manager refused to give me my money back. "We'll see about that," I said. I was blazing mad. I called the company directly and reported the bad behavior of that dealer. I got my money back immediately. The store manager had the consummate gall to call and tell me that I shouldn't have gone over his head. What I said to him alas, is unprintable.

Dad and I went piano shopping again. I played on a German piano which was the best piano I ever played. The price was quite high, but I could afford it. The problem: There was no room for it in our apartment. In that same store there was a Steinway. And it would fit into our living room and also sounded good. I found lots of problems with the action, but the price was only $600. Whoever heard of a Steinway grand selling at such a price? I decided to buy it, wondering if I knew enough to fix whatever needed doing. I knew that I needed help.

I called my former piano tuning teacher, Mr. Rice, and explained about what I bought and the problems I recognized. He told me that grand pianos could be repaired by using common sense for the most part. I had to buy a few, special tools, and he told me how to use them. He gave me a cram course right then and there. By the time the piano was delivered, I had a lot of the parts I needed on hand.

Again, Dad came through. Much of the problem with the piano had to do with action parts which had become unglued. Dad was a good carpenter so gluing a few parts was nothing to him. When I was done, I didn't have a perfect piano, but it was never the less a joy to play. It had one problem which could never be fixed. It only had 85 notes. It was built in 1883 and pianos of that vintage didn't have 88 notes. I wondered if that would be a problem with some customers. In all the years I used that instrument I had only one or two customers who needed to use the missing notes.

Although I never completely lost interest in ham radio, my equipment was so poor that I couldn't talk to enough people. Then too, the technology hams were now using was different from what I knew. I went to what was called "Radio Row" with Joel and found a rather inexpensive transmitter which used the new technology. It was anything but high-powered, running just 4 watts, but that amount of power when combined with the new transmitting system, permitted me to talk to lots more people than ever. My short wave receiver was still very usable.

Top this off with the fact that more people wanted to purchase the loudspeaker I designed, Dad and I decided that we'd form a legal partnership and produce the speakers in larger quantities. All of this happened over a period of a couple of years. We rented a shop not far from our apartment and stocked it with the tools and materials we'd need in order to build our units.

Before getting ahead of myself, it was still summer of 1955—time to go see Grandma. This was her last summer in her little house. She was no longer capable of doing the many chores which needed doing. In as much as Aunt Avis was already helping Grandma during the past few winters, it was a natural decision for her to live with Aunt Avis year round. Since Aunt Avis was still working, there was concern as to whether Grandma could care for herself during the days when Aunt Avis worked. But there were no other options.

It was so extra wonderful seeing Grandma and all her family during that summer. Every time I played the organ, I wondered if it would be my last chance to play it. We had a "garage" sale before we left, and I met a wonderful woman who was looking for an organ like Grandma's. It was the fashion at that time to convert those instruments into home bars. But this buyer promised that she wanted to keep it exactly as it was. That made me feel better!

Then the family all went our separate ways. I had to wonder would I ever see Aunt Avis and the rest of Grandma's family together again now that we no longer had a central place to gather?

In New York at that time there were audio shows which were held in prominent hotels or in the New York Trade Show building—not to be confused with the World Trade Center, which had not yet been built. We wanted to rent space in the 1957 show, but we didn't have the money. What little we had went toward obtaining our supplies and renting our shop. Dad knew so many people in so many fields that he found a woman who was willing to lend us the money at a good rate of interest, and now with that money we could enter the show and still have quite a lot left over. All I can say is that we were "babes in the woods" about how much money was required to run a manufacturing business. There were so many details which had to be gotten through before that time! There was a legal partnership agreement, an accountant to deal with taxes and, well, we didn't really know what else.

Although we had concerns, we didn't forget to celebrate Christmas. It was just great as our Christmases always were. Of course Dad insisted that we go to midnight mass. As the service was in progress, my hands started feeling very warm! It almost seemed that someone was holding my hands! No question about it. I knew Joan was in church with us. She was a Jew, but even so, she was there. Sure enough, when the mass ended, there was Joan. She decided that she'd like to see what Catholic Christmas Mass was like. Dad didn't like that very much, which was always the case when a girl or woman was involved, even though there was no hanky-panky.

After all of the holiday festivities were over, it was back to business. It didn't even occur to us that we needed a company name. After some head scratching, we came up with a pretty good one: "Audiotech Laboratories". We then needed a logo which would be immediately recognizable. My cousin, Sam, who was a decorator of department store windows, designed that logo. That, in turn, led us to find a good engraver who would make the plastic plates to be placed on the front of each loudspeaker, proudly announcing both the company name and loudspeaker model number. Other plates were made to be placed on the rear panels which showed the serial number for each speaker we built. Everyone who saw our finished loudspeaker loved their looks. How could we miss?

By then it was the middle of 1956. Dad came home one night with a surprise! His boss sold him his old, 1949 Plymouth sedan for only $50; so he bought the car without telling anyone about his plan to do it. We were very happy. Among many other things, we'd need that car to be able to carry supplies to our show as needed.

However, that wasn't our last surprise. A much larger apartment on the 4th floor of our apartment house became vacant. Because of something called "rent control", the rent for this unit would be only a bit more than we'd been paying for our smaller one. We moved in as soon as we could.

There was another surprise. Dad was anxious to buy a new (to us) car. That was for the best because our plymouth was not aging gracefully!

I went with dad to check out cars. We found a Mercedes which struck dad's fancy. We traded in the Plymouth and bought the Mercedes. Both of us were quite nostalgic about that old car!

It was summertime. Mom wanted to see her mother and sister, and, of course, so did I. Mom had lived in the vicinity of both Grandma's farm and the little house for many years and knew about a very small group of cabins clustered around a small lake, Hedges Lake. I guess Mom must have tracked down a phone number; so, we booked a cabin which had room enough for about 6 people. Dad got the idea that with so many of his nephews and nieces having pre-teen children, maybe they'd like to rent their own cabins. That's just what they did. Dad found a war surplus survival raft, and we packed it, along with clothes, pots and pans, and who knows what into our car. We had room for Grandma and Aunt Avis who agreed to take a train ride to Albany where we could meet them and take them to our "luxury" resort at Hedges Lake.

When we arrived, all of our clan was there and unpacked in their various cabins. There was no running water, just a pump which was used by all the renters. No running water meant no hot water for bathing. It had to be heated on the inadequate stoves in the cabins. We found that when it rained, some of the roofs leaked so we quickly learned where to place a pot to catch the drips. The owner of this rustic paradise was Mr. Nesbitt. He had no intention of repairing these little inconveniences. He planned to milk the place until he could sell it at some future time.

Despite the run-down condition of this "resort", we spent two weeks there for a number of summers, and those times provided everyone with fun and laughs which we still have when we talk about those great times! There was a pavilion in this "palatial" setting. It was used to hold dances and where people could roller skate hoping they didn't fall because of the roughness which was a part of the flooring.

How can we forget that survival raft and how my young cousin, Joanne, would always row in circles. How can we ever forget the time when the raft met its end? Jerry, the man who was married to another cousin, Josephine, asked if I would take her out for a ride. I was willing. I asked if he'd take the raft and me to where there was an air compressor so the rubber tanks in the raft could be filled. I'd done this job lots of times so knew just how much air was required for proper inflation. As air was pumped in, I felt the firmness of the tanks. I almost had enough air pumped when there was a violent explosion as the raft tore apart! The blast could be heard from a very great distance. Lots of people came to see what exploded. From what I could determine, the kids had dragged the rubberized craft over some sharp stones. I could feel rough places at various points on the bottom of the raftt. Had we fully inflated the craft and gotten it into the water, it would very likely have blown up with Josephine and me aboard. We wore life jackets, but it still would have been a rather terrifying experience! Well, we could, and did, have some good laughs over that incident.

Back at home we continued planning for the time when we would exhibit our loudspeakers and be in the big time. At the same time, my magazine writing had to continue. Letters from readers with lots of questions about sound kept me hopping. One letter in particular caught my interest. It was from a man named Bob Speiden. Along with his letter he sent a phonograph record. From what he wrote, he built his entire recording system in his basement, turntable, lead screw and all, including the delicate cutting head which is to control the movements of the stylus while a disk is being made. All of these items were made with nothing more than a jeweler's lathe and tools which most of us might own. (He was humble and never bragged, but he is one of the few true geniuses whom I had the privilege to know.) The disks he made had great sound most of the time.

He wrote to me with the hope that I could tell him why he didn't always get good sounds on his disks. That's why he sent that sample disk so I could hear the problems he mentioned. I answered him with my best guesses. As our correspondence went on, I learned that he even made his own microphones. I told him that I would be exhibiting my loudspeakers in the 1957 Audio Show, and I invited him to visit my booth. From that beginning we developed a friendship which lasted until his untimely death in 2009.

The time for the show was upon us. We needed quite a bit of audio gear to be used with our loudspeaker systems. A rule in those shows was that the participants had to use equipment which was provided by other exhibitors. We met a lot of the other exhibitors, and we were fortunate to have some of the best manufacturers of sound equipment at the show. We were garanteed great, auxiliary gear.

We were also supposed to use recordings provided by exhibitors. The problem was that there weren't too many good ones. We found a few decent-sounding ones and, regardless of rules, brought some of our own. Stereophonic disk recordings had not quite made the scene, but there were stereo recordings on tape. Stereo brought out tbe possible sound from our loudspeakers.

The show first opened to the press and audio dealers. Nobody had heard of our fledgling company, but a fortunate thing happened. Audio Magazine was willing to evaluate our loudspeaker. A good review could mean lots of sales for us. And they gave us a dandy! Well, it certainly brought in lots of traffic. Our sales brochures were jumping off the tables. When the show opened to the public, our display room was so crowded that people had to stand in line waiting to be admitted. We got raves about our speaker, Model"JA 15". (Those were my initials. The 15 was the size of the cone in our speakers.)

What we needed and got was a sales rep who would show our products to dealers, of which we had none so far. We had lots of folks who wanted to buy our units right then, but Show rules were that we could not make direct sales at the show. There's no doubt that, if we could have been able to do that, we'd have sold more speakers than we could have produced quickly.

Our loudspeakers were quite large, perhaps six cubic feet of inner volume. There were many firms with speakers that size or larger, but we noticed there was a considerable emphasis on smaller units. Stereophonic sound was becoming popular and many apartments could not hold two bulky loudspeakers in their living rooms.

When the show closed, we had picked up a few, small dealers who sold quite a number of units. It was obvious, however, that I had to design a much smaller loudspeaker, or I couldn't compete with companies which already had such units. I built a few prototypes and eventually settled on a design which sounded quite good. When I think back on that design, I can see how many loudspeaker operating principles I was unaware of but still produced something credible and at a competitive price. My dealer rep came to hear what I had and said that I sure had gold there. I'll never forget my comment, "Ya better say that because you've just heard the best loudspeaker in its class." He didn't like that, and later I had to apologize to him. It was arrogant, and I was carried away by the moment. (Eventually I discovered that this smaller model was not the best loudspeaker in its class!)

I later found out that one of my competitors had what I realized was a better sounding unit than mine. I sure wish I hadn't bragged that way. I can say our product was okay if not perfect. We named this model the ME12, my sister's initials. The number indicated the diameter of the speaker we used.

Before I knew it, we were opening our booth at the 1958 audio show. I had to arrange for a way to demonstrate two different models: the one we previewed in last year's show and my smaller model which was being introduced at this show. Let's face it! My original unit had vastly superior sound from our smaller design, but the smaller one sold at a considerably lower price. Dealers seemed to like the smaller design, however; and I referred them to my dealer rep.

As I've said earlier, one rule at these shows was that we had to use only products exhibited at the show. One such firm was Audio Fidelity Records. This firm led the way to introducing stereophonic phonograph records to the public. On the first day of the show, a representative of Audio Fidelity brought in a supply of just-released recordings. I went through the batch to find ones which would best suit what I believed would show my systems to their best advantage. I found a couple of excellent recordings, but some others had lots of background noise, making them completely unsuitable.

It was getting near closing time. There were some important industry leaders in the room. One told me that the president of Audio Fidelity was walking in the door. "This will give me a chance to tell him how lousy some of these records are," I said. A couple of people warned me it wouldn't likely bode well for me if I socked it to the guy. I didn't care. After I was introduced to the man, I started in:

"Hello. I'm glad you're here. I need just a minute of your time; I want to play a couple of samples your company men sent me." I played the first one. I commented on what a fine recording this was and how I was proud to use it. Then I played a sample of a really terrible recording.

"How in hell do you think I can use this? It's fine to use records from vendors displaying in this show, but no way will I play this!"

He said nothing but walked out quietly. When the show opened the next day, my dealer rep came to me excitedly.

"Joe, those Audio Fidelity guys are going all around the show telling everybody that Mr. Giovanelli is the only one around here who has a brain. Because of him, I found that there was poor quality control at my company. I went around to every exhibitor and removed those defective disks so they wouldn't be played. I don't want my firm's name associated with a bad product!"

Instead of being in big trouble in the audio industry, this man considered me a hero! I was making a good name for myself. When the show closed, a couple of important New York dealers ordered two dozen of each model. Fortunately Dad and I trained some people to help us in the event that we had too many units for us to produce on our own. We picked up a few orders, but nothing more from those larger stores. I phoned the managers and each told me the same story. "If you want us to push your stuff, you gotta give our salesmen 15% 'under the table'."

I was really angry. We didn't make allowances for this in our pricing. Besides that, it's wrong for a salesman to expect what amounts to a bribe. I knew that in some cases an inferior product would be touted by a bribed salesman, and a better product might never sell. We were selling a few units, and we were putting a little money in the bank. I knew that if we couldn't come up with a new sales plan soon, we would have to close our doors!

Just about then we got another surprise. For no reason I ever determined, the woman who lent us our starting capital, "called in the loan". We understood that we had at least four more years before we'd have to pay her the principal, but there was nothing we could do. Dad wanted to hang on. He thought we could do a little advertising and sell mail order. I was against that. I saw no way that, with our remaining capital and the cost of advertising that we could manage.

I told Dad, "Look, you're not that many years from retirement. You'll need money to live on. Let me buy you out. All I want is to keep the Audio-tech name so I can use it in connection with my recording business. I've let that go while messing with loudspeakers, but that's got to stop! Please agree to this!"

He didn't answer for some time, but he finally reluctantly agreed. The way I saw it, this was the least I could do for him.

Now it was winter of 1962 and Christmas was at hand. Mary and I shopped for presents for each other and for the family. This would be a very different Christmas for us. Mom had a strong feeling that she wanted to see her mother. Neither Mary nor I wanted to go all the way to Buffalo, New York, where Grandma lived with Aunt Avis. After lots of talking, we agreed to make the trip, stay for a couple of days and return on Christmas Eve.

We all piled into the Mercedes, blankets and all! What a trip that was! As we were driving past Rochester, New York, it began snowing very hard. Flakes were falling so fast that we thought our car might get stuck, but the snow stopped falling just as suddenly as it started, and we arrived at Aunt Avis's apartment rather late in the evening, around 9 o'clock. Grandma was awake and so happy to see us. She wanted to know about all our plans and what we were doing.

There was no room in that apartment for the four of us. I thought about the Christmas story where there was "no room in the inn". In her usual, efficient way, Aunt Avis made arrangements with one of her friends so we could use her apartment. She was away for a few days. We were glad to hit the hay that night.

As previously arranged, we joined Grandma and Aunt Avis for breakfast. Grandma was strangely quiet; she kept complaining about her dirty eyeglasses. We began to wonder if there was something wrong. Her doctor was called. He came and told us that Grandma had a mild stroke. She had trouble controlling her spoon when she ate. She could barely walk, even with the aid of a walker. It was a dark time for us.

We did a bit of shopping. I had the chance to examine a clock which dated from the time of Mozart. It had a complex mechanism, including a fine music box. I probably could have bought the clock, but I wasn't as interested as I would have been if Grandma was well.

Christmas Eve morning we said our good byes. Grandma was almost as animated as she was when we first arrived. Did that mean she was going to recover from the effects of the stroke? No, what we saw was just a flicker of extra vitality, but Aunt Avis told us that later. Once we were gone, Grandma relapsed to what we had seen on the first morning we were with her and had another stroke.

We got home at a reasonable time. We had previously made all of our Christmas preparations, so then we set up our tree. It was getting harder to fine fresh trees so reluctantly we bought an artificial one. We loved setting up the tree and decorating it. By now it was a game in which Dad did his best to sneak into the living room to take a peek at our handiwork. We had to chase him out. Christmas Day was wonderful as all of them were. Dad insisted that we go to Midnight Mass, and when we'd come home, Dad would break out the Italian cold cuts and fresh Italian bread and, of course, a "vaso di vino".

I had not seen Joel and Joan for quite some time and I needed that special help that very few people could supply. I decided to visit them on New Year's Eve, 1962. By then they'd moved to New Jersey, which meant a subway ride and then a bus ride to the town close to their house. When I got there, something was different—an indefinable change in the atmosphere. Joan had a friend there who also needed her help. Joan did her best to find time for me, and I accepted her help gratefully. Something just didn't seem quite right.

I stayed overnight and left early afternoon of New Year's Day, January 1, 1963. I took the bus back to New York, but I somehow didn't want to take the subway. A kind person helped me find a taxi, and I relaxed as we drove into Brooklyn. I couldn't help but wonder if anything was wrong with Joan. She was so different from her usual manner.

I found out later that, at that time, she was contemplating a major life-style change. The gravity of her decision pulled her down.

We were only about a half mile from home and were stopped at a traffic light. I was dozing when there was a sudden crash! I found myself on the street lying next to the cab. There was glass everywhere! The engine was still running, and I distinctly remember yelling at the driver to shut off the ignition.

I wasn't too clear after the accident, but a guy who I think must have been a cop asked me if I was all right. He may have asked if I wanted to go to the hospital. I said no and was driven home. I was resting on my bed and nobody was with me. My family was in another apartment in the building, enjoying a New Year's Day party with some of my cousins. They were expecting me to be with them. I didn't feel well at all, but I had to force myself to get there. I don't remember it, but I must have found the right apartment.

I was greeted warmly when I rang the bell. I remember eating some fruit. People started to notice that I didn't look well. Mom came close so she could take a good look. She saw that I had blood stains in various places and saw slivers of glass. I don't remember anything about walking back to our apartment nor the doctor' being called to check me out. I do remember, or think I do, that my sister, Mary was holding me in her arms. It wasn't something I'd expect, knowing how she felt about those things, but there I was, or at least it seemed so.

The doc said I had bruised ribs and a few lacerations and a probable concussion. I saw the doc in his office the next day for X-rays and for some diathermy. I don't think the diathermy did much for me. Luckily the X-rays were negative.

Because my recording work was not doing well, I took on a couple of custom tape recorder designs which were special orders. My sister's boss asked me to install a pair of loudspeakers in his office. There was also a somewhat complicated sound system for a dance studio run by a friend of Mary's. Because of my association with Audio Magazine, the American representative of a British transformer company asked me to design an amplifier which would employ two of the firm's units.

There were deadlines for each of these jobs, and here I was, laid up and not able to concentrate. There were phone calls from some of the folks who ordered these devices. My sister's boss didn't believe I was in an accident nor did the guy who ordered the custom tape recorder.

I was able to do a bit of work on these projects. Here is a typical mental situation I had to work through: Dad understood how the four speakers should be set up in the dance studio. He had them laid out on the floor for me to examine. I did and told him that it wasn't right. I set them up the way I knew they should look. It wound up that what Dad had done was exactly what I did; I couldn't believe that our layouts were the same ones.

Our family lawyer tracked down the guy who ran into that taxi. His name was La Froscia, who had no insurance and was driving with a suspended license which was earned by committing a few DWI offenses. We couldn't recover any of my medical costs.

All those projects were completed. Mary's boss still didn't believe that I had a nearly fatal accident. I don't think the guy who ordered that customized tape recorder believed me either, but I could be wrong there. Eventually I completed the amplifier and my article relating to it was published. A few readers wrote in with rave notices. One of my friends who is a designer and manufacturer of loudspeakers has the old prototype of this unit, and he said it's just about the best amplifier he ever heard. That's high praise because I built it in 1963 and here we are 45 years later and that unit compares favorably with today's better amplifiers!

Those projects were out of my hair. Given all I went through, I knew that each one was what it should be and I received quite a bit of money for all of them.

Our lives moved on. Mom at her job took a rigorous Government test and this increased her salary tremendously. Dad's boss retired, and Dad took his place with a consequent salary increase. He was tired of apartment house living. I could write a chapter about "some of the odd people and events in our building," but I won't.

Not too far from our apartment house was a vacant, two-family house for sale at a very good price. Dad kept telling us about it. Mom was skeptical. Owning a house has its problems as well as good points. Knowing about their plans to retire in the near future, she wasn't sure she was up to home ownership. One Sunday Dad convinced us to look at the house. So off we went: Dad, Mom, my sister Mary, and I. The realtor was waiting to show us around. The building was put up in 1906, but it was a well-built brick building. Mom noticed the out-of-date kitchen. The wall paper needed to be replaced. Under that paper, however, were plaster walls which was yet another sign of just how well built this house was. There was a dining room which was larger than we'd need. I'm not much for how a building might look with just a few small changes.

The three of them, however, saw how a bedroom for me could be cut out of the dining room space and how, at the same time, it would have more light and airiness. That would mean we'd have to locate a plasterer. Those craftsmen were scarce because of the extensive use of sheetrock those days. I imagined how part of the basement could be finished and I could set up a fine recording studio. The heating plant would have to be replaced. Dad's nephew, Jerry Avalino, knew how to do all of what was needed and, after looking over the situation, offered to do the job for a lower price than he charged others. Dad was a bit put out because he thought he could get the work done with nothing more than the price of materials.

Once the mortgage was approved and we closed on the house, it was ours. I learned how to steam off wall paper and scrape the walls. We found a leaky toilet so I figured I could fix that. I had never done plumbing work, but I looked it over, and it seemed like common sense to me. I bought what was needed and fixed the toilet. Some of the contractors we hired stopped to watch me. I let 'em do that for a while. I figured they might as well know that a blind person could do plumbing work. Then I told them that the party was over and to get back to work.

I think it was early May when we were just about ready to move in. It was a Friday, right after breakfast. The phone rang. It was Aunt Avis. Grandma had a massive coronary. Her chances of surviving this were not good! My aunt said she'd call again as soon as there was any news. She called to tell us that Grandma was now suffering from a bad headache. Another call. Grandma was gone.

How should we react to such news? There were so many emotions. We were supposed to move into our new home that Monday, and we were not completely packed yet. There was the crushing loss itself. Most of my life there was Grandma and the peace she represented. Mom and Dad had their own memories. I don't know how Mary felt.

Calls flew back and forth. We would all meet at the Swan hotel in Greenwich, New York, which was not far from where Grandma lived. Greenwich was where the closest funeral director was so we knew that's where the funeral would take place. We drove there and arrived that night. Aunt Avis got there Saturday morning, and I don't know what arrangements she made so Grandma would be there. I guess that was left to the funeral director. The funeral and graveside service was on Sunday, and we all said hurried good byes.

Then we drove home to finish packing. Moving would be the next day. I have no idea how all of these chores got done, but we made it! We were in our new home. Dad noticed that the previous owner broke a small patch of concrete at the bottom of the outside stairs which led to the basement. He believed that it was the start of a dry well which would be needed in the event of heavy rain.

As Mom and Dad were settling into bed, a hard rain began. Dad asked me to finish digging the well. I found a shovel and deepened the hole. I was told there were lots of stones of various sizes in the front yard, so I had to go out in the pouring rain and locate a bunch of them to put into the hole to aid in water drainage. I finished and was glad to get a bit of shut-eye.

We were hardly unpacked at our new house. After so much stress, we needed a change so on the next day we hopped into our car and took an impromptu trip to Washington, D.C. just to see the sights. I won't describe Washington here; there are lots of books about that city. I'll just say that when I went to the Smithsonian, I got to see old radio equipment dating from Marconi's era. The public would probably not be able to see these things, but one of my college friends was a curator of that section of the Smithsonian which permitted me to have such a great privilege.

The house we had just moved into was a two-family home. We wished it wasn't but renting the first floor was the only way we could meet our mortgage commitments. We advertised with various realtors hoping to find a nice family, perhaps with no children. My folks were fielding calls as I was. I met the nicest family; they met all of the financial requirements. I really liked them.

At the same time, unknown to me, my folks found a very nice couple and drew up a rental agreement (lease) and that was that. I was happy that we rented the apartment but was sad to turn down the family I found. They were Latinos and I was concerned that they would think we were discriminating against them. The wife was very upset because she was desperate to find a home. She believed me after I explained the mix-up.

The couple we rented to were just great. They were with us for quite a few years, and they were never any trouble. Their last name was Core. I didn't get to know the husband Herb as well as I got to know Eilene, his wife. They were very nice—and Eilene had great hands, but I never told her that.

Chapter 23

1963 was loaded with more things than I can count. Shortly after Grandma's death Mom came to me for help. According to Grandma's will, she left small amounts to my sister Mary, my cousin Alice, and to me. Mom told me that Aunt Avis was the executrix of the estate and was the only one empowered to distribute Grandma's assets. She wasn't doing anything about it. Mom's concern was for Alice who was newly married and desperately needed money. I really liked Alice and already knew she was in desperate financial straits. Mom tried to talk to Aunt Avis but got nowhere. Mom said that, because I seemed to be close to her, would I be willing to talk with her about prying the money loose. I was not willing to do it because I didn't want Aunt Avis to think I was hounding her for my share of the estate. I must say also that I had a premonition of something more serious which I didn't want to face nor accept. Was my aunt mentally declining?

Very reluctantly I dialed her number. She answered the call, and we engaged in small talk during which I tried to get a feel for how she was fairing. Her speech was a little more laid back than usual. I forced myself to explain my reason for calling:

"Aunt, I'm glad to hear your voice, but it's more than that. Alice has serious financial problems. I'm not sure you heard about that. What I'm asking is that you release the money due her from your Mom's estate."

"Yeah, well, uh, uh"

"Aunt, do you understand what's on my mind?"

"Hu, hu, well yes."

"When can you get the money to her?"

"Well, I'll do it, uh, soon."

How will I know if Alice got the money? I didn't wanna handle that one; so, I asked Mom to call just to see how Alice was getting along. Mom called, and from what I could hear of Mom's end of the conversation, Alice had not yet heard a thing from Aunt Avis.

I knew what I must do. I called my aunt again. "Hi, Aunt. How's it going?"

"Well, uh, fine. I'm fine."

"Glad to hear it. Look, Aunt Avis, you said you'd definitely get money to Alice and you let her down. I need you to get crackin' on this. When I hang up, please get down to it and send that money to Alice! It's not a problem if Mary and I never see our share, but Alice needs hers now! Okay, what's the first thing you're gonna do when you hang up?"

"Well, yes, I'll, I'll take care of it right now."

"Thanks, Aunt. I'm sorry to be a pain."

In just a few days everybody involved received their rightful shares, and that substantially helped Alice.

As that year moved along, the weather was turning colder and we found to our astonishment that the Mercedes didn't provide very much heat. We often drove with blankets around us. Dad found a good mechanic who improved the heater but it never worked well.

I spent a lot of time with Bob Speiden. (As you will remember, I met him just a few, short years ago.) I'd often spend a weekend with him and his wife, Helen. Yes sirree, she could flat out cook! Bob had a full-time job as a commercial illustrator but always found time to tinker with his cutting head so that he could improve the sound of his disk recordings. I don't know how he did it, but he had a steady stream of customers. We'd gab about such things, and we came up with the simple fact that Bob could record stereophonically—and I couldn't. The cutting head I was using was commercially made and worked well in its day but couldn't be used for stereo recording.

I don't know how they met, but Bob met Howard Holzer who lived on the west coast and worked for a small record company. On the side he ran a small business designing equipment which he sold to quite a few record companies. Bob mentioned the cutting head he developed, and Howard became interested in it. Eventually they joined forces to make Bob's system better looking and making other improvements which made the even better than it was.

Howard made a few prototypes which he eventually planned to sell to record companies. He produced a recording designed to demonstrate the virtues of this new "head". Because, for whatever reason, the record sounded quite bad, and thus no company was interested in buying the cutting head. Bob found out eventually what the problem was, but it was too late. Howard gave me one of the prototypes. Bob made sure it worked properly so now I could make stereophonic recordings. Howard developed a special circuit for that "head," and I built one based on Bob's verbal description of its circuit. I tested it and everything worked just fine. Now I could tell the world that Audiotech Laboratories could make stereo disks. I began to gain a few customers.

By that time I'd written for Audio Magazine for a few years. The owner/editor had shortened the name to Audio rather than Audio Magazine. I asked if I could get a discount if I placed ads for my studio. It turned out that my ads would cost me nothing!

Many more recording studios like mine were opening. How could I compete with them? My operation was in my basement. Most customers would be turned off if they saw that. I was desperate for something which no other studio was doing. It came to me by some sort of inspiration that my customers didn't have to see my studio or me for that matter. They wouldn't know that I was blind.

I could do the work by mail. I developed really complete forms and instructions so the potential customer could fill them out and there'd be no confusion about what they wanted. Later, when I was able to produce multiple copies of cassettes, I developed similar forms which the customers could fill out so I'd know what was needed. These forms eliminated possible mistakes.

Because AUDIO was read all over the country, there was a much larger customer base to draw from than just New York City. Business was increasing. I believe that I'm the only blind recording engineer who made stereo disks. That was all well and good as long as I produced one or two copies for my customers. I began receiving orders to produce 100 or as many as 2,000 copies. The master disk from which these copies would be made had to be perfect. I didn't dare make too many masters until I figured out a work-around the need for a microscope. It wasn't long before that problem was solved.

Because of my magazine work, I was invited from time to time to appear on the one or two radio shows in New York which dealt with high fidelity and its various aspects. It was around 1966 when I was getting off a subway train to walk a few blocks to a radio studio where I was to appear on one of those shows. A man asked if I needed help. He saw I was using a white cane. I thanked him, and we started talking. He told me his name was Hank Robbins and that he was invited to observe the very show on which I was to appear. He was a member of a group called the New York Audio Society. It was a group of audio enthusiasts which met monthly to discuss and demonstrate audio gear. That sounded very interesting.

I did the show. Then Hank and I left the studio, and we had lunch together. I ended up joining the New York Audio Society and attended monthly meetings. The comradeship was fun and often spirited. I benefited, too, from the fact that many audio products were demonstrated. Had it not been for this group, I wouldn't have had some hands-on experience with those products. I used that knowledge to answer questions from some of my readers.

During one of its meetings somebody proposed that the group should have a radio show to promote its meetings and its other activities. One thing led to another, and I found myself hosting the program which we called "Audio Showcase". The program would cover a variety of subjects involving the world of sound. One week might feature the nature of microphones. Another week's show might feature a modern composer and his work. Each show would end with a recording which someone in the New York Audio society thought had excellent sound quality as well as good musical performance. One show was devoted to ham radio, and I interviewed someone who was prominent in the hobby. Another show which was special to me was a tour of my former school, where we could demonstrate how the blind are taught. The climax of the show was a very powerful segment about how students who are both deaf and blind are taught to speak. I ran this show for two years. I only kept copies of these last two shows.

One show featured the highest possible sound quality which could be heard by broadcasting the sound of studio master tapes. One of my friends was the manager of the New York studio of Capitol Records. I asked for copies of some of this studio's master tapes for this show. He couldn't give me complete recordings for legal reasons, but he gave me enough to demonstrate how great a recording from a master tape can sound. The manager told me about one of his engineers, Johnny "Cue". He was called that because he had an almost unpronounceable name, and cueing is an important component of many recordings. Johnny, he told me, was a ham like me and a superb guitarist besides. He would send me the precious tapes delivered by Johnny who lived fairly close to me. He brought them and we gabbed a bit and made a date to bring his guitar and we'd jam. We became great friends for many years.

Having a radio show on a Public Radio station in New York I suppose has a measure of prestige, but it was too much for me. Consider this: I had to find most of the guests, do the engineering, interview them, do post show tape editing, and for no money. Meanwhile I had to keep up with recording work and magazine writing.

Plainly the radio show had to go! I would have loved some "special help", but there was none. As was true so often, I somehow had to suppress any thoughts of that and keep moving.

I wasn't playing much piano. The music scene and my perception of it killed my desire to play.

I wasn't doing very much with ham radio. My present home didn't have enough space for a decent antenna. I'd have to find another aspect of the hobby to conquer. I still had my short wave receiver but because I no longer had much chance to use it, I sold it. At various times I experimented with VHF ham radio. It didn't require long-wire antennas but employed a variety of antenna shapes which could be mounted on TV masts. This sort of ham radio didn't permit transmission of signals over long distances but it was possible to transmit from automobiles even when they were in motion. I recall one radio contact between me and a military aircraft flying higher than 30,000 feet. Because of the very high antenna on the plane, I remained in contact with him as he flew between Maine and Georgia.

It was summer of 1969. My family and I went upstate to see my cousin Alice and her family. Mary and I stayed at her house, while Mom and Dad went to a motel. I had misgivings about the visit. I liked Alice well enough, but there were marital problems. Added to my concerns was that they had two children, the older named Dan and the younger named Kelly. I guess they were about three and five years old. Given all my problems with children, well, I really wasn't sure I even wanted to be there.

One evening after dinner Dan would try to show me things. All he'd say is "Look". Kelly came along and told him: "Dan, he can't see. Give him the ball in his hand so he can see it." Dan did so and I thanked him. Kelly then told Dan to give me some potato chips. Those two kids started feeding me the chips and everybody was laughing hysterically. That was my first experience in which I enjoyed children! How could it be? Kelly was hardly more than a baby. How is it that she was so perceptive?

About a month after that my family was invited to see the beautiful new home in Connecticut that another of Dad's nieces bought. My cousin Ronny and his wife Marilyn drove us there in his large station wagon. I had witnessed Ron's marriage just a few, short years ago. His wife was a wonderful woman. I always notice when a woman has "great hands" and Marilyn's were just that. The house was beautiful. Dianne and Steve, who owned it, were coming up in the world. He held a high position in Pepsi cola and when you get up that ladder, it is virtually mandatory that you reflect your status.

I had my usual mood swing, this one sliding downward. Could Marilyn let me have her hands on the way home? I'm pretty sure no one else in that car would understand so I knew telling any of them about me be would bad move. Could it possibly result in damaged family relations? I had to trust Marilyn.

She was surrounded by lots of folks. There might be no way to get her alone. Mary was there, and she could make things awkward. I don't know how it came about but we found ourselves alone. I had little time to explain what I needed, but she immediately was sympathetic so she acquiesced. Our seats in the station wagon were far from where Mary sat so I hoped she wouldn't notice. We were nearing my home, and Marilyn really made me feel better. All good things came to an end. This ending was caused when her baby girl, Kristen, threw up all over my suit. O well, it was worth sending my suit to the cleaners!

Marilyn and Ronny are truly wonderful friends!

It was the start of 1972. The disk cutting machine that I bought after graduating from college was giving me trouble. There was a slight background rumble on my disks which could be heard when they were played back. I had tried many things to cure it but to no avail. I needed a really professional cutting lathe and they cost thousands of dollars which I didn't have. The whole thing was depressing. All my life

I seem to have been fighting. There was all that time in "that school". Then I had to fight to maintain good grades in college. Now it was a fight to stay in business. Unless I could make significant changes to my recording system, I couldn't hope to keep up with the industry.

Now it was early summer. We all visited Alice again. During the visit we passed a car dealership. Dad spotted a Volkswagen which interested him. He told us about it and, in as much as our Mercedes was showing its age, we thought we might as well look at it. Off to the dealership we went. The car was known as a "square back", a mini station wagon you could say. We went for a short spin and bought it on the spot. They didn't have that model in stock, however, but the manager promised that he'd have one for us pretty quickly. Later we found out that the dealer wasn't completely honest. After waiting a couple of months, Mom was able to check into the problem because of her work related to Customs. Because the car was German-made, Customs could check the dealer and if he really ordered one. The manager didn't do anything about our order till Customs officials pressured him to get the car quickly. Mom and Dad had to make another trip to Upstate New York to pick up the car. They didn't drive the Mercedes but took a bus and drove home in our new car.

I spent quite a few late evenings at Capitol Records watching Johnny Cue do his work. One time I went there with the hope that he could bail me out of trouble. I had completed a live recording of some girls who drove all the way from Massachusetts to record in my studio: my living room. I had to contend with some girls quarreling about how to do certain songs. After mediating those problems, I had a beautiful sounding master tape, but the nature of the music was such that I was unable to make the master disk. So I asked Johnny if he could cut it using Capitol's equipment. It took him quite awhile before he could make the master disk. Without the special equipment in the Capitol studio, even Johnny couldn't make the disk. He did have that special equipment and he was able to make a great recording.

As we were about to leave, Johnny announced sadly that the company was closing the studio. All the equipment would be sold, including the professional cutting lathe which Johnny used to make my master disks. He asked if I wanted it. I said that of course I did but even secondhand these machines sell for lots of money.

A week or so later he phoned me and asked if I wanted to bid on the lathe. All I could come up with was $1500, which was way too low. I was getting more and more depressed. Was there no end to the problems of running a business?

When "hamming" one afternoon I heard about a group of guys who were going to a small airfield in New Jersey to learn about sky diving. That sounded exciting to me. It occurred to me that if they'd let a blind person give it a try, I'd go, learn what I could and then jump out of the plane with no intention of pulling the rip cord of my chute.

I was sick of life. I couldn't help thinking about my life and how simple things like holding great hands or being held could keep me going. Now that all those school situations were behind me, those problems were replaced by the needs themselves. I knew that, one way or another, life had no meaning and whether it came about by sky diving or some other way, I was definitely planning suicide. I remember how I helped two guys from doing that, but there was nobody to help me. My folks couldn't understand my feelings. Certainly my sister, Mary wouldn't help. To top it off, a studio on the west coast put a bid of $3000 for that cutting lathe. I lost again; there went my last hope for saving my business.

I just about had the arrangements set for the sky diving lesson when I got a call from Capitol Records saying that my $1500 bid had been accepted. They said that this heavy machine with all its various parts was easier to pack for a trip from Manhattan to Brooklyn than it would be to pack it up for a trip to the West Coast. The machine was mine! A momentary flash of excitement washed over me—but it didn't last. There'd be so much special work to adapt the equipment for my needs. The delivery date was set, which forced me to cancel the sky diving lesson. I had to wait around for something which I didn't think I really wanted.

Dad arranged for my cousin Ronny and his father to come to the house to help unload the truck. The driver would leave the loads on the sidewalk and that meant that we'd have to unload and carry the equipment down the outside stairs and into the basement where the recording equipment was to go. I didn't wait excitedly for the truck to arrive.

I went into the basement just to sit quietly and think about that missed chance to try sky diving and die.

The room was almost silent except for the ticking of the large, mission-style pendulum clock which hung on one wall. I thought I heard a voice. I guessed it was either the trucker or my cousins. I heard it again.

"Joe."

Who was that? I couldn't figure out where it was coming from.

"Joe, pay attention!" the voice said.

Try as I might, I couldn't tell where the voice came from. It sounded like it was coming from outside my closed door. No, it was coming from where the new equipment would soon be placed. No, it was directly over my head. I heard my name again, and the voice seemed to surround me! What was going on?

I timidly answered: "Who's there? What do you want?"

"We have very little time, so listen carefully. How is it that you got your new equipment when you know the price was too low?

When a company is closing, it expects to get the best prices it can when it sells off its inventory!"

"Who knows? I got lucky."

"No, Joe, I arranged for you to get it! Now don't interrupt. Let's think about a few other things. Where did that idea for recording without using a microscope come from? I put it into your head! How did it happen that on the same night you stole that tone arm that Marjorie showed up? Partly it was because I didn't want you to ever think about stealing.

"How was it that you weren't caught with Esther a few minutes before your big moment when you were in high school. I arranged that, too. You needed success with the talent show. I made sure it wasn't recorded so that fact will come back to you at the right time.

"Let's really go back. I introduced you to Dorothy so you would feel something besides your little world. I took her away so you'd have a taste of feeling sad for others.

"There's more—much more! What about that midnight mass you wish you'd missed? How was it that your hands got almost hot, and you knew Joan was in church with you?"

Stammering I said, "I, I, I don't know what to say." There was no reply.

"Where are you," I asked. There was no answer. I was alone in my room. So many thoughts were whirling around in my head. And then I blurted out, "I think I just met GOD!"

Much of this conversation I paraphrased because I couldn't remember it verbatim, but my last quote was exactly what I said out loud.

That voice—I can't describe it. It was very soft and yet it possessed absolute authority and power. It was a male voice, and I heard both caring and compassion. At no time have I heard a voice which seemed to come from anywhere and everywhere! That voice was to be obeyed!

After God left me, it was as though I woke from a refreshing sleep—except I was fully awake!

I had no time to consider what the full implications of this talk with God were because Ronny and his Dad arrived, followed immediately by the truck carrying my new (to me at least) disk cutting lathe. I quickly examined the equipment which was now on the sidewalk. In addition to the table on which the equipment was to be mounted, there was a very heavy piece of cast iron which weighed a bit more than a hundred pounds. It looked for all the world like one of those old fashioned bathtubs turned upside down. (This was to hold the motor and a very heavy flywheel.) There were a couple of heavy crates which held the remaining parts which made up the rest of the machine. I received a phone call from Johnny Cue that he and his boss were coming to my place to assemble all of the parts and at no charge! I felt excited and vibrantly alive.

Chapter 24

As much as I wanted to play with the new machine, I had to wait a few days for my friends to help me set it up. I decided to call my old pal, Nario, to tell him about my encounter with God. He was truly excited for me. He'd prayed that I'd find Him. He'd tried to get me to one of the prayer meetings he attended, but I wouldn't go. Previously, however, he tricked me into going to one by telling me that we were going to the home of one of his friends who had a great model train layout. He had a great one al right but it was also where a prayer meeting was to be held later that day. Actually, when the time came for the meeting, there were many really wonderful people who were members of the group. Everything they did and said was so relaxed and informal. They all poured their hearts out to God and to Jesus. There was no fear when they talked to either of them.

Once I told Nario about my encounter with God, he had a story of his own. He was going to get married and asked if I'd be his best man. I agreed but only if he'd be my best man when I got married. After a couple of laughs, he invited me to go to another prayer meeting to share my "testimony" as he called it. I thought this was a rather odd way to talk about God; it sounded like I was going to court. During that meeting people prayed and I remembered some of those whom I met at the previous meeting. I was glad to hear them now because it came to me that I probably should start praying to God. Finally, it was time to tell my story. I doubted anybody would believe me because it didn't seem likely that they'd buy my actually talking with God. Surprisingly they all did. Many asked me questions. All I could tell them is what you just read. It was a profound experience but difficult to convey.

The day arrived when Johnny and his boss came to my house and set up the machine. They showed me each part and how it fit into the mechanism. After inspecting everything carefully I saw the microscope, ready to use. They mounted Bob Speiden's cutting head on the carriage which moves it across the disk while cutting the fine grooves. The proper alignment was tricky but it was now ready to try making a test recording.

The test was a failure; the head tended to lift the stylus out of the groove. My two friends were stuck because they'd never had experience with that head. The guys showed Dad how a record groove appears under the microscope. Because some of the grooves on our test disk were good and some bad, it was possible for dad to recognize the differences. It was great how quickly Dad understood what he was seeing. It was a good thing that my equipment now had a microscope. The method I employed to adjust groove dimensions on my previous disk recorder could no longer function.

They left. Now what? I thought about the system at WAER and recalling what's known as a "dash pot". It was used to solve the very problem I had. I'll not try to describe a dash pot pot and how it works. What I will say is that I had to construct one using the largest thimble I could find, a bolt, and a small washer and putting a few drops of slightly heavy oil inside the thimble. What do you know? It worked!

I used that head for a couple of years, but it would quit working every so often. I'd have Dad drive me to New Jersey so Bob Speiden could set it right. Bob had almost the same type of head and his didn't fail. Later, after I was no longer using that head, Bob found a defect in it which made the innards overheat and cause the failure.

Time, as it always does, was moving on. My column was the most popular feature in AUDIO. My business was doing better. I thought a lot about God. How did Jesus fit in? Did I need Him when I'd now met God? Mary gave me a copy of the Holy Bible on cassettes, and I started reading parts of it randomly. I read about David and how he became king. I also read a bit about Jesus Christ but still couldn't place him in the picture.

Then there came a day when one of my regular clients gave me a machine which held three ells which could hold cassettes. he said it was some kind of a duplicator. I put it aside because I had no idea how to use it.

There was another event which seemingly had no connection to the duplicator. I got a call from a man named Jim Jones. He had a dream and was making it happen. He told me that he was setting up a radio reading service for the blind. He said that special radios were needed so the blind could receive the service. It would be broadcast using a "subcarrier" (an FM signal which rode piggyback on a conventional FM station. Listeners to a station using a subcarrier would not be aware of its presence. Listeners to the radio reading service wouldn't hear the station's main programming.

Jim asked if I'd be willing to set up a better studio than was currently being used for on-air broadcasting. I said I'd see, but I wanted one of the receivers so I could hear the special broadcasts and get a "feel" for the project. He brought me a receiver, and I was fascinated by the chance to hear newspaper articles being read from papers which were just printed. Blind listeners could hear these articles on the same day as sighted people would read them.

He told me where to find the studio, and I went there. There was lots of equipment ready to be installed, but someone had to figure out how to do it. The station was on the air al right, but it was running on a small mike mixer and little else.

I'll spare you the details except that I had to interview the two or three people who were keeping the station on the air with a view to finding out how those folks would use the rest of the equipment in the best way. I had a good friend who was great at building electronic equipment. With an understanding of what was necessary, I approached the manager of the station with a price for our building the system. The price was agreed to, but the project had to be completed over a weekend while the station was still on the air.

It took lots of planning before we started but we did get everything complete in two, full days of work. In order to keep the station going, I had to do some engineering so what the volunteer readers read would be heard on their receivers. Everything worked just as it was supposed to when we switched over to the new setup. The station now had the ability to have one volunteer who was reading live on the air and another reader who was in another studio could be reading additional articles on tape so those recordings could be broadcast at a later time.

The station I discovered had a cassette duplicator which looked like what my client gave me some time back. I thought there was money to be made by making multiple copies of cassettes. I couldn't immediately order the system because I had committed myself to writing a training manual to be used by this and other radio reading services for the blind. I don't know how it happened, but the Federal government was interested in promoting these reading services so my training manual was printed in a hard-bound manual for training blind engineers for work in new reading services as they were being built and staffed.

Then I could buy the duplicator. It was just what I needed to make multiple cassettes. I had lots of clients ordering them. I thought I could say I was finished with radio reading services, but I wasn't. I was asked to appear in one national panel discussion and chair another.

Duplicating cassettes was a money maker.

God had additional plans. One day I got a call from a woman who represented something called The Healing Ministry of the Conquering King. She said her name was Sister Gabrielle and hoped I would volunteer to make copies of various sermons related to healing, to be distributed to those who were in need of it. I wasn't very nice to her. I told her something to the effect that I never heard of her group. Moreover, I'm running a business. Perhaps another recording studio would help her but I wouldn't.

She never got excited. No matter how hard I tried to get rid of her, she stayed on the phone and was always calm and sweet. She told me that her group had a supply of blank cassettes so all I had to do was to copy her sermons onto them. I told her that I'd try to help and apologized for being rude. She came to my studio and waited till I ran the small number of copies that were needed. We talked a bit and we made an appointment for her to bring another sermon to be copied.

She told me about a Spiritual Retreat Center and would I like to go there for a weekend? It would be what she called a "working retreat". Anyone there would be expected to help maintain the center in whatever way that was best suited to his or her talents. I tried in every way to get out of going.

"From what you said, this involves getting," I said, "on a subway to Grand Central Station and then finding some way to get to the Retreat Center". Sister Gabriel called a day later, saying that it was all arranged. Someone would meet me at Grand Central Station and get me on a train and then to the Center. I had no more excuses so I went—unwillingly, of course.

I'll never forget that day and that meeting. The person who met me was a woman named Sarah. (It turned out that there were just three Sisters present at that gathering and the rest were a few men and women.) I had tried so hard to suppress thoughts of hands and the rest of it, but Sarah had really helpful ones. There was quite a bit of walking while getting to our destination, and I was able to take her hand. I started wondering if God was somehow behind this trip.

We were greeted warmly when we arrived. Sister Gabrielle remarked that Sarah never looked as radiant as she did then. She asked if I knew why. I told her that all that happened was that I held her hand for a while.

I went to this Retreat Center several times, but I'll condense all of them into one. I just don't recall individual visits, but this sums it up. The first morning when we awoke, we were told not to say a word. We went into a chapel at which time there was a simple service. It was only after its conclusion that we could speak. This was done so we would communicate with God before doing anything else.

After that the work period began. It was like "old home week". The first thing I did was to repair a leaky toilet. Then I rewired a couple of lamps. The wiring could have easily started a fire if I hadn't fixed it. There was a very important visitor there who I discovered was Sister Celeste, who was the head of quite a few retreat centers. I overheard bits and pieces of a conversation which led me to believe that at some point this facility would have to be sold.

After lunch we were told that this period was for meditation. If these meditations disclosed anything to somebody, that person was encouraged to share it. All I could think was that with all the work which was needed, we shouldn't be spending valuable time in that way. In any case, I didn't know how to meditate. Sister Gabrielle said to me that all I had to do was to keep my mind blank and let God enter it. I was thinking along the lines of well, I'm here so I'll act like I was meditating.

The enormous living room was so quiet that we could easily have heard the proverbial pin drop. I couldn't even make my mind be a blank. I took a tiny lead soldier out of my pocket and started to play with it. It was only an inch or two in length. No, it was 6 inches long.

Wait! It was a foot long. How did I think it was an inch or two long? This two-foot long soldier was getting heavy. It was three feet long when I put it on the floor. Lead sure is heavy!

When I checked the soldier again, it was towering over me, and then it was gone but not exactly. Where it had stood there was a kind of steam or mist rising. In fact, the steam was all around me. I was completely immersed in it. It felt something like being in a hot shower, but I wasn't wet. To tell you the truth, it was like being held, but with more power than the combination of Eilene, Joanne or Joan. What was this? I wanted it to go on forever. No way. It was gone, and I was in that living room and people were talking. Even more wild was that I didn't have a lead soldier to begin with!

Then I understood. I just met Jesus! The lead soldier reminded me that Jesus was a man. It took a bit of time to recognize that the rest of that experience was Jesus Christ showering his love on me. He used my need and feelings to show me His love! I was so overcome by this enveloping moment that it wasn't possible to share the full story then.

The next morning we were asked if we knew Jesus and would we ask Him into our lives. We were given a half hour to think about this very important decision. I wasn't at all certain that I wanted to make it. I wanted to be me, not a robot who was supposed to obey God in all things. I'm a person and liked to do things.

During this time I met Sister Celeste and felt very comfortable with her. I would talk about my reluctance to ask Jesus to be a part of me. "Sister Celeste," I said. "I'm not sure I can ask Jesus to be a part of my life. I'm an individual and getting involved with Jesus means I'll be some kind of robot, a carbon copy."

"No, Joe, it's not like that. When Jesus becomes the Lord of your life, you will still be you. Your individuality will be magnified. You'll be a better you than anything you can imagine now. Take that step. You'll never regret it!"

I returned to the group, a bit shaky on my feet. We were asked to repeat a prayer that Sister Celeste would say. I did, and I was immediately calm.

I was about to leave the Center for the last time. I was standing on the porch. I heard Sister Celeste who was now quite a distance from me. She was talking to two ladies on the Center's staff:

"Ladies, when you get in the van to take Joe back to his home, make sure he's sitting between you. Take his hands and hold them till he's back at home." I asked myself how she could know that would be what I'd want at that moment?

I spoke to her a few days later, and she asked if I was afraid. I told her that I wasn't. She replied, "God gave me a gift to see into a person's heart. I understood what you needed and made sure you got it!"

When I arrived home, I greeted my folks with such joy that they wondered what happened to make me act that way. I knew they wouldn't understand so decided to play it cool and keep my own counsel.

Chapter 25

God came into my life, and Jesus showed his power! Where was the Holy Spirit? The Bible tells us that this Spirit is many things: a comforter, an exhorter...

Computers eventually became an important tool for me. As I got more and more interested in these machines, I ran into a malfunctioning printer. The paper jammed. It seemed as though the jam occurred where the paper entered into it. I started to dismantle it to get a better look when I heard the word "plastic". (Perhaps "heard" isn't quite right; rather, I sensed it.) There was no plastic where I was looking. "Plastic" was again in my mind. After examining the printer more carefully I saw that, where the paper would exit the unit, that there was a plastic guide and it was bent over at one corner. Once this was straightened, paper ran through the machine very easily!

At that moment I knew that the Holy Spirit had even more talents than I'd read about!

I got a bit ahead of myself. In the midst of visits to the retreat center, my various jobs and family obligations, Nario was ready to marry. I was in the bride's family living room tying up a few details.

Her father suddenly spoke out: "I'd never believe my daughter would end up marrying a Spick. All they can think about is screwing and makin' babies!"

I thought I knew the family of the bride, Dorothy. I'm almost certain that Nario was close enough to have overheard what he said. I thought he said this probably in the hope of breaking up the wedding. Nario took all this with equanimity. What should I say? I decided to say nothing with the hope it would just blow away.

I was relieved that both Dorothy and Nario were going through with their decision. That was close; the wedding was the next day. I prayed that this would be a wonderful day for the start of their new lives together. Indeed it was. The reception for the couple was in Dorothy's parents' living room. It was a fairly good size room and the wedding party was fairly small. I was surprised to see Johnny Kogler and a couple other people from the days of the boarding school.

Nario asked John and me to do some of the nutty playlets we used do to amuse people. Although we didn't know we were gonna do that, it all worked well for us, and we got laughs. The reception was over and there were no hateful words exchanged. Nario and Dorothy were on their way to many years of happiness.

By now it was near the end of 1975. Mom and I were serving on the 67th Police Precinct Community Council. I rose to be secretary. The Council was made up of a few block associations. Some meetings became heated. At least one of the associations wanted us to have street patrols to keep "certain people" from moving in. I could see that we would end up with vigilante groups. It was true that a few Latinos and Haitians bought two or three houses. The way I saw it, if the new people had the money to buy a home, the area wouldn't become a slum, and I refused to panic. But some of our Council people were thinking of selling their homes. I tried reasoning with them, saying that if we stay, no "undesirables" could move in. A time bomb was ticking and nothing would stop the explosion!

Around that time I got a call from one of the police who were trying to promote groups designed to bring about "togetherness". He told me that a small drama group was beginning rehearsals for the famous musical, Oklahoma. The director, Lois, needed someone to arrange the music. Would I be interested? With everything else going on in my life, I wasn't sure that I wanted to jump into this project. I agreed, however, to meet Lois to discuss the work. She came to my home and shook hands. Yes, she had those very rare and incredible ones. I tried not to think about that as we talked.

The idea was for me to play a few different instruments which would make up a small orchestra. I said I needed a multi-track tape recorder to produce the music. One of my clients, Ron Rothman, had such a machine which I knew he wasn't using. He let me borrow it. Once I had the machine and learned how to use it, I told Lois I'd try to make the background music for Oklahoma. While I knew most of the music, there were parts that were unfamiliar. Luckily Lois had an almost complete recording of Oklahoma which contained the majority of the music. I would, however, have to write a new ballet sequence.

I attended a rehearsal to understand what the cast was going to do as they moved around the stage. Lois walked me around as the cast did its work. I was trying to get a feel for everything related to the show. Lois held my hand as we walked. Believe it or not, I paid attention to the stage business. Then there was the rehearsal with the performers where I could determine their voice ranges. That would tell me in which keys to write backgrounds to individual songs. It took time but I had the work done by the middle of June. There were two weeks of rehearsals in which I at least tried to direct the cast as to how the songs and ensemble numbers should be done.

The night before the performance, Lois called in a panic. She said: "What am I gonna do? Everyone wants to quit. We have advance ticket sales! Do you think you can come and talk to them?"

"I can only try but I'm not known for great tact. I'll pray as we drive to the rehearsal hall."

With all her problems, I wondered if I dared tell Lois that I, too, needed help. I decided not to say a word about that because she had a desperate problem. It was just a short drive to the hall. I felt the presence of the Holy Spirit and was glad because I sure needed someone's help if there was any hope for Lois's show.

When we got to the hall, there was lots of noise—some yelling and others arguing. I told Lois to leave the hall until I called her. When she was gone, I faced them.

"Shut the hell up. I only want to hear from you one at a time. Somebody tell me what's going on. You've stuck it out this long."

"I can't play Jud! I never met anyone like him so I can't act like him." Actually I heard this guy do a pretty credible job and I only had to tell him he was good and he could do it. He did agree to stay.

Next there was the gal who played "Aunty Eller". She wanted a bigger part. I told her that yes, it was not a big one, but Eller is a strong character who had to hold things together near the end of the play. She was a heroine. The actress stayed.

There may have been some other issues, but they were all resolved.

The cast was ready to go to work. They said they planned to give Lois a big bouquet of flowers for all her hard work. Then I called Lois, who appeared briefly and then drove me home. I told her that I absolutely had to talk about a serious subject. There was a scheduled meeting the following Monday and Lois and I would be there. She picked me up and got to the meeting and found no one else there, so we left and Lois asked what I needed to talk about. I gave her a brief explanation.

She said it was no problem holding her hands but being held was something else. She'd do so if her boyfriend would okay it. She recommended that we talk it over with him right then. We drove to his small apartment and he was indeed home. Lois explained that I had a serious matter and asked him to listen. I explained things as quickly as I could but recognized that he needed enough facts before he came to a decision. No, he didn't want Lois to hold me. When I saw her on a few occasions, she did all she could to be helpful.

I found out that, among many talents, Lois was a dance instructor. She was really into that work and could read or write the special notation which permits a record of a person's dance movements to be recorded as symbols so that at any student of this notation could reproduce a dance as though from watching it. She had quite a few students who from time to time perform in a dance recital. By having been in my house a few times, she knew that I had an electric typewriter. She said that she was a lousy typist so she asked me to type the program for the next recital which was coming up in a week or two. I told her I wasn't a great typist, but she still wanted me to do it. I said I would.

I think my folks went to Florida for a few days to help Mary set up an apartment she recently rented in Coral Springs. Her company moved its headquarters there and Mary was a key employee. Thus her boss gave her a good salary increase so she'd agree to move.

The night came when Lois was due. I was quite nervous because I knew that she could not help me enough. I couldn't let this affect my typing. My stomach was acting up. I got a shot glass and filled it with Brandy, which relaxed me a bit. I wanted to do a good job of typing for Lois.

The bell rang and there she was. I greeted her and we started to write the program. She had a special way the paper should be rolled into the machine but she did that. The work went slowly and carefully till it was done. I'd typed it perfectly!

Then when I had finished typing, Lois said: "Thanks for your hard work. That's a relief. Now tell me what will make you feel good." I nervously told her, and she immediately held me for two hours before leaving.

But what about her boyfriend? Apparently he did or said something unreasonable which Lois wouldn't stand for. She felt that this was enough to release her from her promise. She said she'd be available when she could be. She was a busy woman, but she was faithful for more than ten years.

Dad saw us one time, and he didn't like it. I thought it would kill the whole thing but Lois said she didn't care. "I don't need to deal with this, so it's fine with me to help you when I can."

Lois liked directing plays, but it would turn out that she would play a very important role—a life-changing part!

Think about this. I absolutely had to ask quite a number of women for very special help. Isn't it likely that most gals would slap my face or have extremely negative things to say. I can only conclude that God led me to the right ladies!

Mary came home every Christmas to carry out our beloved tradition, which often included listening to recordings of Lionel Barrymore playing Ebenezer Scrooge in Dickens' classic, A Christmas Carol. It was Christmas time, 1980. During her stay I touched her face and felt a lump on her cheek. It didn't protrude so unless that spot was touched and pressed slightly, nobody would see it. She told me that she had a number of those things removed and biopsies were always benign. She asked me not to tell our folks.

She returned to her Florida apartment, and Dad, Mom, and I went to stay with her about a month later. It was a normal trip. Mary's girlfriend, Bea, helped me write customer invoices and depositing checks. Because of business obligations I had to fly home before the folks. Then Mom and Dad came home later and everything was in order. I could do a bit of cooking and could clean up after myself. Mom taught me about kitchen chores almost from the time I learned how to grill a sandwich.

While my business was doing okay, I knew I could do lots better if I could replace Bob's cutting head with a unit which was used in many studios all over the country. The head was called a Westrex. I think they were manufactured by Western Electric. I was beginning to think about that quite a bit now that I had money in the bank.

After much checking around as to where this head could be purchased, I heard about Tom Steele who owned a rather large studio in midtown Manhattan and who used a few Westrex heads in his own work. He also was a dealer selling them. Better still, he designed all of the complicated electronics needed to operate these heads. He called his electronics Ransteele because he had a financial backer named Rand. The entire package cost me $10,000, which I could easily afford. He explained how to install and maintain it, along with very specific instructions how to set up the electrical relationships between the head and the electronics. Once this was done, my records sounded about as good as phonograph records can ever sound.

Once I could advertise that my studio was equipped with this system, business increased dramatically. Life was looking up!

In early April of 1981 Mary called me and said for me not to put our folks on the line.

"Joe, it's gonna take a miracle," she said.

"What do you mean?"

"Remember that little lump you found. My doctor said he wouldn't even try to remove it. He told me that my body's riddled with them, and in time they'll kill me."

"You need to get a second opinion," I said emphatically.

"I went to the best cancer man in the area and he gave me the same report. I'm on some experimental drug and it's not likely to help."

I prayed with her for some time, and we said our usual good byes. I did not tell the folks. A week or so later I got another call in which Mary said it was getting very hard for her to walk. Then the folks were told.

Our neighborhood was changing. Those who bought homes were great, but an apartment project was being filled with less than desirable people. We knew of a couple of children who were raped on an apartment house roof and thrown over the edge to their deaths. The folks and I decided it was past time to leave.

It was in July that our house was listed and people came to view it. Because of the changing neighborhood, nobody even came close to buying it. Dad had his heart set on moving to Bethpage, Long Island, because of the excellent, championship golf course there. We went to a Realtor there and found virtually no available houses.

Because Mom and I were still members of our Block Association and the 67th Precinct Community Council, we knew many people, and we mentioned our plans to move. A family of three heard about the house, came to see it and immediately were ready to buy it. We had our lawyer draw up the contract and our bank immediately approved the mortgage. We began packing.

The listing Realtor wanted to sue us because he was cut out of the sale. My lawyer took care of the problem easily because the Realtor showed our house to so many people and could not sell it; we did it on our own.

Meanwhile, Mary talked to Mom and asked her if she could come to Florida to help her. My sister would be bedridden very soon. Mom knew I'd be alone and having to deal with the many, unpacked boxes, keeping up with my mail and more. She called my Aunt Kitty to ask as to whether Aunt Avis would be willing to stay with me and help me get through many necessities. Aunts Kitty and Avis were long-time friends before Kitty married my Uncle Art. Aunt Kitty answered: "Oh no! Don't even consider asking. Avis has slipped a few cogs and she'd only be a liability to Joe."

Mom told me this, and I felt just awful. Aunt Avis was such a kind lady and had got me through tough times. Would I ever see her again? Would she know me?

We were almost packed. It was two nights before we could leave. We were all in bed when our home security system went off. We heard a bang as the built-in siren screamed. We could tell that the break-in was in what would be the tenant's apartment. As we packed, we had moved quite a bit of our belongings there. Dad and I dressed hurriedly and found the tenant's door had been forced open and some of our things were moved. The siren scared the burglars off before they took anything. Before we could go back to bed, we reinforced the door. On the next night we were again awakened. There were a couple of nuts near our house firing guns in the air. We sure were glad we'd be out of the area the next day!

While the movers were carrying out our furniture, the son of the new owner came to say good bye and visit me. He was interested in electronics. I showed him how the house intercom worked. He enjoyed that, and we talked more about electronics in general. After that I handed him his very own set of house keys. The boy's personality quickly changed. He strutted around his new house and tried to order me around. I told him I had lots of things to do and to get lost. He tried his new imperious game, and I ignored him. Then his father came along and started asking, no, demanding, that Mom show him all the lovely flowers, plants, and shrubs which she had grown in the garden since we'd lived there.

The van was full and we said good bye to that house forever. I really didn't want to move. I had my recording system set up very well, and it was a chore to take it apart and have to set it up again in our new house. Faithful Johnny Cue was there for the tear-down and setting it all up. I can't say I liked the new house. I said so before we even bought it, but Dad was insistent. The rooms were smaller and the background traffic was louder because we were on a main street near the road. Luckily I was no longer interested in "live" recording because the traffic would ruin any such recordings. Shortly after we moved in, Johnny came over to set up the recording system. It was a big job so he stayed overnight in order to fix things so they worked right. How could I ever thank him? We got enough of our furniture and belongings unpacked so that I could find the main items I'd need. Mom and Dad had to go to Florida immediately so they could help Mary. There was food in the house so I could manage. Also my cousin, Joe Mesiti, lived a few towns away. He and his wife, Carmen, often picked me up, took me to their home for dinner and an evening of relaxation, and then brought me back home.

Years ago in Brooklyn I had joined a ham radio club which featured special speakers, and other events, including what's known as Field Day. Groups or individuals set up their stations away from commercial power sources. Antennas were erected, generators set up. The stations were prepared to operate. The basic plan was to contact as many stations as possible during a 24-hour period. I was a part of these events since 1963. I had to skip this summer's Field Day what with all the plans for our move.

Fortunately Joe Marrone, a member of the ham club, lived a few blocks from me and was of inestimable help during this time and later on.

It was the last week of September. Mom called me from Mary's home in Florida and told me to get down there immediately. She sounded on the edge of hysteria. I was pretty sure I knew why I needed to be there. Mary didn't have much time left. I called her old friend, Bea Resnick. She was aware of Mary's condition, so I invited her to fly down with me so she could spend a bit of time with Mary. I guess it was Joe Marrone who took me to Kennedy Airport to meet Bea and leave for Florida.

Bea once went with us to Grandma's house, and we often walked together to the general store nearby. She was always good company.

Once on the plane I did something I never do. I ordered Champagne with breakfast. Then she let me hold her hands as we winged our way south. I did not know yet just how important that would be.

Dad met us at the airport and drove us to Mary's apartment building. He said very little during the drive. Dad immediately took us to Mary's room, and we said our hellos. Mary was her usual self, and happy to see us. I went into the living room where Mom was. There was no greeting, Mom began yelling at me to do something.

"Get started. Come on, move!"

"Mom, what do you need?"

"You just stop stalling and get to it!"

"Mom, if you don't tell me what the hell you're talking about, I can't do a thing for you. I'm here to do what I can but can't do anything till I know what's up!"

"Papers! Mary's papers!"

"I can't read any papers unless you have time to read 'em to me."

"No, money. Mary's got money somewhere."

Here I was, in sunny, semitropical Florida, where people relax in their retirement. What to do. Who'd know about Mary's finances? Well, Frank, her boss would probably know something. I was somewhat prepared. I brought a few local phone numbers with me which might come in handy. I hunted through my few index cards and found Mary's office number and called it.

Frank himself picked up the phone.

After we briefly chatted I got to the point. I needed to know if Mary made out a will, where her bank was and the like.

"Joe, I'm lost around here. I can't believe Mary won't ever work for me again! She knows more about my business than I do."

Frank then told me that he thought he had a power-of-attorney form which Mary never signed. This would permit Frank to take care of whatever needed doing in the event that she became incapable of doing those things.

Shortly after that, Rene Rodriguez came by with the papers which Mary had to sign. I didn't think it was important to have Mary sign them right then.

I wanted Bea to have the time for "girl talk" and who knows what else. After all, Bea probably wouldn't have another opportunity.

Bea left the next day. When I checked in on Mary, I found that her mind was not as clear as it was yesterday. I told her about the "power of attorney" documents and asked if she was willing to sign them. She said she needed to read them because there were too many crooks. She tried to read, but kept losing track of the line she was on, and never could read the whole lengthy, legal document. I asked if she'd sign it anyway. After all, being her brother, she knew I'd never do anything to hurt her and her interests in any way. She refused to sign it. All I could do was wait another day for Mary's mind to hopefully clear up.

I learned just how complex caring for her was. All that she could swallow was crushed ice. Her appetite was gone. She needed medicine late at night. Mom gave me the job of sitting with her and giving her the meds. That first night was pitiful. Mary would ask me repeatedly if the meds were safe and not poison. Eventually I managed to give her the pills and wash them down with some ice water.

The next day was even worse for Mary. She was barely conscious. We were losing her fast. I think the date was October 2, 1981. Dad called a priest to administer Last Rites. I recall the priest asking her if she understood that she was dying.

Weakly she asked: "I am?"

After he left, Mary's boss came to say his good bye, and left in tears. Then Rene Rodriguez came in for a special reason. He knew Mary very well, so we asked him if he could forge Mary's signature on the power of attorney document. You can imagine that he didn't want to do it, but he cared for Mary and the rest of us so consented. He signed her name, and neither Mom nor Dad could tell that Mary hadn't signed the paper. Without that signature, we couldn't pay any outstanding bills or withdraw money from her bank account nor do any number of small chores which were required. We were not trying to cheat her!

She had another visitor whose name I've fortunately forgotten. He told us he'd borrowed a considerable amount of money from Mary but said that he didn't intend to pay it back because "We were very close, and I know she'd want me to have the money." We understood he was generally rather charming and had pulled the same stunt on other lonely, dying women. Dad and I threw him out. Very few things gave us so much pleasure!

Now it was Sunday, October 4. Mary was in a coma. We didn't think Mary would be with us much longer. I knew that when that happened, I wanted to leave Florida fast. Mary was a very private person. We had no choice but to look through her possessions to see what might need to be done, what we wanted to preserve and what should be discarded. There was no point to giving her medicine so I went out onto her balcony and sat there for a couple of hours reading the Braille version of Guideposts magazine.

We ate a quiet and somber supper. We moved into Mary's bedroom to say our goodnights. As we finished, there was a moment when she missed taking a breath, then she drew in a long one, let it out with a great sigh, and she was gone. I looked at my watch. It was 11 PM straight up. I was asked by my folks to call Hospice. If that wasn't done first thing, there would be a police investigation, and who wanted that. The supervisor of the hospice group was the person who came. She may have had another person with her who stayed to check Mary. She stayed with us, offering comfort. I held her hand, and we talked.

"You seem like such a caring person," I said. "What does it take to do your job? I know that everyone you work with is leaving this world."

"When we interview a prospective volunteer, if we find that this person has never lost anybody of significance, she is immediately excused."

The next morning we packed up our suitcases and packed two brief cases of Mary's things. Dad told me to get them safely home. There were many bottles of medicine and Mom assigned me to emptying all those bottles and flushing their contents down the toilet. There was so much meds that it took me nearly 45 minutes to get rid of them. (I didn't know that this was not the proper way to dispose of medicines.)

We ate a quick breakfast at IHOP and boarded a plane. Once back home Mom and Dad did a bit of straightening the house and completed funeral arrangements.

The Funeral Mass was held in St. Jerome's Roman Catholic Church, which was the church Dad attended ever since I can remember. Dad knew a fine priest there, and asked him if he would celebrate the Mass. After a short, graveside service, most of those who'd gathered there went to Ronny's house where we would eat the meal which customarily follows a funeral. We were treated so very nicely. It was one of the two or three times in my life that I had a little too much to drink. I wasn't drunk but knew I shouldn't have any more.

Ronny grabbed me and said we had things to do. I needed a special timer and other odds and ends from Radio Shack, and he took me there and I bought what I needed. Ron wanted to keep me from thinking about the events of the day as much as possible.

My folks stayed for a couple of days and returned to Florida. Mary's rent was paid up through October so they used the time to do many things related to packing things up and discarding more of Mary's possessions, giving many items to Hospice to help with its money raising events.

I had lots of mail, which I asked Joe Marrone to help me with. I had quite a few orders. Some were for making masters which required the use of the microscope. It was amazing just how quickly Joe learned how to use it. Joe was a God-send because he addressed and shipped out masters and other orders.

Quite a few boxes still needed to be unpacked when my folks came home to stay. It would take a very long time, if ever, before life would be normal.

Chapter 26

Dad was in a dark mood. Friends called him for a game of golf, but he ignored those calls. Golf was the reason he wanted to move to Bethpage. There were many good golfing days before winter set in, but Dad ignored the game and his golfing buddies. Christmas was coming. He wanted nothing to do with it. He wouldn't even let me play carols on the piano.

Word got around to Dad's family about this and my cousin, Adrienne Karoly, was determined to do something about it. They arranged a Christmas day feast at her home. We were invited. Dad made it clear he wasn't going. He was the driver; so, if he wouldn't go, we were stuck. Another of my cousins was going.

He came to the house unannounced just to take us to the party. Dad tried to get out of it, but my cousin was having none of it. Knowing he'd be dragged into the car, he relented and reluctantly came with us.

What a wonderful Christmas gathering it was. Adrienne did as many things to cheer us as anyone could. Mom and I were sad at losing Mary, but we knew life must go on. Dad just sat there.

Adrienne showed us a large doll house which she and her husband built. It was even intended to be lighted and equipped with doll furniture. She asked me about lighting it, and I said that I knew nothing about it nor about the lighting fixtures required. I asked her to show me how it was supposed to be done. It was too bad that this was about as far as the project ever got. Somehow the two of them never got around to completing the doll house. Nonetheless I was glad to examine the little house. It took my mind from the gloomy mood which would still be there when we returned home later.

The only times Dad was almost normal was when I had a master disk to make and he was called into service to check groove geometry using the microscope.

The cutting stylus was nothing but a specially shaped sapphire wrapped with fine wire. It was too tiny for me to replace when that was needed. The tiny wires had to be fitted into small clips. They also were too small for me to install. The clips were needed to supply heat to the stylus. The stylus was heated while recording because heating the grooves as they were made would make them play back with less noise than they would if no heat was applied.

This head weighed a lot more than the one which I got from Howard Holzer. That extra weight made it mandatory to use what's called an "advance ball". This ball rested on the disk just ahead of where the next groove was to be cut. Occasionally that ball would begin to flatten just a wee bit, and that produced a small amount of added noise when playing back a recording. That meant that the ball had to be replaced and I couldn't do it. Dad learned how. It was rare when this had to be done. Occasionally the head would jump up and down so again I needed a dash pot. I had lots of friends who were in the recording field and one of them had an unused dash pot. Having it was one thing. Getting it to stabilize the head was something else. I got it to work after a lot of tinkering. I think I used slightly diluted auto transmission oil.

Believe it or not, heat could build up inside the head. If this was allowed to continue, the head would be damaged. To counteract this, helium had to be pumped into it. Helium tanks were leased along with the main pressure regulator. The amount of helium used was quite small, so two additional regulators were needed. Dad took the glass covers off those regulators. We figured a way to mark the faces so I could check the position of the hands which would provide a way I could monitor the amount of helium left in the tank as well as the pressure.

The final regulator was a plastic tube with a tiny float. This had to be adjusted so the ball just floated above its resting position when the helium was turned on. There was no way for me to check this. I had to count on dad to adjust that. Once done, it would not need to be touched.

From this you can see that I couldn't record masters without Dad's help. In a way I didn't like that but in another way it was good because it gave Dad a sense of purpose.

Dad and I often took long walks around the town. I asked him to show me landmarks so I could get around by myself. I won't try to describe the layout of the streets except to say that they were such that I just could not learn to travel in town alone. Again I had to count on Dad so I could take walks. There was a man my age who was also blind, but he had no trouble walking around town. I found out later that he was in my school at the same time I was, but I never knew him well.

I think it was the summer of 1982 that Mom suggested a trip to Maine. That suited Dad so we planned to drive to Bar Harbor. Aunt Avis would meet us at a convenient place and join us. Dad didn't like that. "All she'll do is smoke and keep her head in a book," he said.

What a wonderful trip that was! The shops were really interesting because they carried odd items. I found an air compressor which I could use as a vacuum pump to create better suction for the recording head, which would lessen the chances of fire. As I said earlier, there's always a small risk of a flash fire if care is not taken.

Our trip was extended to visiting the Canadian province of Nova Scotia. The people were so friendly. I never had to worry whether or not I would be accepted when people saw I was blind. Believe me this was often a problem. On the trip I observed Aunt Avis closely; I could see that she sometimes didn't make sense but most of the time she was fine. She knew I wanted to hold her hands, and they were very available during the trip.

Life was pretty good. Back on the home front, I don't know how it came about but one of my cousins knew a couple which held a Bible Study in their home. Through that cousin arrangements were made for me to be picked up and brought back from the study. The couple's names were Ray and Dianne Melograine. They were well versed in their understanding of the Bible. Before each study began, we were expected to sing hymns. I knew a few hymns but not any of these. The Melograines were members of a Pentecostal church, which explained why I didn't know the hymns. Ray played the guitar which was used as the accompaniment to the singing. Ray also liked to play songs other than hymns. I started teaching him better chords than he knew. I even showed him better chords to use in the hymn sings.

Most of those in the small group knew one another. I heard a bit of gossip about a pastor whose name was David Munizi. He was apparently being vilified by the board of his church. As I recall, he was accused of stealing money, and lots of the ladies didn't approve of how his wife, Angela, dressed. If I heard it right, he was forced to resign. As an arm of the church to which he belonged, he ran a radio show. I'll never know the entire story, but the body which governed his church and others in his denomination permitted him to take all the items related to the radio show with him.

A couple of weeks later Ray announced that he'd talk to Pastor Dave as he called him, and he very reluctantly agreed to start a new church, his own church. Ray and Diane were backing the idea as well as others in our Bible study. The church would be held in Ray's living room. It turned out that Pastor Dave had a following in his former church, and they didn't believe that the church treated him right. When the first service was held, a few members from his former church came to this initial service.

All I remember about that first service is the humility which Pastor Dave showed. He told us that he thought he was finished as a pastor and here he was, leading a service in the room with all of us. "If this is God's will, we're starting an adventure together."

Life runs in parallel directions. At this time I was reading a magazine which was on cassette, the purpose of which was to describe products and techniques useful for blind people. A man named Bill Grimm was being interviewed about his new company, Computer Aids. He was selling software and computers which could aid blind people in finding jobs and doing tasks which were more easily done than on a typewriter.

This sounded very interesting. I could type and hear the name of each key as I typed it. With this equipment I'd know when I made a typo and could erase it and re type the character. I called Mr. Grimm and he gave me a careful description of his products and services, and I was so impressed that I plunked down $2,000 and sat around excitedly waiting for my equipment to arrive.

When it came I was to call Mr. Grimm so he could tell me how to unpack and set up the system. Well, when the equipment came, I opened the box and examined its contents. It looked like I could set it up al right and indeed I was able to do it. I figured out how to put a floppy disk into what Bill Grimm called a "drive". When I turned the computer on, low and behold, I heard the word "Hello" emanate from the little loudspeaker. I called Mr. Grimm and told him what I'd done. He was pleasantly surprised, so he explained how to connect it to the Epson dot matrix printer and the basics of writing and saving a document. I experimented and, to my horror, I couldn't understand much of what was spoken via synthetic speech. By repeated tries, I began to catch on. It was not long before I started writing letters to my readers using the computer instead of a typewriter. I have seldom used a typewriter since. Eventually I replaced the original Apple II Plus with an Apple 2E. A couple of guys in my radio club showed me a bit about programming and I found myself staying up nights working with this new technology.

I have to digress. Sighted people find it hard to imagine a blind person using a computer. It's possible because I can use my ears to hear the computer "talk" to me rather than seeing what is shown on the screen. Making a computer "speak" is a complex process but it is how blind men and women can use computers. The door was open for us to do many things which were not possible without computerized speech. We can now play games, write books, edit music files and so very much more. As you read this, you may have thought these developments were revolutionary. Actually they were evolutionary. In the 1939 New York World's Fair Bell Telephone Laboratories demonstrated synthetic speech. I heard the demonstration and was amazed that a man typing on a keyboard could have his typing be heard as understandable human speech. The U. S. Navy developed rules which were the basis for early computerized speech.

Bill Grimm didn't develop the use of speech completely on his own. A small California company called Street Electronics designed a rather small metal box which contained the equipment for generating speech when connected to a computer. One or more companies were doing work similar to what Bill Grimm and his company, Computer Aids, was doing. As software for the sighted world grew more complicated, it was no longer possible for an individual like Bill Grimm to keep up with these advances. His company became GW Micro and is a leader in making blind people more productive through the use of computers. Other companies were started so that the field of computer technology for the blind has become very competitive. This means that the software products which we use will be more powerful; otherwise a software provider might fall by the wayside. As time passed, book publishers began using what are known as "scanners" to transform the printed page into computer language. It wasn't long before enterprising people and a few companies got into the business of writing special software programs which permitted a blind computer user to employ scanners. We could read, by means of scanned information, textbooks, and other books, which were or are not yet accessible on talking books, Braille, or other media. We blind people were catching up with the sighted world in obtaining information. As the Internet blossomed, blind people could use that resource to do research, download music and a host of other content. The computer didn't affect just my life, but those of many, many other blind men and women.

We blind people also use touch screen tablets! At this writing the Apple Corporation has done the most to make its devices usable by us.

I didn't skip church or Bible Study. Ray's living room was now too small so we rented a church in a nearby town. The New Life Christian Fellowship was on its way!

Along the way Lois would come to see me. Of course, Dad didn't like that much, but I just had to overlook it because I needed Lois's friendship and help.

I had my small ham station up and running and was able to keep up with friends from our radio club and many other people who I never met but knew because we'd talked quite a bit. Bob Gunderson was on the air and through what are known as repeaters we were able to chat. Many of the guys from "that school" were on the air, and we had many pleasant discussions. I remember telling Bob Gunderson about my interest in computers, and he said that they were too complicated and that, in the long run, it would be a passing fad!

It was approaching 1985. My business was doing well. The number of letters I received in connection with "Audio Clinic" increased in number. One day I got a call from a man I didn't know. He said his name was Gary Greico, and he heard I knew quite a bit about computers. He told me he was blind and expected me to help him because he deserved it. I never minded sharing what little knowledge I had with anyone but I didn't like a guy I didn't even know telling me he knew I should help him because he deserved it.

Well, not quite. I'll put an end to this right now.

"Mr. Greico, I don't know who the hell you think you are, but believe it or not, I do not have to help you. You sure haven't shown any consideration for me or if I have time to help you."

"Look, Mr. Giovanelli, New York State VRS says that in order to find work, I needed special computer training. I figure that when you help me, I'll be ahead of early VRS Training and the sooner I can find a job. So when can we start?"

"Gary, who said we'll work together? Sounds to me like you need an attitude adjustment before you'll shut up long enough to learn anything I could teach you."

"Okay, I'm sorry. Would you please help me?"

"Al right, Gary, but if you give me any lip, forget my name and lose my phone number because you can count on me to do the same."

We made arrangements to get together weekly, and I showed him the basics. He was as good as gold. He was a very fast learner. I showed him the inside of my computer and how things plug into the main circuit board. His equipment arrived from the State, and he was anxious to try it. His trainer told him not to do anything until he came to show Gary how to take the machine apart and install special parts which were needed. I told Gary that he could install everything himself and would then show the trainer how good he was. To that end I went over to his house which was in a town nearby. I saw what he had. It was a different make of computer than mine, and I never had seen it. He showed me everything which was sent to him. I looked it over, and had the machine apart almost immediately. The way parts plugged into the main board was pretty much how my computer worked; so, I popped everything in its place.

I showed Gary what I did and quickly unplugged everything and had Gary reassemble it. He had no problems, and what a confidence booster this was. The software Gary had to use was unlike mine, but he was trained on the software, so he knew how to get it going. Before long he was hearing really good synthetic speech. He was very, very excited. His training would be speeded up. I had no more to teach him, but we have remained friends and, in fact, still keep in close contact.

I learned more and more about computers to the point where Bill Grimm asked me to take over a newsletter which he tried to run and was not able to get started. It was to be a magazine on cassette for blind computer users. Bill called the magazine BAUD, standing for Blind Apple User Discussions. A baud is the name of a character used when working with computers. Luckily I added more than double the number of cassettes I could make at one time. I began to wonder how much luck was involved and how much God was involved. I thought more and more about Him and what he was doing in my life.

The BAUD newsletter required a subscription just like other magazines. I charged 24 dollars a year and before long I had 300 subscribers, so this was a money maker. It was work, too. I had to write articles. I asked readers to write some articles about what they knew and could share with other readers.

I'm really bad at remembering important days and dates, but I know it was April when something important happened. I was in church. Ray Melograine was the one who brought me there on this particular Sunday. When the service ended, he asked me if I'd mind going with him to a funeral home so he could pay respects to a friend of his. I wasn't keen about it. I didn't know the deceased.

He said: "Joe, if I have to bring you back home first, it will be way out of my way, whereas if we go to the funeral parlor, it will be almost on the way to your house."

I agreed, even though my mood was not great and a funeral hall wouldn't lighten it. When we walked in, I heard a lady praising God!

"Thank you, Lord. My husband's at peace. He's no longer in pain. What could be better than my husband's being in Heaven? I loved him and still do, but I'm unselfish enough to let him go, but I wish he was here! I just wish I'd thought about it because I would have given him a going-away party."

The woman was obviously at peace. She almost radiated love! I left with a light heart. I was blessed and was so glad I was there to witness this.

Chapter 27

I can't say that I was at peace. I had never been able to shake what happened to me in boarding school. I hated to mention the name of the school and the names of some of those kids—well, I still hated them. I couldn't recognize that I got through these things and was making my way in a sighted world. I awoke a few days after hearing that peaceful woman in the funeral parlor. I prayed more or less like this:

"Father God, I recognize your hand in so many of the events in my life. Your Word says that I must forgive people 70 times 7. Heavenly Father, I can't even come close to forgiving those people I lived with in that school' while I was growing up. They put me through so many physical and mental hoops. I hate 'em all, and I'm not supposed to. I can't carry these things in my heart any longer, but how can I let them go?"

His quiet, reassuring and loving voice actually spoke to me: "If you truly want to forgive these wounds to your spirit, it's easy. I'm going to remind you of each boy and girl and then I want you to say out loud, in a firm and convincing tone of voice: 'I forgive you.'"

I thought I couldn't do that, but as God spoke each name, it was so easy to say "I forgive you." I said that with conviction because I felt it deep down in my heart. Boy, God had a long list of names, some of which were forgotten or buried wherever hate is stored.

When it was over, God's voice was no longer heard, but I knew that even if I couldn't hear Him, that he was still there. A great weight was lifted from me. I was now proud to tell people the name of my school. During my travels I'd occasionally run into one of those people, and they felt like long-lost pals. I was never ill at ease as we gabbed about old times. To think I could have had this relief much sooner, but hate and pride are serious conditions of the heart. When a person calls on God rather than hanging on to these destructive things, life can and will be sweeter. I could see that I had said some hurtful things but know now that God forgave me.

Life has several dimensions. Audio began sending me CD players so I'd understand what would soon be well known to the public. It taught me that if this digital revolution was embraced, my investment in phonograph recording gear would be lost. I would follow trends and sell the equipment at the right time.

I became more active in our church. Pastor Dave's wife, Angela, was a good pianist and led the worship. She wanted other musicians to join her, so I was asked to play keyboard bass. About the same time a pretty good guitarist joined us.

When summer came, Mom, Dad and I spent some time in Virginia. We did it on quite a few occasions—enjoying such places as Luray Caverns, Williamsburg, with a visit or two to North Carolina thrown in. We all enjoyed those outings. It's possible that Aunt Avis went with us on a couple of trips, but I just don't remember.

We never know when a chapter will end. We heard that my dear aunt passed away. Mom went to Buffalo to take care of funeral arrangements and other matters which come up after a death. I don't need to tell you how I felt. Back to my story.

In September I was again at home, involved in the many tasks you know about. My church wanted to have a late summer picnic to be held in Bethpage Park. Because I lived in that town, I was the one who secured the necessary permit to use its facility. It was a beautiful place, with trees and flowers and lots of clean air, and it had many walking paths, picnic tables and benches. When I got there and was relaxing at a picnic table, I found that a woman was sitting next to me. We talked a while and introduced ourselves. Something about her was vaguely familiar. I confess that I was taken with her. Our talk took a strange turn.

"June, you remind me of someone."

"Who?"

"Well, I don't know. I think I never knew who she was. At the risk of making a fool of myself, uh, uh, I mean, well, you remind me of a woman I saw in a funeral home."

Silence. It seemed like forever until she spoke again:

"Joe, it was me. I saw you there and thought to myself that guy was really handsome."

After a nice lunch, I asked June if she'd like to take a walk. She agreed. She took my hand and we started on what would end up as a rather long hike. I learned three things: She liked to walk just like me. She was really sweet and kind. And she had incredible hands!

When we returned to the group, the guys ribbed me about love at first sight, and had we set the date? They knew something that I didn't. I thought the proposal was where it begins. No sir, it's that first "test drive" that seals a man's fate! I won't say I forgot about her, but I led a busy life. When I'd go to church, I'd be up front with the other musicians.

One day when our service ended, I ran into June. I took a chance:

"June, may I sit with you at next week's service when the sermon begins? I'm through playing by then."

"My neighbor, Ruth, always wants me to sit with her. I don't want her feelings hurt. She's a bit sensitive."

"Thanks anyway."

When the following week's service began, after the praise portion concluded, Pastor Dave walked to the podium, and June came to me and led me to our seats. What a help it was to have her near me.

A considerable length of time went by. The pressures of my various jobs was getting to me. My spirits were flagging. I vividly remember getting up one Sunday and praying, "God, I'm sorry. Please forgive me, but I have nothing to offer in worship. I'm not bringing my keyboard bass to church. My tank is empty. I need your help."

There was an arrangement in which a different person picked me up and brought me home from church. June was newly assigned to do this and that day was her first time. She noticed that I didn't have my keyboard with me, started to say something about it, but stopped. I had little to say during the ride to church, a drive of about 15 minutes.

After the service as I was getting into her car, she asked, "How'd you like coming to my house for dinner. I have this nice meat loaf ready to put in the oven. I made it for Ruth, and she turned me down at the last minute."

I'd never been invited to a girl's house before. It sounds silly now, but I'd lived at home for so long that I was afraid to tell Mom that I wouldn't be home for dinner. I thought, "Gee, I did ask God for help. Hmmm, she said she's got meat loaf and its one of my favorites. She could have had chicken, which I really hate.

"June, I'd love to have dinner with you. May I use your phone to call home so my folks won't worry?"

That was no problem. She put the meat loaf in the oven and we made small talk. My heart was heavy. I wondered how I could continue doing all the things I was working on. I loved all of this, but somehow my work was no longer enough. I was glad I was holding her hands, but I needed the rest. I hardly knew her so there was no way I could ask about that!

O man! What a great dinner. I'm sure the entire meal was great, but all I remember was her meat loaf. She used such great spices and who knows what else. It seemed to me that God was lurking around.

After the meal June got serious.

"I can tell that something's weighing you down. Can I help?"

"No, I don't see how you can". I squeezed her hands.

"Let's see what's going on. If I can't help, we'll pray about it. God cares about you, and somehow, well, so do I."

I thanked her for allowing me to hold her hands as many times as I had. She never objected. I poured out quite a bit of my story and how it all started with a boy's hands and how I found out that girls' hands were better. The flood gates opened. I told her about needing to be held and I couldn't control my tears. I'll never forget what happened next:

"Joe, that's quite a story. Either this is the most unusual pickup line I've ever heard or you have some major needs. Let's give all this to God so He can help us." She put an arm around me and squeezed me. Then she asked God for guidance as to what she should do, and to lift the burden which was crushing me. She said that if I'd come to her house next week after church, she'd pray and read some Scripture and see what she could do.

After church the next week I was at her house. She told me that God showed her that she could be of help to me. She must have held me for more than two hours. What a relief it was. I think I cried for most of that time. We saw each other frequently. Something was bothering me for a long time—something which I knew was important but which had no meaning. I asked her what love was.

Nothing flustered her: "Love, well, there are several kinds of love. The best kind is God's love." She picked up her Bible and read the first 7 or 8 verses of 1 Corinthians, Chapter 13. What it comes down to is that His love has no strings attached. No matter what a person does, God's love remains constant. Paul (who wrote 1 Corinthians) tells of many things which are love and many things which are not.

"But June," I said, "you're telling me things which are about love, but what is it?"

"You'll know. Don't worry about it. You'll know what it is when the time comes."

Almost from the time we ate that first meal together in her home, she was showing me love, not by words but demonstration. She showed me love in action. Slowly I understood, no, felt love. I realized that I loved June!

The oppressive weight was lifting. I had my keyboard with me at the next service. For some reason, happily, June was the only one taking me to church from that time on. When it was the month of January, one of the guys, who I called "Uncle Jim". kept singing "It's June in January". That song was popular in the late '30's, and Jim was old enough to know the song very well. Sometimes another guy would try to imitate wedding bells. I didn't know why they were doing those things. I had no plans to ever get married. Apparently I was the only one who didn't know I would.

Again as always, time moved forward. At this point it was a bit less than a year since June lost her husband. Early in our relationship she told me not to rush her. I thought I understood what she meant, but I wasn't rushing her. Marriage was the last thing on my mind.

CDs were being played on the radio occasionally. I knew it was time that I should sell my disk recording system. One of my Jamaican clients was always interested in my equipment when I was doing work for him. I asked if he'd like to buy my setup, he definitely wanted it. He had a small studio and he was sure that the addition of a machine like mine would impress his customers. I asked for quite a bit of money for the system, and he readily agreed to it. I could hardly believe it. I was going to get most of the money I had invested. It was good that I sold the system to a Jamaican because people in Jamaica were not ready to use CDs. I wrote a very long instruction manual for the system. There was none. The only manual was in my head.

When that job was done, the buyer and a couple of helpers came, dismantled everything and left. I found out just a bit later that the system was reassembled and working properly. It was sad to see all that space in my basement empty. Disk recording was my life, and it was very likely that I'd never make another phonograph record. It didn't dawn on me, but a large chunk of my business was gone.

It was raining one afternoon as June and I drove to an out-of-the-way restaurant which was seldom crowded. As we ate, we started talking idly about our future. We sort of dreamed about what it could be like in our own house. How would it be furnished? There'd have to be room for my Steinway. It was kinda fun, even though it was nothing more than idle dreams on a rainy day. It seemed as though any time June and I talked seriously, it would rain.

Now and then after church was over, not only did I have the guys riding me, but Angela gave us the business. As she'd walk by us she'd say something like "Did you two hear bells?"

It got to a point that when Dad saw June coming to pick me up, he'd yell, "Here's that damned dame!" I had no idea how I could handle him. I didn't want June to hear him, but I was afraid she might already have. Well, nothing to be done! She did hear him, but it didn't matter. Very little fazed her.

I owned a satellite receiver, and I found something which recently came on the air. It was called "The Home Shopping Network". This was the first time I was exposed to what sighted people took for granted. I was exposed to men's bracelets, computer accessories and so much more. I decided to make a ring for June just for kicks. I measured her finger so I'd know how large it should be. I braided some copper wire and soldered a dime onto the wire and gave it to her after church. I know it couldn't have been pretty. One of the guys saw that and told June that he'd make one with a quarter instead of a dime. He told me that he was gonna steal June away from me.

I'd occasionally heard about something called "cubic zirconia". Apparently it looked as good as a diamond. I remember that it was described as being in a high Tiffany setting. I thought it would be a nice gift for June. It was only $30 or $40, so I ordered it to give to June just for fun.

One day I asked Lois to come to my house because I needed her advice. She came, and we sat together a few minutes. Then I told her that I had a really heavy-weight decision. I told her about June, and that I really cared about her. "I've lived at home all my life. Could I really leave home after living there so long. I know Dad resents June. She's as fine a person as I've ever known, but should I marry her? How will my folks handle this? I'm not sure if they can do it with good grace."

Lois didn't skip a beat: "Go for it!"

I'd see June at church in a couple of days. It was raining as June drove up. On a whim I grabbed the cubic zirconia ring, all nicely boxed up just the way it arrived. Then it came to me. I could use it to propose to her! I was really nervous during that service. I started to get cold feet. After the service as we drew near June's house the rain came down even harder. I figured God must be telling me something.

When we finished our meal, June and I sat together. Then I got up, turned to face her, knelt in front of her and asked, "June, uh, will you marry me?"

She grabbed me, kissed me, and said she would. I suddenly realized that it was Valentine's Day! I handed her the ring. When she saw it, she loved it. It had so much sentimental value for her that she decided it would be her engagement ring. (Eventually I did give her a real diamond.)

The next Sunday at church, I thought it was high time to get back at Angela for all that riding they gave us. As the service ended, I asked Pastor Dave if we could have a serious talk.

He took us to a secluded spot and asked what was wrong.

"Pastor, I have to confess that I made a terrible mistake. I hope you can somehow forgive me."

June was a pretty good actress: "Yes, Pastor, he did, and somehow I made one and that made things even worse than they were."

If I hadn't known better, I would think June was on the verge of tears. Pastor Dave sounded worried as he asked what was wrong.

In perfect unison we said: "We're getting married!"

Pastor Dave was so excited. He was running and jumping around the church yelling: "There's gonna be a wedding! There's gonna be a wedding!"

June wanted to tell some special friends. I'm not sure if we headed right to my house to break the news to my folks. I think it was a couple of days later. And I think it was raining. I was glad June was with me. I didn't know what would happen when I told them.

We got to my house, we sat for a couple of minutes and then I simply said, "Mom, Dad, June and I are getting married."

Dad was silent. Mom spluttered something about whether I could support her and whether I could be nice to June. June must have said something, but what I do know is that she left us quite soon.

Mom seemed to accept our coming marriage, but Dad wouldn't speak to me. Would he ever accept that life is always changing? He certainly couldn't accept that Mary was gone. I hated the thought that Dad would be even more unhappy than he already was.

If I wasn't with her, we'd talk on the phone. I reminded her of Dad's attitude and told her that I'd let her back out of the marriage if she couldn't deal with my family.

"Joe, your father is scared because he thinks he's gonna lose a son. Give it time and he'll find he's gained a daughter."

I was sitting in our living room a week later when Dad walked up to me and asked:

"Joe, how about a brandy?"

"I'd like that, Dad." He served the brandy just as he had many times before the marriage announcement. He even cut up a few slices of Italian cold cuts! I was relieved that he came around.

By this time June had met quite a few members of Dad's family, but I wanted her to meet Aunt Kitty and Alice; those two were the only family mom had. Uncle Art already left us.

I knew aunt Kitty had cancer but didn't know how sick she really was.

I phoned Alice to see if June and I could come and see them. Alice said that it was a matter of days when her mother would leave her and that even then Kitty would not recognize me if I did come there! She went to the Lord a day or two after the phone call.

There was so much to plan. Where could we find a hall? Who should we invite? Once we found one, thanks to June's stepdaughter, Kathy, we then knew what all the costs would be. We could invite just 40 people. There'd be hurt feelings on the part of those who couldn't be included. There were clothes to buy.

Where should we go for our honeymoon? I mentioned that I wanted to see Bermuda. My cousin, Helen, loved it. June was delighted because she knew some people who lived there, and this would give her a chance to see them. I suggested that we take a cruise there, and again June liked the idea. I'd think idly sometimes that, if I ever married, I'd want to take a cruise or maybe see Bermuda. I'd never have guessed that I'd be able to have both experiences.

We went to a travel agent to find out when a Bermuda cruise would be available. One was scheduled to sail on April 18. We called Pastor Dave to see if he could perform the ceremony. Angela picked up the phone and June asked about that date.

Angela said: "Oh no! Dave would never perform a wedding ceremony on Good Friday, but he would be able to do it on Holy Thursday."

We could adjust our plans; we'd stay an extra day in New York and sail on the 18th. We'd marry on April 16, 1987, just a few days after my 58th birthday.

When possible, I'd bring some of my things to June's house, where we would live. On one such trip I found that there was no way my Steinway would fit. I was really sad about that, but it wouldn't change my mind about our impending wedding. Just about then I was driving with a couple of my friends to attend a meeting of our radio club. Ed, a member of the club, was with us, was quite excited. He had acquired something new, and he made a recording of it which he wanted me to hear. He was an exceptional pianist and what I heard was a recording of his playing his new digital, electronic piano. It sounded very good, not as good as my Steinway, but I realized immediately that it could easily fit into what June and I would call our "music room". What I also realized was that I wouldn't ever have to tune it. The Steinway was fine, but its design was such that it was very difficult to tune.

I was so happy that everything was falling into place. Nario was truly happy for me, and he definitely agreed to be my best man.

But as the day drew close, I had misgivings. I thought about the vows I would take. We would be "one person", and compromises must be made. Could I make them? Could I really be there for June, regardless of our circumstances? We'd be seeing a lot of each other. Would we get on each other's nerves? How many fights would we have, like Mom and Dad often had? Had I matured enough to handle these things?

Now it was here, the day of our wedding. I was packed and ready.

It would be a simple matter for me to change into the clothes I'd wear. I was nervous. There was a bit of extra time, so I decided to modify a cassette recorder which I planned to use for taping the events of our honeymoon. What do you know? It worked! I ate a quick lunch, changed into my wedding duds and just then there was a horn blowing right outside the house. The limo was there to pick up Mom, Dad and me. We were on our way to the church!

Chapter 28

What a ride that was! I was cushioned in the quiet comfort and elegance of a Lincoln Town Car. I felt rich, not with money but because of my new life. All too soon we arrived at the church. We took our seats and suddenly I was really nervous. I hoped it didn't show on my face. Again I had doubts that I could go through with the wedding. I loved June, no question, and I'd committed myself to her. Would I have time for myself? I wanted to experiment with arranging and putting orchestral music arrangements together. Would I have my own space? I reminded myself that June and I had talked about these matters, and she said that she also sometimes needed her own space.

I finally realized that God was with me in the form of the Holy Spirit. Maybe I should talk to Him. I bowed my head in prayer and told Him what was troubling me. It seemed that something was always making me feel that way. I silently poured out my heart. When I said the "amen," organ music was playing. June was in the church and was walking to the traditional "Here Comes the Bride". Our moment was at hand. Where were my questions and doubts? They vanished and peace filled me. I knew I would walk into my new life with June with a profound joy I had previously not known.

The ceremony was the traditional one, and the word "obey" was not omitted. We both knew this was not a dictatorship but an incredible partnership which is only granted to those who desire to commit their lives to each other and to God. When we kissed after being told we were really married, our lives together began in earnest.

As we walked hand in hand outside the small church, we were greeted by a church filled with so many who loved us and wished us well. I never felt such an outpouring of love and friendship. I had a quick flashback to those boarding school days where the only outpouring was of hate and that was now replaced by something inexpressively more powerful than hate! It was as though we were in a world where everyone cared for us.

We drove to the reception which took place in a fine catering hall in Eisenhower Park, Long Island, New York. June's stepdaughter, Kathy, knew the owner of the establishment and arranged for us to have their best server who was gracious in everything she did. As we were preparing to be served, there'd be that expected tapping on wine glasses, and I pretended reluctance about kissing June.

Two of the guests were clients of mine, and they combined to video everything about our wedding to make it memorable. We'd only get married one time, and this time there would be a recorded memory of everything that took place.

I planned a surprise for June. Only Ron Rothman, one of the two videographers, knew what it was. Many times June asked me to sing to her. I had sung in a chorus, but I'm not a solo singer. I really worked hard to both sing and play two songs which to me fit the occasion. Ron helped me to the piano and positioned a mike which I could use so I could be heard throughout the reception hall. I warned the young boys present that if they weren't careful, they'd be where I was standing. I then sang a tune from the mid-forty's called "It Could Happen to You". June was shocked just the way I hoped she would be. Then I told those present something they may never have heard. I explained that people had it all wrong. I then sang a pretty but obscure tune called "Girls Are Made to Take Care of Boys".

"Girls are made to take care of boys. Made to share their sorrows;
Made to share their joys.
Made to lead and guide them
With ever a patient hand.
Made to give affection
In the right direction.
Always understands.
Boys may think they take care of girls
Just because they pass on their fashions and their curls.
But I've always found
It's just the other way around.

If you love the girl and declare you do,
She'll be there to take care of you."

Most ladies in the room were very moved. June's step-daughter had a rather strong exception to the sentiments of the song. She was a "Women's Libber", so, she missed what I believe to be the true meaning of the song. When I decided to sing that song, I thought back on just how often it was a woman or a girl who got me through rough times. There was a subtext which was that the song was a thank you for all that June did for me as we courted. June understood what I tried to tell her: that I recognized just how important she was for me.

The evening was over. We said our good byes and my cousin, Ron, and his wife drove us to the Edison Hotel in Manhattan, which would be our home for the two days before we sailed to Bermuda. When morning came, we arose and ate our breakfast in the Hotel dining room. June found it amusing that our first errand was to shop for the digital piano which would replace my faithful Steinway. She had lost two previous husbands, and she laughed about this new way to spend a part of our honeymoon.

June was anxious to go to the Good Friday service in St. Patrick's Cathedral. I wasn't altogether happy about the idea, but it was something she'd wanted to do for a very long time. How could I refuse her request? But I couldn't help thinking about my problems with priests many years ago.

When we walked in and found our seats, an organ, orchestra and choir were just concluding Bach's Mass in B Minor. I thought I was in Heaven. Just for that one performance I was happy to be in such a sacred building.

The service was celebrated by the Archbishop of New York. I remember that he was an excellent speaker. What really impressed me came when Holy Communion was about to be served. The Archbishop invited us to receive, but it was a different invitation. "This is the Lord's table," he said. "This is not a Catholic table. It is for all Christians who know they are right with God." June and I felt really blessed as we received the elements.

After the service ended, we went outside, and, what can I say? It was raining! While we were dressed for that, as we neared our hotel, the shopping bag June was carrying was soaked through and her camera and strobe crashed to the ground. We could no longer take any pictures other than outdoor or otherwise well-lit scenes. I tried to fix the strobe, but it could not be fixed.

After a leisurely dinner, we went back to our room. From out of the blue June asked me to transfer many items from her purse into a briefcase. I was concerned about doing that because this briefcase was like a thin, flat suitcase rather than a case which opened at the top. The one I was charged to carry would have spilled everything if it were to be opened when held vertically. It was fine if it was opened on a flat surface. June handed me a bunch of "stuff", and I put it into the case. It would have been much easier if most of those items were in her purse which would have made retrieving them much easier. I thought to myself, "Well, ladies do have some strange ways."

The next morning we went to the hotel diner for a great pancake breakfast. June was helping me with the pancakes, spreading syrup and butter. Some rowdy young boys started carrying on about the poor service and ran out of the diner. After finishing breakfast, June found that her purse was missing. Those boys took advantage of June's helping me to steal her purse. The dining staff gave us free breakfasts and called the police, so we'd at least have a case number. I knew darned well that the purse would never be returned.

We went to our room to take stock of our situation. June thought about it and told me what was in the purse—two or three credit cards, a little "mad money," and all of our traveler's checks. She said that the cruise tickets were also there. The first thing to do was to call the companies which issued the cards to report their loss. June then told me that all of the envelopes we had made out to tip certain people on the cruise ship were also gone.

I carried more cash than June lost and that was a help. My credit card was with a company different from any June owned, so no problem there. The card could be used on the ship. But losing the traveler's checks and the boarding tickets for the cruise might present a major problem. This all was taking quite a bit of time and we were late checking out of the hotel. Someone from the staff came to the door and told us to stay as long as we needed to.

Then we remembered the briefcase. June laid it flat on the desk and opened it. The first thing she saw was a list of the serial numbers for all the traveler's checks. She told me they were drawn on the Barclay Bank, which made me very happy because I knew that was a British bank. I hoped that there would be a branch somewhere on the Island because Bermuda was part of the British Commonwealth. She dug a little deeper and there were the boarding tickets and all our carefully prepared envelopes for our dining room servers and whoever else was to be tipped at the end of the trip!

We were saved!

As far as I was concerned, our anxieties were over. Now I understood that the Holy Spirit directed June to have all those items moved into that briefcase. It was with a light heart that we checked out of the hotel and hailed a cab to take us to the dock from which we would board our ship. It was raining of course.

But June was not light-hearted when we boarded. She was very quiet. I got to thinking how little I knew about women, but I took her to the ship's gift shop. The woman behind the counter described her merchandise in a rather cool and bored manner. She mentioned a bottle of perfume from BAL Maine called Ivoire. I asked the lady to dab some on June so I could check it out. I don't know a thing about perfume, but I rather liked this one and bought it on the spot. It wasn't cheap, but June loved it. She began to perk up.

I felt I needed to relax for a bit, so we went to our stateroom. June said she expected me to yell at her for her carelessness. I could never have done that. She was helping me with my breakfast. It told her that the guys who grabbed her purse were undoubtedly pros. Giving her a bad time was the last thing on my mind. The event was taxing, and I was glad she was there to help me relax for a short time before the dinner hour. June smelled great as we walked into the ship's dining room.

Dinner had its little surprises. Our server's name was Joseph, a young man who was no more than 18 years old. He was from Italy and was homesick and the cruise had barely begun. We ordered our meals. When our food was delivered, June got exactly the same things I ordered, not what she ordered. Rather than complaining or asking for what she'd ordered, she ate it. At least she liked the meal. We were to learn that this would be the pattern. From what we could figure, Joseph (Giuseppi) lived in a home in which the man was king. We could have complained, but we liked him and didn't want him to get into trouble. We read our menus carefully so that June would enjoy what I chose.

The next day was Easter Sunday. We had a wonderful breakfast and were anxious to enjoy Easter worship. The worship service was held in the ship's movie theater. We were a bit suspicious when June read the activities schedule for the day. Worship was set for 10 A. M. The first movie of the day was to be shown at 10:15. Was this a mistake on the schedule? Alas! No mistake. The best we could say of the service was that it was short.

O well, it didn't matter. God knew our hearts and knew we wanted to observe the day. Besides, June had brought a couple of small bibles to use for devotions. We went to our room to read about the great events of that first Easter. We couldn't. The Bibles were in the purse which was stolen from us. We wondered if the robbers ever used our Bibles.

As I remember it, we docked at Hamilton midmorning on Monday. The first thing she saw as we pulled into the dock was the Barclay Bank, just a block from where we anchored. It wasn't long before we were able to replace all of the stolen traveler's checks. The rest of the day was devoted to sightseeing. I wanted to hear a good steel band. Bermuda is not the real center for such music, but one nightclub boasted of a good band, and it was.

June called her friend our second day on the island, and he took us to lunch in what seemed to be a modest restaurant, but actually it was where the various political figures of Bermuda often dined. There were so many interesting sites, but we particularly remembered a perfume factory where we bought a couple of bottles of Frangipani (probably misspelled) perfume.

It was time to leave the island, and we boarded our ship to start the trip home. The schedule showed that there was to be a talent show, and June persuaded me to enter it. We were pleasantly surprised that there was a piano I could use to practice. The show began, and when my turn came, I told a little story about how I met the cruise director one time in New York. When I asked him how to get to Carnegie Hall, he said: "practice!"

"That's what I did, like this." I played "London Bridge is Falling Down" with plenty of wrong notes. Then I changed gears and played it as a snappy jazz tune, immediately moving into "Over the Rainbow".

When I first started playing, I heard some gasps from the audience because of all those wrong notes.

It appeared that this would be a terrible performance, but I turned the audience from pitying me to cheering me! What a difference this was from how it was in my boarding school days! So that nobody would feel bad if they didn't win a prize, everyone was given a nice Cross pen. I kept that pen until I somehow lost it a couple of years ago.

I know June enjoyed herself, and I sure did. But it had to end sometime, and then we were back at June's house where we planned to live. Yep, I carried her over the threshold!

There were so many details in starting our lives together. She worked part-time, and I had my magazine column to write. I won't go with details about work and housekeeping, except to note that we had no trouble dividing the chores. I loved setting up our breakfasts and learning how to use a dishwasher. We were so happy to be together, but there was a cloud just beyond the horizon. When it hit us, our lives would change. June didn't own her house outright. Half of it was owned by her three step-children—Kathy, Kevin and Richard. When I first moved into that house, we were told not to worry about anything. Without warning June was told in no uncertain terms that they wanted the money for their share of the house. Richard (Rick) kept coming around threatening us. The threats were veiled, and I decided that there was nothing to them but "mouth".

We were given a day on which the money had to be paid or we'd be sued. That was no threat, and we knew it. Because we didn't have the funds, we had to mortgage the house. Mortgage interest rates were quite high at that time. We took care of that but knew that, given the high taxes on Long Island and the mortgage payments, we would sooner or later need to sell the house and move. We could stay there for a time. I think it was a year before we had to make a move.

Meanwhile we often visited my Mom and Dad or had them come to our home. When I was at their house, I loved playing my Steinway. Besides, I had it rigged up with something called a Pianocorder. It was the modern equivalent of a player piano, and it included the ability to record my keystrokes as I played. I could record one part and play another part of a song. That made it possible for me to play more complex music than I could without the electronic help. Because I knew we'd have to sell the piano, I hired a very good re builder to get the instrument in its best possible shape before I sold it. I wanted top dollar.

A bit of time went by. I wasn't feeling just right. Even so, I decided that I wanted to make a recording of my Steinway now that it was at the top of its performance capabilities. I had a buyer for the piano who would pick it up the next day. Even though I wasn't feeling very well, I was determined to make the recording anyway. Mom and Dad had doctor's appointments and would be out of the house all day. When they returned, I still had a bit more to record and I had to work while dinner was being prepared for all of us. After a good meal I finished the recording, packed up my equipment, and June and I went to our home. I really felt miserable.

The next day I couldn't pass water and I ended up requiring a prostate operation which kept me in the hospital for a week. Truly that procedure was about as uncomfortable as I've ever felt. I was so glad to be home again. To celebrate, June bought some Italian cold cuts and Italian bread. What a meal. It was great to feel normal again.

Meanwhile June had a plan involving Dad which she was ready to carry out. Dad gradually warmed up to June. She "sealed the deal" one evening when she asked Dad what he most liked to eat. When he said it was lobster, June said it was one of her favorites. June knew all along that Dad loved that, so she told him that the two of them would go somewhere special and enjoy a good lobster meal and leave Mom and me behind because neither of us liked seafood. As it worked out, we went someplace where they could have their lobster dinner, and we'd have something more to our liking. Dad loved June from then on.

Our lives ran smoothly, but we heard reports that Dad would go for a walk and just stand in the middle of the street, oblivious of traffic. Mom told us about an evening when they went out to dinner and how Dad couldn't remember how to start his car. He figured it out, and they got home without incident. I was wondering if I'd soon have to take his car keys away from him.

We began to give serious thought about selling the house and relocating. So many of the places we liked turned out to be too expensive for us. I suggested we move to the Poconos, but June vetoed that one because of the cold winters. I suggested Virginia because I'd been there a few times and found the people to be friendly and laid back. One of the subscribers to BAUD lived in Charlottesville, Virginia, so I phoned him to ask if there was a Chamber of Commerce or other agency which could send us literature about that area. We got letters from restaurants, banks, Realtors, and more.

I guess it was in the late autumn of 1988 when we made up our minds to drive to Virginia to get the lay of the land. We decided to use a Realtor named B. J. Banton. He said he grew up in the very area we were interested in and would be glad to show us around. When we arrived and asked for Mr. Banton, the woman we asked told us that she was B. J. Banton. That gave us a good laugh. She did know the area and drove us to many homes which would give us an idea what was available and prices we could expect to pay.

As we were driving away June commented, "This place is like a perpetual vacation!" And indeed it was. We had a good idea of the size of our new home and knew what we'd have to pay for it. Then when we got back home on Long Island, we found a Realtor and had her check the value of comparable houses so we'd know roughly what we might get when we listed our house.

Many things were taking place. We began noticing how Mom would start to cook something and got into a book and forgot what was on the stove. We started talking about bringing Dad and her to Virginia to live with us. By then it was perhaps the first or second week of February. We went to Dad and Mom's house for a Saturday lunch. We needed cold cuts and a few other things. We told Dad we'd write out a list. He really was forgetful by then. He refused to take the list and got in his car and drove to the deli. He returned quickly with everything we needed. He didn't forget anything. We told them about our plans and my folks were excited for us. Somehow that simple lunch was one of the best I ever had. We were all so close as a family.

Early the following week Mom phoned to tell us that Dad was not well, and that she had called the rescue squad. When they came, they found Dad to be fine. A week later, June and I were having breakfast on February 28, 1989. Mom called to say that Dad was rushed to the hospital. The hospital called us a short time later, asking that we come in as soon as possible. I wondered if the worst had happened. We got there and were asked quite a few questions about Dad. I didn't know why but June knew that Dad had passed away. She had lost two husbands to death. She was all too familiar with hospital routine under those circumstances.

When Mom heard that, she said, "So finally the son of a bitch is gone." She took a short breath as if she tried to take those words back, but they were said. I mentioned that there was always a certain amount of tension in our home. Could Mom now feel a sense of greater peace? Funeral arrangements had to be made: with the Church, the cemetery, and with all of Dad's family and friends. There was nothing remarkable about the service; it was a conventional Catholic Funeral Mass, followed by a short graveside service.

The weather was beautiful on the day of the funeral. I thought that after the funeral June and I would host the meal which follows a funeral. We had plenty of food which could be readily set out. When it was over, I told the people that June and I planned to have the meal at our home. After a family discussion, one of Dad's nephews came to me and almost pleaded to handle the meal at a local restaurant. My thought was that a meal at home would feel more intimate, but he said that a few family members would have trouble driving home after dark as would be the case if we managed the meal.

It was a strange feeling for me. When other members of the family passed on, Dad was always the one who was consulted; he was the eldest. I was not the oldest then, but this was clearly a decision that I alone must make. In truth there was no choice but to let Dad's nephew take charge. The family, too, that so loved Dad, wanted to pay for all our meals. He chose a very good local Italian place.

We ate and drank a little wine and talked about our adventures with Dad. Then the day was done, and we all went our separate ways. Various people urged June and me to take Mom with us wherever we moved. We had already planned on that. For now, however, Mom wanted to be in her home by herself. Whatever she said or how she acted toward Dad, she needed time to grieve. They were together for so many years.

As June and I drove home, I knew there were many things which I should have told Dad—about how much help he'd been and that I should have thanked him more than I did. Why the hell couldn't anyone in my family show emotion and say nice things to one another? Nobody knew how the others felt about anything! Where was the affection everybody needs? At least I could truly say that June and I never failed to show how much we cared about each other. If only our lives would remain just as they were, we'd just sail into the setting sun together!

No time to think on these things. Sometime soon June and I would have to go back to Virginia to find and hopefully buy a home—a larger one than we planned for because Mom would live with us. It's more than just Mom; it's bringing some of her furniture and books. At the same time I had to help Mom with Dad's affairs. I had to find a buyer for his Squareback. That was easy to do because one of the members of our church needed a vehicle. I needed to go through his effects and figure out who in his family might like certain items. Mom had all of his papers so she could work on insurance matters. Once she had a partial handle on things, I'd do the phoning.

When we write a book, we do it sequentially, but life isn't handed to us in that way. While we planned to move, handle Dad's affairs, and start doing some packing, our pastor left the church because he was called to Florida to do some special ministry. Of course his wife, Angela, was also leaving, I became the worship leader. Pastor Dave's replacement was a different sort of man. He was devoted to God no doubt but he lacked the personal skill for handling people. His services were very lengthy. Church members asked if he could shorten them, but this made him lengthen them further. I never knew why, but he singled out both June and me as "trouble makers". One of the musicians thought that he should be the Worship Leader. I wasn't about to argue with him, so, I told him to take over.

As luck would have it, Marilyn Macintosh, a long-time friend of June's, called me with an urgent problem. For unknown reasons, the pastor of her church resigned. His wife was the organist so, of course, she was leaving, effective immediately. She asked me to fill in. I agreed to help until I moved or if her church found a more permanent musician. The atmosphere in my old church was very different and I was no longer content there.

However, June decided to stay with our original church, which made me wonder how I could get to Marilyn's church. What happened was that Bill, Marilyn's husband, drove me. I loved the atmosphere in my temporary church and I managed to play for worship. I had to teach myself enough about their electronic keyboard, but I got through that. I continued playing and worshipping there until we moved to Virginia.

Some time before this I obtained what was then considered to be a good laptop computer. I recognized that unpacking after our move would surely be a nightmare. I thought about this long and hard and came up with a system for putting records as to the contents of each and every box we packed into the computer. The information on the outside of each box had a number and the room in which the box would go. This corresponded to information stored in the computer. If it worked as planned, we could locate any item, find the box which contained it and locate the item fast.

We were busy all right. I had to keep up with writing "Audioclinic". It was too much; I had to sell my computer newsletter, BAUD. God was with me because I found a buyer almost immediately.

There was even more happening. My cassette duplicating business was doing poorly. For whatever reason, fewer people needed that service. My duplicators were getting old and I questioned the wisdom of spending quite a bit of money to rebuild them. I talked seriously to June about this, and she came to the inescapable conclusion that it was the right time to retire on disability. By doing that, June reasoned, I could recover more money from Social Security than I would if I simply retired. I was not yet 65 and wouldn't be for five years. It was pride which kept me from making that decision sooner. I absolutely hated to give up. But I had to do it, of course.

We went to our Social Security Administration office and we had wonderful help in filling out all the required paper work. The hardest thing I had to endure was the special eye doctor who was appointed to check as to whether or not I was truly blind. He wasn't likable and he asked lots of trick questions designed to trap me if I was a fraud. At one point during the examination he apologized for what he just did. I didn't know why he thought he had to do that. Well, it turned out he was shining a bright light directly into my eyes and I never knew it. That was his last trap. He said that nobody with sight could have withstood the light.

I was officially retired. I filled out the appropriate forms which should have told New York State that I had closed my business and was no longer working at my Long Island address.

Both Mom's and our homes were listed through a Realtor. Now we were packing in earnest. My friend, Joe Marrone, came to Mom's house to help me pack up most of my electronics parts.

It was time to go to Virginia to buy a house. We didn't know how long we'd have to be away, but we made sure Mom could take care of things while we were gone. We were concerned as to whether Mom would help us with finances because we needed a larger house than we originally planned because she would be living with us. There was no problem there. Mom was more than generous when the time came.

We made hotel reservations in advance and off we went. It was a 480 mile trip which meant that we arrived late in the evening. The next day Mrs. Banton drove us around and we saw various houses. June loved one which had a swimming pool. I wasn't sure about that house. We'd have to fence off the pool area, and then there's the maintenance of the pool to consider. Once we looked around the house carefully, neither of us wanted the place. There was junk all over. I checked out the appliances and the furnace. I saw too many clamps on pipes, which meant that we'd have to re pipe the basement. It would be an awful job cleaning up the place. It wasn't worth it.

We saw a wonderful house in a mountainous area and the price was great! Well, it needed to be great. There was no road leading to it. We'd be stuck inside all winter and it would cost us thousands of dollars to have a road put in.

Then there was a really sad place. A grandmother lived there, but her children knew that she was no longer able to live alone in a large house. As we walked through the house, the grandmother followed us, telling about all the things which were wrong with the house. The price was too high, and some major repairs to the house were needed so we passed it up. We couldn't get that poor woman out of our minds.

The next day we searched again. The first house we saw really was nice. It had just about everything we could want. I thought the price was too high, but it was one we might come back to. At the end of the day we did come back. We met the wife of the owner, who said that her husband was absolutely firm on the price. We really did love the house. We saw how Mom could have a small apartment and be independent when she wanted to be or could come eat with us when she wanted to.

But we were stuck because we wanted to pay $25,000 lower than the asking price. Just then the actual owner came in. We told him how much we liked the place, but we needed a lower price. He immediately came down to meet our counter offer. The house would be ours!

A few details were taken care of, and we knew we had only a fixed amount of time before we would either close on the house or lose it. When we got back with Mom, packing had to be rushed even more. Meanwhile, nobody was interested in either of our houses. One day, however, we found a buyer for our house. We set a closing date. Time was pressing us. Mom had to find a buyer. Two days later she found one. Our lawyer was able to set up both closings for the same day. We know God's hand was behind the scenes!

I'll never forget that day we closed. We began working on the closing of our house. Mom's house would close next. June had used this lawyer for years so we thought he'd properly represent us. No!!! We got a young gal just back from her honeymoon. It seemed to me that she must have just received her law degree, and we were her very first clients. June read me the contract. It was printed on a standard form so who would expect a problem? There was one. The lawyer interchanged the buyer and the seller's names. She had to start over and re type it while we waited. Mom was with us, of course, because we had to close on her house once ours was sold. Finally, we had everything signed and sealed.

We had this same woman as the lawyer representing Mom at her closing. The lawyer representing the buyer of mom's house was a solid-seeming guy. All was moving along very smoothly. My mind started to wander a bit while the two lawyers grappled with minutiae. Then I heard the lawyer for the buyer say that a number of clauses would have to survive the closing. Our lawyer started to agree, and I started to see red (even though I don't know what red is).

"What in hell are you trying to pull? Maybe you may think you can fool an old lady, but you can't fool me so quit trying. Nothing will survive the closing! I'll let those clauses survive inspection but when all that is settled and we close, it belongs to the buyer who will assume all future aspects related to that home!"

Another lawyer who happened to be in the office, said, "Joe, you can come work for me any time!"

"No way I'd work for anyone who's dishonest."

On our way back home, Mom wanted to know why I got so mad. I had to explain that if I allowed that language to stand, she could be sued for years.

The two of us figured it was best that Mom shouldn't make this long car trip and then have to deal with unpacking. June arranged with Kathy for Mom to stay with her for a few days while we sorted out most of the mess of unpacking. She would fly down a few days later.

Real property laws in Virginia were different from those in New York State. Most of the details could be managed by faxes. Even the payment for our new home was wired. We knew that we owned the house without personal contacts with Virginia lawyers. Yes, we owned our home free and clear!

I won't detail our last day in New York. The buyer of our house was supposed to be there to help us but didn't show. Of course, she didn't have to be there, but she did promise to help us with last minute packing. On the other hand, when we drove to Mom's house, the buyer was there and really pitching in and was just the nicest person!

Finally the moving van was full, and we were headed to Virginia. The van driver knew how to find our hotel and would meet us there at 8 o'clock the next morning. June was remarkable. She remembered where the hotel was because we stayed there on our previous trip to Virginia. What really amazed me is that June knew exactly where to find our new home, because she recalled the various local roads and because she studied all the maps she could find. The woman always amazed me with the way she handled so many of the details about traveling.

Both of us were leaving family and friends behind—but we were at peace.

CHAPTER 29

When we were in our Charlottesville, Virginia hotel room, I wondered how we'd get into our house. There was no way to get our keys. June hadn't considered that either. We unpacked the few things we'd need. What do you know? Right on the dresser we found our house keys and a Jefferson Cup—which is a silver cup which was cast to remind people of Thomas Jefferson who was born in Virginia and was the third president of the United States. In it there was the remote to open the garage door and a note from Mrs. Banton welcoming us to Virginia!

We awoke refreshed. After a good breakfast we met the van driver and our little caravan drove the 25 minute trip to our new house. We had a surprise! We didn't have electric power. June had previously arranged for the power to be on, but it wasn't. She wanted to call to find out why we had no power, but the phone wasn't working either. I had arranged for phone service but, as I said, no service.

I waited until June could find a phone. The van driver and his helper located a manual release for the garage door so it could be opened without electricity. Most of the furniture would need to be brought into the house through the garage. They began bringing items into the garage. June returned with the makings for a quick lunch and opened the door from the garage which led into the kitchen. Then June showed the men where furniture and cartons would go.

It took lots of time but we were moved in. I set up my laptop and I could tell June in which boxes we could locate items without the need for opening any boxes -but the right ones. I was really glad that my database worked as I designed it.

July 4, 1989. We were in our wonderful new home. Over time we unpacked all of the myriad of boxes, and picked up Mom at our local airport. Kathy was just great with Mom.

We planned to visit the local churches until we found one in which we'd feel comfortable, but we only went to one church, The Palmyra United Methodist Church. The people were so friendly, the pastor was excellent, and the music was absolutely outstanding. I wondered how it could be that a small rural church should have attracted so many good musicians and singers! I knew almost immediately that I wouldn't be a featured performer, and I didn't care.

While driving from our old homes to our new one, we talked to a number of "hams" and found that there was a good ham radio club which met not too far from our home. I attended a meeting and joined.

June saw me use my various pieces of ham gear and recognized how useful this hobby could be. She often traveled late in the evenings to various religious functions. If the car broke down, she realized that she would have no way to tell me she was in trouble. For this and other reasons June decided that she wanted to have a ham radio license of her own. My club offered study courses for this very purpose. Of course, I could also help her learn the information needed to pass the government exam. She struggled with the study materials, especially the ability to both send and receive Morse Code. Technical matters were not her strong suit but she doggedly plodded on and received her license.

It was really great to be able to talk to her while I was home and June was out driving. (We didn't do everything together.) The club guys got a kick out of some of our communications, like when June would tell me that she was about to pull into the driveway and would I come out and help her with the groceries.

As hams working together we participated in community service events such as helping with communications for the multiple sclerosis 150-mile bike tours. We helped find bikers which broke down on the course or made sure that a rest stop was properly supplied with water and food. That doesn't cover many things we did, such as assisting in hurricane preparedness drills.

We often thought we'd like to do a bit of traveling, perhaps staying overnight. We'd want to bring Mom with us, of course, so we considered buying a motor home. It just happened that the father of our auto mechanic had a motor home to sell. It was a 25-foot, cab-over Shasta. I think it was a 1981 model. After a couple of test drives we purchased it.

Mom's legs were not strong but she could get in and out of the vehicle. We learned how to prepare the home for winter if we didn't plan to use it. We often did, however, when we took a couple of trips to Florida. People were amazed at how well June drove that machine. She always loved driving. She could study a map and memorize routes we'd use: either in the motor home or in our car. I was continually amazed at June's abilities in so many areas of life. I can't remember how many years we owned that motor home, but we loved every moment we spent in it.

Life was so good; God was so good. As I got to know more and more church people and others in our area, I found opportunities to record many concerts and sell cassette copies of them. I worked out special order forms for each type of concert, but I used a common theme: Be sure to keep the printed program because this, along with the recording, will be a memory you'll always treasure. I remembered that long-ago high school talent show, so I well understood what it meant when there was no way to preserve a priceless moment in the lives of those with whom I came in contact. It was the main reason why I began recording here in Virginia.

No longer did I still own a high-speed cassette duplicator. I wasn't dealing with too many copies of each concert. It was a rather simple matter to make a few copies with the equipment I already had. I never really liked cassettes for many reasons. They were, however, very convenient to use so they were popular. I wished I could make copies of the concerts I recorded on CD's, but at the time they were introduced, recording one required a million dollar setup. Later In the mid '90's almost anyone with a computer and the proper additional equipment could make a CD.

I was on the radio one day when one of the guys from our radio club in New York told me that he could record CD's. He sent one that he made. It was impressive to say the least. He had a spare CD burner he wasn't using and he sold it to me. I didn't know how to use it. At one time when I lived in Brooklyn, I helped a boy in high school. I taught him recording basics. We remained in contact. When my "burner" arrived, I phoned him to ask what he knew about recording on a CD.

He gave me the name of a piece of software he thought I could use. I bought it and, by using my scanner, read the manual. I did some hard studying and figured out how easily I could record a CD.

The Lord is the best planner of all. A year or so before this venture into the world of CD's, Dave, a friend who was in our local radio club, insisted that I should learn Windows. I thought that Windows was so visual that I couldn't learn it, but it wasn't true. I needed to get some screen-reading software made so that a blind person could get a good picture of the important items which are present on a Windows screen.

With that screen reader and Dave's help, I learned how to send and receive email and a few other things. I learned about software which would permit me to copy recordings to a digital format for editing. This made it possible for me to remove long pauses, applause and more. The edited copy was such that it could easily be put onto a CD. Once I had the burner and the proper software, I could make CD's. From then on, I stopped making cassettes and used CD's exclusively. They were cheaper than cassettes and the sound was much more like the original recording.

We were, I guess, members of Palmyra United Methodist Church (PUMC) for a year or two when the teacher of the adult Sunday School was resigning. A long-standing member of PUMC asked me to become the new teacher. She believed that the current teacher was introducing material into her classes which was not according to the Holy Bible. I told her that I'd give it a whirl. I didn't know how Adult Sunday School worked; so, I joined the class to hear the final lesson taught by the previous instructor. I heard some things which I understood were not scriptural, but I at least knew the format of the class.

For the first few weeks June read me the material in the quarterly lesson book the class was using. I found a few lessons which didn't strike me as proper. In those instances I made up my own lessons based on the lesson title for a given day. Eventually we found out that there was a special teaching manual for each quarter's work, and that there was a Braille copy available. We bought those as necessary. I noticed there were some lessons which June would love to teach; so I asked her to do those. That gave me a break from teaching once in a while. June was a superb teacher and was truly loved by everybody.

The time came when the Braille version of the quarterly was no longer available. By then I learned how to use a "scanner" to put the text of books into my computer. That made my work easier. After scanning the contents of a quarterly, I wrote my lesson based on the quarterly and then "printed" the lesson from my computer to a Braille printer. That's a printer not unlike the printers used by sighted people except that it embossed Braille onto heavy sheets of paper designed for Braille reading. The Braille dots do not stand up to repeated readings when standard paper is used.

I taught that class for a number of years until I felt that I was getting "burned out". I'm pleased to say that my replacement was a very special person. Not only was he a great teacher, but a fine wood worker.

It wasn't long after we moved into our Virginia home that June began something which was always in her heart but which she couldn't arrange. June always wanted a Bible study in her home, but it had never worked out till now. June could easily have taught Bible study, but she was content to be the hostess. I don't know how she managed it, but within a few weeks she lined up a teacher from one of the many small churches in the area. Some of the students were members of our new church and as time passed, she had others come from other churches. Even though it was a Bible study for women, when it came to singing songs of praise, June asked me to accompany their singing. After that was done, I disappeared into the basement to putter around.

As you already know, all of my ham radio work made June decide to become licensed to be a ham operator just as I was. Previously I had been a member of a ham radio club on Long Island. Just before I moved away, Johnny Cue gave me a complete radio setup which would permit me to talk to my friends from that club. What a wonderful gift that was.

For quite a few years Johnny and I spent many happy hours on the air. The last time we spoke, he said that he felt absolutely lousy and signed off. His daughter called a few days later to tell me he had died!

When my new radio friends discovered that I had equipment which would allow me to talk over great distances, a group of those guys came to my house to install an antenna suitable for use with my new equipment. From then on I talked to my old friends in New York as well as to many strangers I would never meet, but we were never the less united by our common interest in radio.

June had said that being in Virginia was like a perpetual vacation. In 1991 it still was. I couldn't have been happier. I thought it was high time I got started doing orchestral arranging and recording my work. I had a recorder or two and my Roland digital piano plus another keyboard. I experimented with what I had and came up with a few semi orchestral sounds, but I had difficulty keeping to the exact beat. That was and still is very necessary if the sounds I created would hold together. I heard about something called MIDI which appeared to be an answer to my problems. Even when a note was slightly off the beat, it could be edited so it would be "right on".

I asked June to take me to what I hoped was a good music store so I could learn about this MIDI. When we arrived, a helpful salesman showed me a device called a Sound Canvas. It was a rather small metal box which had a few buttons on the front surface and a few places to connect various devices. It could, however, produce numerous sounds: piano, bass fiddle, harp, chorus and so many more sounds. The salesman showed me the buttons to press so I could hear any given sound. It seemed to be just the ticket, but it cost $600. Normally I would have talked with June about spending the money but this time I didn't do that. I bought it on the spot! June didn't get mad, but she was a bit unhappy with me.

I couldn't wait to experiment with the Sound Canvas. Although I could connect my digital piano to this device and play various instruments, I could not record them as an "orchestra". I was frustrated. From time to time I'd mess with it but just never got anywhere. June admired my persistence but was pretty much convinced that the $600 investment was a loss. I talked to God about this, of course, but I received no direct guidance from Him.

One day I telephoned Gary Greico, the guy I taught computer basics to a few years before. He's a good pianist and I mentioned my problem. He didn't know anything about it but he had a friend who was actually doing what I so badly wanted to do. He put me in touch with him, and through him I learned that I needed software called a "MIDI sequencer". He told me to buy it. It didn't cost much. I did. When I got it home, I installed it on my computer. However, I couldn't make heads or tails from the instruction manual.

When fooling around and getting nowhere with the Sound canvas, the light dawned. I wasn't supposed to use the buttons on the Sound Canvas to play a given instrument. I was supposed to enter a specific number into the software, and the software sent the number into the Sound Canvas. But how could I know what number to enter? I asked June to look at the instructions for the synthesizer and there it was: a table of numbers which correspond to specific instruments.

I learned how to record what I played by using the software. I was ready to try a short recording. I remembered a promise I made to God long ago that if I ever could record my musical arrangements, the first song I'd record would be the Lord's music. So I decided to record "Forget About Yourself and Worship Him". It took me very little time to record the song. The instruments I chose were a Harp, string bass, guitar and flute. When I played the song, it sounded exactly the way I pictured that it should. I was on my way.

I ran upstairs to find June. I brought her down to hear my creation. "Now I understand what that unit does. It's amazing!" She encouraged me to do these orchestrations from then on. It took me a year, but the rewards for me are beyond words! I couldn't have been happier and contented. Eventually I could record my music from the computer and onto CD's and I was able to let my mind try more complex musical arrangements.

Life moved on; it was 1995. That was a great year. I guess the highlight of that year was the planning a surprise 90th birthday celebration for Mom. So many of her friends and members of Dad's family, who loved Mom, couldn't come to Virginia; we realized we'd need to bring the party to them. We doubted that Mom would want to travel to Long Island without an obvious reason. What we did was to ask Ann, a niece of Dad's, to send an invitation to all of us to attend the 50th anniversary of her husband's parents. There was no such event scheduled. That was a big enough event to make Mom willing to take the long trip to New York. Rather than June having to drive the nearly 450-mile trip, we decided to fly.

All went smoothly. We boarded the plane, made our connecting flight in Baltimore and arrived at Kennedy Airport. We'd arranged for a rental car. It was raining when we jumped into that car. We had a rather long drive to our hotel. The dash lights went out and came back on. They went off and stayed off. It was a difficult drive for June. With those lights off and her unfamiliarity with the car, she had a hard time locating such things as the windshield washer button. We managed to get to our hotel.

The next day, Mom's birthday, dawned bright and beautiful; it was a glorious fall day, October 15, 1995. We drove the few miles to the large restaurant which was catering our party. When we walked in, Mom saw people she expected to see for the "anniversary". Eventually people began wishing Mom a happy birthday. Quite a few had to say that before she knew she was had.

There were some wonderful moments for Mom. Many years earlier when Mary and I were little kids, Mom had Tommy, one of my many cousins, come to our basement apartment. She shooed us out of the room and wouldn't explain why we couldn't play with Tommy. He had a terrible time learning to read. Dyslexia was a word most people never heard, but Mom, always in a book, learned about it. In short, she got Tommy passed his reading problems. After all those years, he never forgot how my mother gave him the gift of reading. He became quite successful. He was at her party to thank her.

Another thing Mom loved was an edition of the New York Times, dated October 15, 1905 (her birth date). It had all the news events covered which occurred on that special day.

The party was over and time to say our farewells. Luckily we left before some of the other guests. June couldn't get the car to run unless her foot was on the accelerator. No way she could drive unless that was fixed. When we went back inside, my cousin Ron, his wife, Marylyn, and their son, Joseph, were still there. Joseph was in high school and was the champion auto mechanic in his school. He was able to get the car running at least temporarily until we got to our hotel. June and I knew God's hand was in that.

As we drove to the hotel, the car was "acting up". She managed to park it before it just plain quit running. We planned to fly home the next day, but that rental wasn't gonna get us to Kennedy Airport. We called the car rental agency and told them we had a "lemon" and that we were gonna take a taxi to Kennedy Airport. The rental folks tried to balk, but June told the man on the phone that we had a 90-year-old woman with us and how the press would love to get a story of how a rental agency wouldn't help us. They paid the taxi fare. It got better than that. The company had to retrieve the car and refund the entire rental cost.

We thought we'd arranged with the airline to have someone meet us because we needed a wheelchair for Mom, who could never walk the great distances involved in getting to our departure gate. Yes, we thought everything was set, but there was no help. We had to pay outrageous sums to porters so they'd do the least things. We got to the departure gate with less than five minutes to spare!

We weren't done with transportation problems yet. We arrived at Baltimore to find that our connecting flight back to Charlottesville would be delayed. A plane hit a deer when landing, blocking the use of that runway, the runway our flight needed. Eventually, we got home; but we figured that in the long run it would have been easier on June if she had driven. Considering how Mom was surprised and loved her party, the trip was worth all we went through to make it happen.

It was 1997, getting close to our tenth wedding anniversary. We were at a church outing and were returning home. Suddenly a policeman stopped us. He asked to see June's driver's license. Because she appeared drunk, he made her take a Breathalyzer test which she passed). He explained that June was weaving in and out, crossing lane lines erratically. My guess was that June was getting sleepy.

We did a lot of walking and I noticed that her pace was slowing down. It was so gradual that I hardly was aware of this change. Occasionally she asked me to button a blouse. Those buttons were so small that I had to play with them a while till I understood that she would have trouble with them.

For our 10th anniversary we drove to Virginia Beach to spend a quiet weekend. We got someone to stay with Mom. It was a marvelous time. Here in Virginia the weather is often quite warm in mid-April. When we drove home, June had no problem. I never thought about those little situations she had a month before.

Now it was early June. June had one of her friends over, but she had a short errand to run so excused herself and got into our Olds 88. Mom and June's friend, Nancy, and I were all in our living room. We heard a quiet boom. The noise didn't seem to be that close. Then we heard an insistent horn blowing. Nancy and I went out to see what the horn blowing was about. We had to walk around the house and were dumb-struck! June had driven part way around the house, knocking our propane tank off its foundation. We could smell propane. Just a bit further on was the car, which hit our deck so hard that one corner sliced through the passenger side and ripped it open like a can opener. June was unhurt. It was no problem getting her out of the car. She was shaken but was otherwise fine.

I went into the house, took my address book and my cordless phone. We each carried a folding chair, got mom, and quickly walked down the driveway for about three hundred feet. We sat down. I called the propane company and our insurance company. It was amazing how fast the emergency people from our propane company arrived. They had the tank remounted on its foundation, refilled, and reconnected to the house.

This was a narrow escape from an explosion which could have killed us and destroyed our home. They hardly left when our insurance agent came with camera in hand and took pictures of our car and the deck. Both were total losses.

Mom had to have an eye operation the next morning, and she could not get there without a car. Our agent helped us to find a rental car and also recommended a particular sales lady at a car dealership in nearby Charlottesville. The rental car was delivered in a very short time. There's no way to convey to you the kindness shown us by everyone. June and I thanked God once again for the place in which he put us and for His help in this bad time.

Mom was operated on successfully, and that was a relief. The insurance company would only permit us to use the rental car for a few days; thus, it was important to buy a new car quickly. I installed my ham radio set in the rental, and we were off to the car dealership. The woman who was recommended to us was another amazing lady. When we got down to business, she said she had a really good deal on a Lincoln Continental. I have to tell you that I've ridden in a few of those, and I loved them. They were so comfortable and it had all kinds of technical gadgetry. I told her that we couldn't afford a Lincoln. She showed us quite a few other cars, but many of them had to be ruled out because we weren't sure Mom could sit in the back seat. We could have afforded one of these, but none of them rode well.

Nothing seemed right. When we got back to the dealership after a test drive in one of these compacts, the sales lady said that we really needed to take the Lincoln home overnight and come back in the morning. She even had already transferred my radio into the Lincoln and had it properly connected and ready for use. When we came back to the dealership the next morning, the sales lady had worked up a price for the car and also found out how much the insurance company would pay us for the ruined Olds. The Lincoln was not a brand new car; it was a 1991 model, which reduced the price such that, along with the insurance money, made it possible to purchase the Lincoln.

With so much going on, I never had the chance to find out from June how such an accident could have occurred. She said that Nancy parked in such a way that it was hard for June to get the Olds out of the garage. She eventually managed it, but had to make a very tight turn. She accelerated and then lost control. Her hands froze on the steering wheel, and she could not lift her foot from the gas pedal. Thus she continued to pick up speed until she hit the propane tank and then the deck. I began to remember some of the other things I noticed about June and figured I'd have to watch her closely.

We drove many miles in the Lincoln with no mishaps. Time moved on, as it always does; and it was now September of 1997. There was what's known as a "ham fest" in Virginia Beach; we decided to go to it as we had for a number of years. We'd be gone for about three days which meant we had to take Mom with us. We knew a nice lady who we asked to help us with Mom when we were touring the various radio exhibits.

On the last day of the ham fest we saw all that we wanted to, met Mom and the other gal whose name I have forgotten. We stopped to pick up some funnel cakes at a stand on the board walk. We were moving very slowly, and June wanted to park, but she couldn't stop where she intended to. We grazed a concrete wall and scraped the car just a bit. It was not very noticeable. She finally managed to move her foot to the brake, and we stopped. The funnel cakes were just great, but I'd have enjoyed them more if June hadn't had another problem driving.

The trip home was uneventful. It was a good three hour run. I was nervous all the way home. I talked with June when we were alone. She knew she had some kind of condition. We made an appointment with our physician and everything appeared to be fine from his perspective, but he recommended that June see a neurologist.

The neurologist found nothing obviously wrong but an X-Ray

showed an abnormal growth at the base of her brain. He suggested that we consult with a neurosurgeon. We found out that the University of Virginia Hospital, located in Charlottesville, had one of the top brain surgeons in the country.

By the time we had the consultation it was January of 1998. His recommendation was for June to enter the hospital for more extensive tests, and, depending on how they came out, surgery was a very likely option. The day came for June to go into the hospital. Fortunately one of the few ladies in our ham radio club was a registered nurse who worked at this same hospital. She volunteered to drive June there and, once she was settled, drive me home.

I'd ask different people from our church to take me to see June. She was there for more than three days and still no word from the surgeon as to whether or not he considered surgery warranted. Eventually the doctor said that he would do it.

Chapter 30

When I visited June shortly before she was wheeled into the operating room, I found her in an almost giddy mood. She exuded great confidence. I knew June had prayed, but in this instance she was almost laughing! I learned later that she was given steroids to mitigate brain swelling. That produces these effects.

After the operation I didn't see the surgeon. I found that he never does see post operative patients. Another doctor met me and said that June came through the operation very well. It wouldn't be long before she could come home. I also found out that the delay of June's surgery was because the surgeon was praying long and hard beforehand. All of June's neurological tests showed no reason for her symptoms. He didn't see how the growth would create June's deteriorating condition. He performed the surgery only because he found no other options.

It was time for June to come home. It was necessary, I was told, to have a kind of "daily companion" to help June with bathing and a few exercises to strengthen her.

What a great day it was on that Friday when June came home!

Our church family knew about June's hospital stay and also knew she would need a wheelchair for some time while she recovered. The men got together and built a ramp which June could use to enter or leave our home. They worked very hard and very quickly so that by the time June came, it was complete. When she came from the ambulance, we pushed June's chair up the ramp and into the house. I didn't tell her ahead of time about the new ramp. You can imagine how surprised and happy she was, both for the ramp itself and for the love which went into its construction.

June could even walk as long as someone helped her. It wouldn't do for her to fall. June felt really good and dutifully did everything she was told to do. Sunday came, but we couldn't go to church; it was just too soon. A few people visited. It was a beautiful day.

I called Bill Stevenson, a ham radio club member, because I had a radio which I liked but didn't have the space it required. Bill and I had common interests in weather forecasting using this kind of radio. He was eager to have the set and was going to pick it up the following morning.

It was bed time. Everything was peaceful and still. I was sound asleep when I heard a terrible crash. I struggled to understand what had happened. June had fallen and banged her head against a wall very hard as she fell. June said she wanted to go to the bathroom and didn't want to wake me; she "knew" she could do that with no help. She seemed unhurt, but was that true? I helped her to get to the bathroom and then walked her back to the bed.

Once settled, she said, "Joe, I'm scared!"

"Relax. I'm sure everything is fine. We'll see how you're doing in the morning."

To tell the truth, I was scared, too. That was a nasty blow, and it was only a short time since her surgery. Would her brain have healed sufficiently so that a jar like that would not result in further damage? No matter how it turned out, I knew that I'd better get some rest in order to face the new day.

It was about 5 A. M., and I heard June's voice. "I can't get off the toilet."

"Oh June, you should ask for help when you need to do something like this. That's what I'm here for."

I walked into the bathroom as I spoke. It was only a few steps away. She said she felt all right but a little weak. I tried to help her stand up, but she was dead weight and wasn't able to help herself. I told her that I was going to call 911. She didn't want me to do it, but I did. I had a hunch as to what was happening to June. The rescue squad came quickly and June was placed on a gurney. She was put into the ambulance and was on her way to the University of Virginia Hospital. I knew I couldn't ride with her because I'd have no way to get back home. That was the right decision.

All I could do was wait for a call from the hospital. Bill Stevenson would be here soon. I called him on the radio. He was already on his way over. He came at about 8 o'clock. I was so glad he was here. He worked as an anesthesiologist at the hospital; so I acquainted him with June's problem. He had contacts which allowed him to call directly into the operating theater and talk to someone about June.

June was on the table being prepped for another brain surgery. X-rays showed that she had a subdural hematoma (bleeding in the brain). I asked Bill if I should have called 911 immediately after she fell. He said that if I had, June might have gotten to the hospital and nothing would have showed up on the x-ray. He said that I called at exactly the right time. Bill said he'd stay with me until we knew the outcome of the surgery. We knew she might not survive.

In a surprisingly short time Bill heard that June was out of danger. He had to leave, but I remembered to give him the radio I'd promised him. I didn't know how to thank him for his companionship during this ordeal.

In a day or two I was permitted to visit June in ICU. She wasn't responsive, but I was told that she was doing well and would survive. I thanked the two nurses who were monitoring June's progress and helping her. One of the nurses started to cry. I couldn't imagine what I must have said to offend the woman. I asked if something I'd said was offensive.

"You didn't say anything bad," she said. "It's just that most people come in here and complain about the bad care a patient was being given. You're one of the few who have come here to thank us!"

In a few days June left ICU and was placed in a conventional hospital room. She was able to speak with a very soft voice because she was very weak. This was nothing like the recovery which June had after her first brain surgery. I was told that June could not come home immediately; she'd have to be admitted to a nursing home for physical therapy. There was no telling how long she had to stay.

There was a bed available at a nearby facility, which was about 20 minutes from my home. June didn't stay in the hospital very long, probably not for more than a week. Then she was admitted to the nursing home. One of the ladies in our church set up a schedule of men and women who would drive me to the home twice a week so I could visit June. What would I have done without my church family? I needed their help to do grocery shopping. Mom could cook, but she couldn't do the shopping. I made out shopping lists using my computer and whoever it was who was assigned to shop with me could look at the list I printed. Things went on like this for perhaps a month or two; I can't give you a time frame. I got to radio club meetings, and to church, and did a bit of music arranging and recording.

Martha Rossi and her husband, Al, members of our church, invited Mom and me to go to dinner with them. That was great, especially for Mom because she had so few chances to get out of the house. They came over at the appointed time, and we were off to have a nice dinner. We were walking on our gravel driveway and were chatting about nothing in particular.

Mom was talking but not watching her feet. She slipped and fell hard. When we tried to help her stand, she was in terrible pain. She broke her hip. We called 911 for an ambulance. The three of us followed the ambulance. We got to the University of Virginia Hospital and Mom was checked by a doctor in the emergency room. God was with us. One of the top hip surgeons in the country was visiting this hospital and teaching other surgeons. He would perform the hip surgery.

She made a spectacular recovery. She was 93 years old. people that age don't live too long after breaking a hip. Like June, Mom could not come home; she was admitted to the same facility in which June lived. She needed lots of physical therapy before she could walk, and when she did, it was with the aid of a walker and a wheelchair. She would never walk unaided again.

The way I recall it, Thanksgiving was close at hand; both of my ladies were homesick, but neither of them was ready to come home and live as they once did. They'd need lots of care—probably round-the-clock. I wondered if there was a way to get them home by Christmas. The administrators at the nursing home said they could possibly come home but I would need some training because it was likely that I'd have to care for them at times.

I had to learn to walk with Mom as she used her walker. I'd have to learn to push June as she sat in her wheelchair and how to transfer her between the wheelchair and the toilet and back. And I'd learn how to undress her and transfer her from her chair into her bed. I had to get a hospital bed for June so working with her would be easier for me or one of the aides who I'd have to have on hand all the time.

I could see that there would be no such thing as privacy. It was getting close to Christmas by the time I completed my training. My teachers were wonderful. None of us knew whether I, as a blind man, could learn all of the many things I'd have to know, but they took up the challenge. I worked hard till everyone involved was satisfied that I could do whatever was needed to work with Mom and June.

I hired a couple of aides and they were lined up at my home awaiting a two-car caravan taking them home. It was December 23 and my gals were in our living room, and they were so glad to be there.

Some of the details of the next few days are hazy. I knew I rushed things so they could be home for Christmas. I didn't have enough aides. Judy Surber, another member of our church, was a retired nurse and seemed to be able to solve almost any problem. She talked to many of the nurses and convinced them to be temporary aides. She convinced one of the supervisors to work for me on Christmas Eve and Christmas day. I remember having to pay extra for her services, but at least I was covered for the moment.

These aides were wonderful. They cooked meals for us. June, alas! no longer could swallow properly and had to use a feeding tube which was inserted into her stomach. I had learned how to feed June. Technically aides are not supposed to do that work; supposedly they're not trained for it. Some aides knew how to feed June, and I taught most of the others how to do it.

Everything seemed really good, but the world is not a perfect place. There were times when an aide didn't show up for her shift. I had to be that aide. I was trained to work with my ladies, but it was awkward when I had to bathe them. I felt almost embarrassed to bathe Mom, but we both knew there was no other choice. This was less of a problem with June as you can imagine. If their needs were many, I'd get tired. Moving people is hard physical work when they can only provide a minimum of help.

There were three 8-hour shifts. If an aide didn't show for the 11 P. M. to 7 A. M. shift, I might have to stay awake all night. Even at night either woman might need to be taken to the bathroom or needed to be turned in her bed among other things. Each of my gals had a call bell which they used to summon help. I eventually learned to nap at night, ready to jump when a bell rang.

Occasionally some object was lost. I hated the idea, but I had to wonder if the item was stolen. Many of the aides lived from paycheck to paycheck. Even though I paid them a bit more than nursing homes paid, the money was never enough for the person to live well. I really couldn't blame an aide for stealing. I have to say, however, that in all the time I had my loved ones home, I only know of one item that was actually taken.

The aide involved was a rather young person, little more than a teen-ager. Another of my aides was her aunt. I hinted to the aunt that something was missing after the niece's shift. The aunt vehemently denied that this could ever be true of her niece. About a week later, the aunt gave me a bottle of perfume which she said was under June's bed. I thanked her profusely for finding it. I had a cleaning woman work in June's room, and I know she would have found that perfume had it really been under the bed.

It wasn't long after that when both aides quit. That meant that I had to struggle to find two other aides. If it wasn't for Vicki Davis, I never could have located competent, trained help. She was the chief of my staff.

When I started using aides I did not know that Virginia and Federal work rules were involved. Not only did I have to pay each one, but the expenses added up when I had to match their contributions to Social Security. The paperwork was incredible. None of it was hard if just one person was involved, but overall I must have had 40 aides there at one time or other. It was necessary to keep strict track of the hours each one worked. That includes noting when an aide missed her shift. Had it not been for Martha Rossi, I would have had to give up having June and Mom home. There's no way to show her how much I needed her and appreciated all her efforts. In all of this, her husband, Al, was ill with Leukemia, from which he eventually passed away.

I also received help from the county social services people. They knew that, unless circumstances changed, I would eventually run out of money. I couldn't let that happen. I had to face the fact that June and Mom would need to go on Medicaid. In order to do that, however, they would have to live in a nursing home. I hated that thought.

It was even more complicated than what I've explained. June owned our home jointly with me. She also was partners in various other investments. In order to protect myself and to provide for June's care, I'd have to ask her to sign over all her assets to me. June's mind was sometimes not too clear, but I had to convince her that this was my only choice or I could lose the house. June was having a good day when I presented her with these needs. She never hesitated; she trusted me to do the right things by her. I even had a clause added to my will that June could not be prevented from living in the house.

Besides the aides, both women needed various kinds of therapy. In addition to physical therapy, June required occupational and speech therapy. The latter was done in hopes that she could again learn to swallow. These people were more than professional; they had hearts. June asked one of them if she could somehow take her to a church service. The therapist did it on a few occasions—which cheered June immeasurably.

There was another concern. I no longer could have much physical contact with June. All I could do is to suppress my need. A few times Vicki put June in a place where she could hold me. I could not ask for this very often because it was a strain on Vicki's back to have her put on a couch. Many aides who do the sort of work that my ladies needed had back problems because of awkward positions they had to assume in order to maneuver their patients.

All of these things were physically and emotionally draining. Finally, I had to face the idea that I would burn out if life continued as it was. I had to put them in a nursing home. I started looking for a facility. The one I used before my ladies came home was filled. I found one in another county, about 35 minutes from my house. It was sad for me, but because of this decision, I'd have to dismiss my aides. I hoped they could find new jobs. Some were past the point where they could work in a hospital or in a nursing home. Working for me was much lighter duty than other possible jobs.

It was in mid 2001, I think, when the time came for the move to the Louisa County nursing home. My church family came to my aid once again. A caravan of two or three cars carried all three of us to the nursing home. The cars were filled with wheelchairs, walkers and clothes, plus medicines which the two women needed. We entered the home and settled each one in a separate ward. Neither June nor Mom wanted to be in the same room, but the rooms were near one another.

Chapter 31

My life would change again. Whereas before this moment, there were almost too many people in my home. Now I was alone. I would have to do the cooking and vacuuming. I kept the house cleaner so my place would always look presentable. It was too quiet when I got back home from dropping off June and Mom.

How could I stand this new life? I sat around for a couple of hours. I couldn't get myself in gear. I couldn't continue like this.

By doing something, the house wouldn't feel so empty. I had been sleeping in the bedroom in the basement. I decided to sleep upstairs in the bedroom in which Mom slept. She had been using my old bed so it would be familiar. After making up the bed, it was time to prepare a meal. I wasn't very hungry; yet I knew I must eat. Whatever I had, it was not a great dinner. I could have cooked something fancy; blind people can cook and do!

It was necessary for me to begin doing routine but necessary tasks such as food shopping. I had to inventory what foods were on hand and make a list of what had to be bought. It meant that I had to have someone from my church go with me to do the actual shopping.

When I finished shopping, I'd ask the person who went to the store with me to help me put items into the freezer. I'd write down, using a Braille note taker, the items in the order in which they were stacked. If an item was used, I'd delete it from the inventory, thereby keeping the order intact. I made labels to put on salad dressing bottles, canned goods and other foods. They were held in place by rubber bands so the labels could be re-used. I also wrote down the instruction for the preparation of frozen food, noting both the microwave and conventional oven instructions.

I used a timer so I could know when a meal was cooked. I counted on other tell-tale signs as to the progress of my cooking. Sometimes I would use the loudness of sizzling food. Sometimes I'd detect progress by the smell of the food. One of my best "friends" was a George Foreman grill. I learned how to use it to cook steaks, chops, sausage or other goodies. I could also use the grill to make my grilled cheese sandwiches. You can see that, if I had the patience, I could cook up a pretty fancy meal!

Because of being so involved with the my ladies' care, I had little time to make up musical arrangements, but now I had lots of it.

My church friends continued their loyal support. One lady, who was not well enough to help me in other ways, took charge of scheduling men and women to take me to see my ladies twice a week. It was good to see them. Mom would often ask me to play piano for her. She had to be wheeled into the recreation room where the piano was. Sometimes June would wheel herself and the three of us would spend most of a visit with my playing whatever they asked me to.

June and I used to study the Bible daily. She could no longer read her Bible; so she asked me to read it to her. A Braille copy of the Bible would take up more than a bookshelf but I had a kind of computer which permitted me to read a document by using a line of 20 Braille cells. As I finished a line, I'd advance the document so I could read another 20 characters. I had a copy of the RSV Bible stored in the unit—along with my frozen food lists and cooking instructions. It's amazing how much information can be held in this device. I spent many visits reading to June. Occasionally Mom would listen as well.

We talked about all matter of things from church happenings to music. June and I held hands, and that helped me. But I wished she could do what she was so willingly before, but now she was lying in bed. I tried not to think about that. During one of these visits a flash of insight came to me. What if I sat in her wheelchair and removed one of its arms. If I moved the chair right next to her bed and locked the brakes, all I'd have to do was lean back. She could put her arms around me. June seemed to be happier than I was. It weighed on her that she couldn't do anything useful and now that had changed. I knew, as did June, that the Holy Spirit showed me how to solve my dilemma.

June was getting weaker. Her voice was much softer than it once had been. She occasionally lost reality, but when this happened, it was almost beautiful. She thought she was giving breakfast to homeless children. Then she would be back to normal thoughts and conversation.

During one visit she told me that Mom accepted Jesus as her Lord and Savior. Over many months June talked quietly to Mom, explaining step by step the process of salvation. Mom hadn't seriously considered church or worship ever since her pastor made fun of her clothes when she was a little girl. It was too bad that this thoughtless act pushed Mom's thoughts away from God. Nobody ever told her that it was best not to focus on people because they were not perfect; she should have focused on God, but, as I said, nobody told her and her life took a direction away from religion. After almost a lifetime of meticulously staying away from true worship, she finally knew what it felt like when the Holy Spirit became a Presence for her. Mom was transformed and had a more peaceful attitude.

During another visit she said: "I wish I'd been more demonstrative, more affectionate with you two children. I'm sorry for that." I didn't ask for further explanation, but I think she understood what I needed. Had she given freely of affection, would my life have been different? Only God knows.

At church some of my friends wanted to see me more involved with music. Judy Surber started me on that road as one of the services was coming to a close. The organist started playing the postlude. Judy grabbed my hand and led me to the piano. "Play along with the postlude. The piano will add a lot to the sound of the organ alone."

Somewhat reluctantly I did. From that time I played the postludes with both of the organists. I was also asked occasionally to play at times when there would be special music. The music director would suddenly tell me that I should play the prelude. I had to think fast to come up with something to play. It was more than flattering that my music was being noticed. I knew that it was a way for me to worship in a very special way.

I continued to record community choral concerts and by that time I could offer them on CD's. It was always at the back of my thoughts that I was providing a way to preserve memories which, without my recordings, would have been lost.

I was glad to have other things to do than visiting my ladies. Seeing June and Mom as they were was really hard for me to handle, and I knew there was no other choice but to do whatever I could for those two people. In other words, it was the right thing to do to help them, but in order to do it, I needed distractions at times. The rides to and from the nursing home often provided distraction. Those rides gave me the opportunity to get to know some of the church family who I didn't really know otherwise.

Take Chuck Johnson for example. I wouldn't have met him if it wasn't for the times that he was scheduled to take me to the nursing home. It turned out that Chuck graduated from Syracuse University in my graduating class. He studied at the engineering campus whereas I studied at the main campus. It was wonderful to talk about old times. It was even better when he told me of his hobby: restoring antique cars. He had a 1903 Franklin which he was working on at the time. It was fascinating to learn how cars of that era operated. He finally was able to get the car running.

Then there were Clark and Mary Lee Weaver. While I didn't know either of them, there they were, worshipping in our small church. She knew about me and my interest in music, which led her to ask if I'd accompany her when she sang "Right Now". A casual listening to the song would lead you to believe that it's a pop tune, but in reality it was a song which invites its listeners to come to know Jesus and the benefits of doing that. I hadn't heard of the song, but she had a recording which I studied so I could learn the tune.

We were scheduled to sing it one Sunday as "special music" during a regular worship service. We did it, and it was very well received. I liked the tune so much that I orchestrated it for use on one of my CD's. It was a background track, or an accompaniment; I hoped Mary Lee would sing the melody. I invited her and Clark to my house to hear the track. She loved it and willingly sang it for me. As she sang, I added her voice to the background, and we had a complete selection. It's one of my prized arrangements.

Mary Lee asked if I'd be willing to do another arrangement of the "Summer Time". She always wanted to record her singing of that Gershwin song but she could not locate a commercial background track. I wasn't sure I could do the song justice, but I worked hard and managed to provide a decent background against which Mary Lee sang. What I didn't know was that she had a definite reason for doing this. She was dying from the ravages of cancer and wished to make a recording of "Summer Time" while she still could. It was her hope that when she left us, that I'd collect her recordings and put them onto a single CD. That recording was played while people were coming to her Memorial Service at the church.

Another driver who I hadn't known prior to my need for rides was a woman with the rather odd name of Iscella. When I met her, she was willing enough to take me to see my gals, but there was something which gave me the sense of her being cool and somewhat distant. I wasn't too sure I was gonna like her, but she was a driver and I needed those. I treated her just the way I treated anyone. After all, she did something wonderful for me, and I was grateful to her and said so.

The next time she was scheduled to be my driver, she was different. I'm not sure in what way she was different: less controlling? I wasn't sure, but she was sweeter somehow. We talked about that one time and she said that she sometimes felt a need to protect herself from new acquaintances because she'd been deeply hurt by someone—so she took time before letting her guard down. She eventually came to be one of my best friends.

I soon discovered that it was best to have the same person take me shopping because she learned my buying habits and could move more quickly through the store. She'd remind me of things which I might have failed to write down on my list. The person who shopped with me was Flo, who I met when she first joined our church. June had her and her husband Bob over to our house for coffee. Also, Martha and Al Rossi joined the church at about the same time and June threw out the welcome mat for them. Martha continued to help me with paper work.

It's one thing to talk about loving or serving God; it's quite another matter to live that service. Those who drove me to the nursing home or to shop were truly dedicated to Him. I don't know when I saw so many people in a small town who walked with God. What a privilege it was for me to be among them!

I was happy to read the Bible to June or play for Mom. When Mom was no longer able to be in the "rec room," I would sometimes bring a keyboard into her room and play for her. Mom's mind was still very sharp and clear. Her hearing was failing, leading one to think that her mind wasn't good. Mom took a sudden downturn and was taken to the hospital. She slowly slipped out of consciousness and eventually died on March 8, 2003. She was almost 98 years old. I had to tell June about her passing, but she wasn't sad because she knew that Mom belonged with Jesus.

Because Mom and I knew that her time would eventually come, funeral arrangements were made in advance according to her wishes. Similarly, I talked to June about her desires so even her funeral and burial were planned.

First there would be a grave-side service in Brooklyn, immediately followed by a meal at Bea Resnick's home. Bea was the woman who flew with me to Florida to see my sister, Mary, and to say goodbye to her before Mary passed away.

The funeral director said that, if it didn't bother me, I could ride with him in the hearse going to Brooklyn. He knew it would be easier for me than finding another way to get there. I got the word out to Dad's family and to my Cousin, Alice Martin. Alice was all the family Mom had.

We got to Holy Cross Cemetery and just about everybody was there, just waiting for Mom and me. I went into the cemetery's office and presented the deed to the grave in which Mom was to go, and there was a problem. The woman in the office said that Mom wasn't a Catholic so couldn't be buried with Dad. I was shocked. The cemetery administrators knew in advance that Mom was to be buried there. Surely they have said something to me! Now What?

"Ma'am," I said, "really. What do I do now? My funeral director is here. My family and friends are here. The Deacon who will conduct the service is anxious to proceed. You could have phoned but you didn't." I restrained myself from saying more. I doubtless would have been sorry if I had. She relented, and I could sign the necessary papers. I wasn't finished with the funeral.

We gathered around the grave and the Deacon RAN through the service. He read the service in record time. Very few of us could keep up with him and answer responsively in the way we should. As soon as he intoned his last words, he ran out of the cemetery, no doubt running off to another "quickie" service. Mom deserved better.

The meal following the burial was wonderful. I hadn't seen most of the family for a long time, what with my living in Virginia and they were all still living in the New York area. Many things were shared about memories of Mom. Lots of folks asked me about June. Most of the people had met her at our wedding and the two subsequent receptions which were held for us. It took our original reception, one Mom and Dad held in the basement of their house and one which June and I held in our back yard. The latter one had 75 people in that small yard. All were terrific. These were some of the memories we shared during that meal.

Then it was time for the funeral director to drive me home.

My visits to the nursing home now were totally concentrated on June. She was not improving, and I knew that it was only a matter of time when I'd have to say goodbye to her. We talked about that one day. I told her, "June, please know that I love you. It's because I do that I say to you that, when the times comes for you to go to Jesus, run to Him like you're doing a 50-yard dash. Don't look back at me. Don't even think about me. You have something much greater to come to than what you're leaving. Can you accept this?"

"Yes, I do. This will make it easier for me when I leave."

I found time to arrange and record music. I had a recording of a concert given by Peggy Lee and George Shearing. Toward the end of the CD, Peggy sang a Mildred Bailey tune, "All too Soon". I could tell that June was slowly slipping away. I knew that I would record my own arrangement with my singing the poignant lyrics of that song. The loss of June would come "all too soon".

I remember a visit, perhaps around the beginning of April, 2005. She invited me to sit on her wheelchair and arrange things so she could help me. When everything was set, she said, "Get all you can from this. Be sure to really feel all there is." I thought she was telling me more than her words themselves.

June was no longer able to digest food; the feeding tube was withdrawn. June's 50-yard dash would soon begin. She had a brief stay in the hospital for a final check to see what could be done for her; there was nothing to be done. She was returned to the Louisa County Nursing Home.

Meanwhile, Iscella urged me not to stay in my house alone. I knew I was already a burden on my church family. I tried to resist the idea of leaving my house. Iscella suggested that I visit a few retirement facilities around Charlottesville. I said I'd go with her. I told her that if my audio system couldn't fit into one of their apartments, I wasn't moving. I didn't want to live in a place like where June and Mom lived. The rooms were cramped and there was little to do except lie around.

One morning Iscella, her husband, Ernie, and I drove off to look around. I liked one which had a fine grand piano which was pretty well in tune. There seemed to be lots of things one could do besides sitting around. The rooms were tiny. I wanted space to do things if I didn't want to do scheduled activities. We found a place called Branchland. The rent was very reasonable and the apartments were spacious. There were few scheduled activities. Only evening meals were served, and only five nights a week. As I walked the vast halls, I didn't see anyone. I felt like I was in a ghost town.

We found another one called Our Lady of Peace. I loved the name. I needed peace. I wondered if Our Lady could really give me that. I saw a few apartments and was impressed by the size of the rooms. The bedroom was just a tad larger than my present master bedroom. All of my bedroom furniture could be fitted into one of those bedrooms. The living room turned out to be 21 by 12 feet. I calculated that my sound system would fit and that the room's size would support good bass down to 32 Hz, the lowest note found on most organs.

We drove back to my house. It looked like I had just found a home. Iscella was surprised because she thought I went with her just to patronize her. Despite my desire to stay in my house, where I had great ham radio antennas, I knew I could not continue to ask the church people to drive me wherever I needed to go. I had to move. We drove back to fill out an application. I was told there was a waiting list of between six months to a year. I liked that idea because I could continue living in my present home where everything was familiar. Looked like my immediate future was planned. On another visit to June I told her about my moving away from our home and going into a Place called Our Lady of Peace. June could barely speak. I left fairly quickly, not wanting to tire her.

I was home one evening in the middle of April, 2005—April 14. I had just put the finishing touches to my arrangement of "All Too Soon". The phone rang. It was a nurse. I waited for dreaded news. The nurse told me to hold on. "June wants to talk to you."

I was so glad that she wanted to make the effort to talk to me. She could just barely talk. Would I understand what she wanted to tell me? I could hear the nurse handing the phone to June:

"Joe, I love you, but it's time for me to go to the arms of Jesus."

"Run that 50-yard dash whenever God tells you it's time." The nurse took the phone from June's hand.

My next visit to the nursing home was on Saturday, April 16. When Iscella took me to June's bed, June was still. She didn't show any response to anything I said. All I could do was sit with her and hold her hands. Those hands were more beautiful than I had seen them. I knew I'd soon lose her. I wondered how June could have fixed it so that her hands would be really special.

Iscella and I left her at about 1 P. M. There was little said as we drove to my house. Just as I got the door open, the phone was ringing. It was a nurse calling from June's room. She passed away at 1:10 P.M., April 16, 2005—our 18th wedding anniversary!

I was numb. I had no feeling of grief even though I just lost the one person I ever knew who gave me tons of happiness. I knew that if I could marry her again, I'd do it, even while knowing that it would end just as it did this time.

Chapter 32

How could I grieve? I'd done that for almost eight years, watching June gradually slip away. What I did feel was relief. June was with God; her suffering was over for eternity. I knew I did all I could to help her. I got the answer to my question which I asked myself before we married: "Could I truly live by the vows I took?" I was tested in many ways, and I got past all of them. I could say in good conscience that I past the test as to whether I could really keep my vows.

I was glad I finished my CD with my farewell to June. Somehow, though, I didn't want that disk to close with a goodbye. I chose to close it with "Here Am I, Lord". Just like I did with Mary Lee, when I asked a soloist in our church choir to sing the song. The funeral for June was held on Long Island. I asked Marilyn Macintosh, one of June's best friends, if we could use her house as a kind of meeting place for all of us who attended the service. She readily agreed; I was sure she'd want to be a part of June's start of eternal life.

The service for June was all I could have hoped for—much more than the awful manner in which Mom's service was conducted.

I rode with the funeral director to Long Island, once again riding in the hearse. After the service ended and the meal where we all talked about June and got re-acquainted with one another, I rode back to my Virginia home. It was a rather solemn ride, but Franky Sheridan, the funeral director, knew how to break a somber mood. It was pouring rain. First he asked if it was too warm, and I told him that it was. Then he asked if I'd like some water. I said that would be good. He gave me some by opening the window next to where I sat. I got some water, all right, from the rain and was cooled off. We were driving at highway speed, so you can imagine how the rain poured in through the open window. I just had to laugh! That silly gesture was a real help.

Back home my church wanted to hold its own memorial service for June, a time for sharing what June meant to so many people in the church. At the service the choir sang some beautiful anthems, and Pastor Mike preached a marvelous sermon. June talked about wishing she could have had a "going away" party for her husband, but she never arranged one. I wanted June to have a party to celebrate her homecoming. She loved balloons and liked to use them to celebrate events such as birthdays or other special occasions.

As we left the sanctuary and were ready to go into our Fellowship Hall to have our party, everyone in the church had a balloon and all 70 were released at the same time. For me this was the highlight of all the events which were held in honor of my wife. When I imagined all of those balloons rising in the air and gradually getting smaller as they soared, it seemed as though I could see June's soul being freed to go to its final rest. As I write this, I'm still moved by the memory.

As difficult as this time was, I realized that life must and does continue. It's something like a book with pages and chapters. June was no longer with me; nobody can ever replace her, but her chapter was written. When we read a book, when we finish reading a chapter and start reading the next one, we don't forget what happened in the previous chapter. We look forward to the next one, anxious to see what will happen. This is exactly where my life was—at the beginning of a new chapter.

I was no longer married. I wore my wedding ring for all my married life. It was time to take it from my finger. I certainly didn't discard it; I kept it and sometimes look at it, reliving parts of this previous chapter!

How would I spend my time now? How will my new chapter begin? It was going to be perhaps six months or more before I'd move to Our Lady of Peace. I hated the thought of leaving my house where I had all my electronics and music gear set up just the way I wanted it. I was leaving the place where so many memories of our happy marriage were made!

I heard about antennas buried underground which were supposed to be superior to antennas which were in the air. I read about some experiments with underground antennas so I figured I'd try one. It was incredible. My regular antenna was 250 feet long, strung high in the trees. In some respects the underground antenna worked better than my main antenna.

I love to read books, and now I had time for that. There are books printed in Braille, but reading Braille is slower than a sighted person can read even when reading aloud. This is well known and the Library of Congress has a few studios which are used to record books and put them on cassettes and in other formats.

Time was, as always, moving. It was the beginning of summer when I got a call from Our Lady of Peace (OLOP) that there was a vacant apartment. I thought I would have more time to enjoy my home, but I had to move quickly, or I'd be paying rent for an empty apartment. Iscella and some other people in the church took charge. They planned the move, even to the placement of furniture and my audio equipment.

One of the guys in our church, Gary Ziemer, took me to my new home to teach me where to find the most important areas in the building. This was very important because this building is large and is six-sided. The lobby is furnished with chairs, sofas, love seats and small tables with lamps on them. Could I find my way around all of these things? Could I find the three corridors which branched off this lobby at odd angles and not right angles which would have been more familiar? There is a panel of mailboxes and elevators in the lobby as well. How would I find my own mailbox among the hundred or so boxes? I solved that by putting a Braille label next to my apartment number.

As Gary walked me through these areas, he helped me find ways to navigate to where I needed to go. All of this had to be repeated on the floor below (where the dining room is located) and the third floor where many special activities are held. As I grew in the understanding of what would soon be my new surroundings, I recorded the navigation cues I discovered. I could later replay these recordings when I had to go somewhere which was not yet familiar.

Moving day was almost at hand. I enlisted some of the guys from my radio club to help me take down my various antennas. I had some good radio equipment which I knew could not be used at OLOP, but I found a buyer for it right away. I had to fight off a growing sense of sadness for a home and also a way of life. I couldn't yet guess what living in a retirement community would be like. I knew there was no turning back. Moving day was on July 11, 2005, now only 24 hours away. I filled suitcases and a couple of briefcases with small items which I knew I'd need soon after I arrived. Some of my great church friends came to help pack other items, such as kitchenware and clothes. How could I ever thank my church family for all their support?

When I awoke the next day—moving day—I knew that I would not spend one more day in my home; I'd never see it again. I was about to walk into the unknown. I didn't feel confident. I can't tell you how many church friends came to my house. I was about to climb into one of a caravan of cars plus a small van. I didn't even eat breakfast. My people even took care of that. The caravan was rolling. I kidded with the others traveling with me that it was really great to know how many people came along on this ride to be sure I couldn't come back. They laughed and so did I. I needed a laugh about them. I'd rather laugh than cry.

When we arrived and checked in, we walked to my apartment. The minute I walked in the door there were even more people greeting me and wishing me well; they, too, were some of my church family. They brought some items with them and had already started setting up my apartment with familiar things. There was a crowd which almost overflowed the big living room. Some of the guys put furniture into place and put up some of my pictures. The gals were arranging the kitchen, asking how I'd like things to be placed so I could locate them. We broke for lunch, which they supplied. Somebody said a beautiful grace, asking God to bless me and all those in my new home.

As the afternoon was well advanced, it was almost impossible to think that I could live here. Low and behold—I found that the bed was made, towels were out, dishes in the cupboard. The only things not done was to set up my computer and stereo system. That job was facilitated by one of the men in my Adult Sunday School who had built me a set of shelves which could accommodate a great deal of equipment in an easily accessible way.

Just as my helpers were leaving, there was a knock on my door. The woman who lived directly across from my apartment, Sadie, offered to escort me to my first meal in the dining room downstairs. I had a hazy idea of how to get to it, but I gladly accepted Sadie's help. When dinner time came, there was Sadie. As we walked to the elevator, she said, "I like holding hands; do you?"

Well, one more surprise. All I said was "Yes!"

The dining room was large. I had no idea of the number of tables there were. Most were tables which seat four. A few could seat six. The place settings were just like one finds in a fine restaurant, with cloth napkins. A menu was set at each place. Somebody offered to fill out mine, and when the food was served, it was enjoyable. When the meal was done, someone else walked me back to my apartment.

It was time to explore my new home in more detail. When you come in, there is a small hallway. If you walk straight down the hall, it runs right into my bedroom—a surprisingly good sized room. If I hadn't known better, I would have expected one of those tiny rooms I'd seen in nursing homes. If I took a right turn just past the front door, I'd enter the small kitchen. There was a refrigerator with an across-the-top freezer, a small countertop space, some cabinets, a dishwasher and a nice sink. If you stood in front of the sink and looked straight ahead, you would see a pass-through into the living room. The idea is to prepare a meal in the kitchen, place it on the pass-through and go into the living room and pick up the meal. There is also a fine, four-burner electric stove with a large oven. It's possible to do some limited cooking but with very little work surface. I wouldn't want to do it. If you again started at the entrance door and walked a couple of steps along the hall, you'd see a nice closet on your left, followed by the bathroom door.

Back at the front door, if you walked down the hall bearing right, you'd walk into the living room.

That's sufficient detail for anyone to have an idea what my apartment is like. I saw a couple of larger apartments in other retirement centers, but I couldn't afford to live in them.

I am known as an "Independent Resident". I'm only entitled to one meal a day, but I pay extra so I don't have to prepare any meals. There are also Assisted Living residents. They require minimum care, like being reminded about medications, which are dispensed from the nurses Station. Most of these residents require either walkers or wheelchairs so they can move about the facility. If a resident needs very special care, there's a Skilled Nursing facility for them.

Finally there is a very excellent unit for Alzheimer residents. This is a wonderful place in which those who live there are encouraged to do as many activities as they can handle. There are mental exercises to help to slow the progress of this disease. A resident can remain at Our Lady as his or her physical or mental condition changes. In other words, a person can stay here from room to tomb. The staff is wonderful.

As my first full day at OLOP began, it was breakfast time. I found my way to the dining room. Both breakfast and lunch are served buffet style. I thought selecting my food and bringing it to my table would be a challenge but it was not. The servers proved to be wonderful people who are glad to help.

I knew there were scheduled activities, but I did not know what they were nor when they were held. It didn't matter right then because I needed to set up my computer and wire up my stereo system. I did most of it, but Ron, a friend from my radio club, came over and helped get the work done more quickly than I could manage it on my own. I found there was one important advantage for me in moving to Charlottesville. The ham club met very near to my new home, and some of my radio cronies lived very close by.

Except for meal breaks, most of that first day was spent in wiring my electronics gear. When dinner time came, there was Sadie, ready to bring me to the dining room. She did that for many nights even though I knew very well how to find the dining room. Although it was wonderful to have Sadies's company, I wanted to get to meet and know other residents.

I found the piano in the lobby and played it one evening and it wasn't long before I had an audience. I introduced myself to whomever was present. Word got around about my playing and the Activities Director asked me if I'd be willing to play at definite times. I agreed, partly because I knew there were many others to meet. I'll never forget Edna Predmore. She was my number one fan. She grabbed anyone she could find and dragged them to hear me. The main lobby was quite crowded on Thursday nights at 6:30 P.M.

I joined a Bible Study run by Chaplain Gayle Richey, who also conducts many of the Protestant church services. There was a pretty good organ in the Chapel, donated by a resident after his death, which happened just before I came to live at OLOP. I worked hard, studying the many controls and learned to play it. I still play it both for church and for memorial services and group hymn singing once a week.

I was adjusting pretty well to my new home and to my new life. Though I didn't have enough space to perform many electronics experiments, I received permission to have a small ham station here. It helped me stay in touch with my ham radio friends in the area. I was able to participate in radio drills for emergency preparedness. We hams can often operate when electric power, cell phones and regular telephones fail. If there was a real emergency, we would have the proper training to maintain communications with hospitals or other organizations.

Life was quite routine by early October of 2005. I was playing piano one Thursday night when a new resident came to where I was seated and asked if I knew how to play "Come Back to Sorrento". I did. Next she wanted to know if I could play it in F Minor; she loved to sing that song, and her key was F Minor. I played an accompaniment to her singing, and I found out that she could really belt out a song. When I asked what her name was, she said it was Vail, "just like Vail, Colorado."

I couldn't help wondering if she would be a minor part of this new chapter or would she be its central character. I started seeing her at various activities held here. There was a game called "Word Quest" which involved defining words with varying difficulty. Vail also loved the game. She and I were usually on the same team, and we were hard to beat. It wasn't long before Edna became jealous of Vail. Because of this, she gradually faded out of the picture—my picture at any rate.

The Christmas Holidays were here.

Before the actual Christmas, OLOP put on a great party filled with music and good food! Residents could invite a few friends, so I invited Iscella and Ernie.

There were so many residents and guests that it was spread out among a few rooms. Vail ended up in the same room as where my friends and I were. Late in the evening when Vail went off to get a glass of wine, Iscella told me to stay close to Vail because she would become a major part of my life!

I don't remember much about that first Christmas here. I do remember New Year's Eve. Vail invited me to her apartment for a drink and conversation. I admit that I was lonely so I accepted her invite with thanks. She showed me around her apartment which was more or less like mine. She told me about her many treasured family photos and mementos. She was fascinating. She had traveled around the world; she'd lived in many countries and was fluent in French. She also has somewhat more than a passing knowledge of other romance languages. She told me about her life, the bad and the good. In some ways I could identify with her.

She asked about my life. I told her bits and pieces while we held hands. She sensed that this was something very important to me. I told her more than I wanted to. She was so kind and understanding and I needed understanding. Could she possibly ever hold me? I said just a little about that and it didn't seem to bother her. She was, and is, a truly wonderful friend. She has a car and drives me to places which I otherwise could not go. I loved walking as did she, so we began walking, increasing our endurance until we could easily walk two and a half miles a day at a brisk pace.

As recollections come to me, it was early March. We were walking our two and a half miles and our talk turned to the matter of religion. I mentioned that there was a Bible Study and invited her to join us if she was a mind to do so. She didn't seem interested. As our walk and talk went on, she said that she had lots of confusion about God and His place in the scheme of things. She wasn't too sure about her mother's beliefs. She said that her Mom developed an interest in Eastern thought and she even wrote a book about Yoga when that system was not yet popular. The walk ended as did our discussion. I don't know when the next theological discussion took place, but I do know that I explained my belief in a loving Father and how wonderful it was that He wanted to let us know that we were His children. I explained Who Jesus was and that He had a mission when He was right here on earth: to arrange things for those who believed so He would be able to live with them forever. She listened very carefully and had questions. I suggested that she read certain Bible passages which explain matters far beyond my power to do so.

As time went on, she became more and more convinced that this understanding of God made sense. She felt something deep in her heart that she wanted to declare that Jesus was truly Lord of her life. She confessed her sins to God as Rev. Gayle witnessed. Then Vail invited Jesus to come into her heart on March 27, 2006! She joined our Bible

Study. The weekly lessons include some rather searching questions. It wasn't long before Vail answered with a conviction and understanding that were often far better answers than I might have given! What a wonderful feeling that was for me!

There are quite a few singers and musicians who come to Our Lady of Peace to entertain us. Their efforts are genuinely appreciated. Vail and I believed that some of us could also entertain the rest of the residents. We started planning a musical program which featured a musical trip around the world. Vail knew enough songs which originated in many lands, so we eventually had a sufficient number of such songs to fill an evening's program. We presented this and it was immensely successful. Who else might be able to entertain us?

There was a wonderful woman named Jean Soroka who in her day was a fine violinist. Among her many credits were being a violinist and featured singer in the Phil Spitalny women's orchestra which was on radio for many years besides doing national tours. Jean had parents who were dedicated missionaries. Jean could no longer play her violin well. Fortunately Jean had a few recordings of her playing as well as recordings of her student orchestras. I found a couple of broadcasts of the Phil Spitalny show. Once the materials were assembled, we wrote a biography of Jean's life, featuring some of the recordings. The program was very well received, especially when Jean played a short violin selection.

One thing leads to the next. We were asked to perform for the folks in the Alzheimer unit, which we did and continue to do. They are an incredible bunch of people. They truly love music and love us as well. When we began performing there, I found an article about music therapy which said that the last thing that Alzheimer patients lose is their love of music. We've found this to be true. We've seen a few patients nearing the end of life who could at least mouth the words of the songs which Vail sang.

However, one thing plagued me about all our work. The pianos were seldom tuned. An untuned piano is an anathema for most pianists. Vail and I were determined to do something about that state of affairs. My next door neighbor was a fine musician in his earlier life. He knew so many songs. Even though he could no longer play very well, he had an electronic piano which sounded remarkably close to a real one. I thought that we should have such pianos at OLOP. These electronic pianos do not need to be tuned. Upon checking some music shops in Charlottesville, I found one which carried the Yamaha Clavinova, the instrument we wanted. This dealer was willing to help us by offering a deep discount on one of those instruments. He went so far as to deliver the Clavinova to OLOP for a 30-day trial.

Vail helped me to set up an account to raise money in order to purchase the instrument. Little by little the residents gave us money and we eventually had the money to purchase the Clavinova. Once we had the money and bought the instrument we donated it to OLOP. That made one out of the three pianos I had to play. Eventually somebody donated a nice instrument which was similar to the one I use in my apartment, a Casio Privia. About that time I came into a small amount of money as did Vail. We purchased another Clavinova and donated that to Our Lady of Peace.

I began using it immediately after it was delivered. I can say that, with these three instruments, I had some peace whenever I sat down to play one of them. As I said, one thing leads to the next one, and so I found myself volunteering to play once a week in the main lobby of the University of Virginia Hospital. Doing that is a wonderful experience.

Most people who pass through the lobby or are sitting on chairs, are waiting for something to be done for a loved one. Very often they are in moods of despair. They come to me as I'm playing to thank me for brightening their mood. I always include hymns and praise songs. These move the spirits of many of those who are within earshot of the wonderful Yamaha Grand piano. Oh yes! This fine instrument is kept in good tune.

I find time to continue doing some experimenting. I designed a somewhat portable sound system with very inexpensive parts, and yet it performs better than many commercially-made sound systems. I demonstrated it at one of the Ham Radio club meetings and people seemed to like what they heard.

Since I arrived on this planet, it has rotated 29200 times, more or less. I'm astounded to realize that, after that much time, my excitement when a good piece of music is played has not flagged. I recently attended a performance of the Charlottesville Municipal Band (an amazing group of musicians). One of the selections the band played was Glenn Osser's "Beguin for Band". This exciting piece really "grabbed me!" I start rubbing my hands together. My breathing was almost suspended. It felt like I'd lift off the seat. I was wrapped in the music, and the music was "in me!" It's the kind of high not attainable by liquor or drugs. It was the same emotions I felt when hearing Tchaikowsy's Fifth Symphony for the first time or "Music Out of the Moon" way back in high school! I'm still thrilled beyond measure when I play that album!

In closing I'd like to share something that has given me great peace and comfort that happened years back with June. June and I were happy in the church we were attending. She had many friends in many other churches so we'd go to one or another of them on occasion. At one of those churches the Pastor asked if he could pray with me with a view to God's restoring my sight. I thought about that for a second. I never asked God to give me the gift of sight. I gladly let the Pastor pray for this. He hoped for a miracle right then and there, but there was none. I decided to ask God for this gift, which I did a few times. The last time I prayed for sight, I heard God speak to me, "Joe, it's best that you do not see. You will glorify me far more by being blind and showing that you have a full life. When you show people your love for Me by word and action, I will be glorified".

I do not feel I need sight. I am completely at peace.

The End

Afterword

So you thought that the book ended, but there are a few more words. Now that the book is complete, I had time to think about the book and my life as a whole. What did I leave out? What did I say that perhaps I should not have said?

Two thoughts keep recurring. "Reach out and touch someone. That's a line from an old ad by the telephone company. Touch... What does it mean? In the context of that old advertisement, it meant that lives intersected—with no physical contact. A call from a good friend can brighten up our day. It's certainly true of a physical contact. It can calm you, excite you and probably do even more. Holding hands is a touch which can last longer than a fleeting moment and can be more calming or exciting than a fleeting touch. It's meant so much to me and you know. if people think about that simple act, they might discover that it has more power than we might want to admit.

In one of his letters, Paul tells his readers to give "a holy hug". He knew how powerful a hug can be, especially when the people involved are receptive. Imagine how it would be if the hug lasted for a time. The power to comfort and calm each other would be vastly stronger than it is with just a quick hug. I've known the truth of that for many years. All too often people don't really feel things but walk away from a touch or a hug unchanged. It's a pity; they miss too much!

Still reflecting on my life, I cannot forget that I am sightless. In one way I'll never know darkness nor will I know light. What happens when some mystery is revealed? We say that light was shed on it. The revelation might come in the middle of the night when you're in bed. There are no photos to stimulate your eyes, but you saw the "light". John, the Gospel writer, tells us that Jesus was a light. In his Gospel

Jesus said that we, that is everybody, can be a light if that light isn't hidden. Please excuse my paraphrase. When we "reach out and touch someone," we can be a beacon for someone. So, thinking about what I have written and what my life was and now is, I can only say: "LET THERE BE LIGHT!"

Joe Giovanelli, Monday, April 1, 2013

Appendix A

Braille and Arithmetic Notation

The Braille system which most blind people use was invented in France by Louis Braille in 1834. It is a system of raised dots which can be felt by a reader.

Each Braille character is contained within a "cell". A cell can contain up to six dots, arranged in two, vertical rows having as many as 3 dots in each. It is the presence or absence of dots in a cell that determines what the character represents. Just as with printed characters, the Braille reader scans a line of Braille from left to right.

Writing Braille can be done in a couple of ways. One employs a slate which is a board slightly longer and wider than a sheet of 8-1/2 by 11-inch paper. The paper used for writing Braille is much heavier than that used for printing. Good writing paper can be 20 pound stock. Braille paper is 80 pound stock. The paper is held in place by a clip at the top of the board.

There is a "guide" which is used to locate the Braille cells and to aid in punching the correct dot within a cell. Cells are rectangles and there are small niches on each of the long sides of a rectangle (cell). This permits the writer to locate each dot.

What I've described is the top surface of the guide. There is another part of this guide which could be called the lower section, or surface. This guide is hinged at its left edge so it opens, allowing the paper to be sandwiched between the surfaces.

The bottom surface has many depressions which are where each dot is formed. The device which punches the dots is called a stylus. It looks for all the world like a miniature awl. The point, or writing tip, is placed in the nitch that determines what dot is to be punched. Firm pressure on the "handle" of the stylus forces the point to penetrate the paper. The amount of penetration is limited by the depth of a depression on the lower part of the guide. If there were no depressions, the stylus tip would completely punch through the paper and a dot would not be formed.

We had to learn to write right-to-left and move down one line at a time. In order to read what was written, the paper is unclipped from the slate, turned over so that the dots then face the reader. Now the reader can feel the dots and will be able to read from left to right.

Learning Braille sounds daunting. Actually children learn it quickly, probably because they are exposed to it starting in the First Grade.

The second way to write Braille is much faster. It uses what could be called a Braille typewriter. It has six keys, one for each dot in a Braille cell plus a space bar. Rather than laboriously punching out one dot at a time, a person presses more than one key simultaneously, depending on the number of dots required to form a Braille character.

The paper is rolled into the machine much as is done with a typewriter. (Remember those?) The little depressions which permit the punches to penetrate just the right depth are on top, or above the paper, and the punches come up from below the paper. The Braille can be read as it rolls out of the machine, making it possible to correct mistakes.

Arithmetic

It's appropriate to say just a bit about numbers and arithmetic. Numbers can be written as a part of the Braille code. But how does a blind student "see" how the numbers in multiplication or addition are laid out. This is done by means of another kind of slate. This one has many rows of eight-sided holes. There are what are called "type" which have only 4 sides, but they are made in such a way that they can be inserted into a given hole in 8 different ways.

The surface of a type is flat, but with a straight line raised above one edge. With this arrangement the orientation of the raised edge shows the student what number (from 1-8) is represented. If the type is flipped end for end, you'd see that, rather than this raised, straight edge, there are 2, raised dots.

Again, the orientation of these dots determines whether what is represented is a 9 or a 0, or various operators such as the multiplication sign, division sign, etc. The type are placed into holes in a way which looks just as a sighted person would write a problem, such as division or multiplication.

This system for writing numbers is not used nearly as often as it once was.

Appendix B

Clock work.

When I was a kid, most clocks were not run by batteries or by being plugged into an electrical outlet. Rather, they were wound up and the tension of the "main spring" forced the gears to turn the hands.

I was fascinated with clockwork at an early age. At first it was the ticking of a clock. When Dad showed me how to tell time, I began to wonder what made the hands move slowly around the dial. I hounded everybody I could find asking if they had an old clock. I had quite a collection which I took apart. I destroyed many of them, but during the destruction I began to understand how the hands were moved. I figured out that there had to be a means by which the gears wouldn't just rotate at high speed. The hands would end up whirling around the dial and wouldn't indicate the passage of a time.

I began to see how the mechanism worked. There was what I later found out was called a "balance wheel". It's mounted between two" pivots just as is true of all the gears. On the upper surface of the wheel there is a tiny pin that meshes into a fan-shaped gear which was at the end of a lever. (I learned that this part is called an "escape lever" or an escapement.) I found that if I pushed the lever a bit, it would jump a bit more and stop. If I started to push it the other way, it would jump in the opposite direction. Two pins on the escape lever engage with one of the gears in such a way if the lever is pushed, one gear tooth at a time will pass by the escapement. When this lever is fitted to the roller on the balance wheel, it would be rotated when the lever pushes against the roller. With the assistance of a very thin spring wrapped around the shaft of the balance wheel, it will make the wheel move far enough so that the lever would push it even further. The wheel would turn in the opposite direction. The wheel will rotate back and forth, not unlike the way the agitator in a washing machine does.

Thus, rather than whirling around, the slow release of the gear teeth will produce a very slow movement of the hands.

The sound of each tooth being released is partly the cause of the ticking of the clock. The rest of a "tick" is the result of the roller passing among the teeth on the fan-shaped end of the escape lever.

It was with that understanding that I replaced the balance wheel in our alarm clock.

As I think about clockwork, I can hardly believe that I had that all figured out when I was just 8 years old. It is for this reason that I included this information here.